MEN AND PLACES

J. H. PLUMB

MEN
AND PLACES

LONDON
THE CRESSET PRESS
1963

Printed in Great Britain by the Shenval Press
London, Hertford and Harlow

TO DANTE AND SELINA

CONTENTS

PREFACE

The essays in this volume have appeared in various American, British and Canadian journals over the last ten years and I am grateful to the following publishers and editors for their permission to reprint them. American Heritage Publishing Co., The British Council, Longmans, Green & Co., The New American Library, The Oxford University Press and the editors of the *Daily Telegraph*, *History Today*, *Horizon*, *The Listener*, *Times Educational Supplement*, *Times Literary Supplement*, *Toronto Quarterly* and *Wine and Food*.

J.H.P

PART I

THE EIGHTEENTH CENTURY
SCENE

THE WORLD
BEYOND AMERICA AT THE TIME OF
THE REVOLUTION

FOR the farmers in the lonely valleys and hills and plains of America and the fishermen scattered down its endless coast, Europe in the eighteenth century had little meaning. Few realized that their lives were tangled in a web of forces—diplomatic, social and economic —that stretched from London to Moscow, or that their fate might be settled on the burning plains of India or amidst the hurricane-swept isles of the Caribbean. But it was so. For nearly a century Britain had been locked in a struggle with France; on its outcome the fate of the world depended.

And there were more subtle ties than these. When Benjamin Franklin walked the streets of London and Paris, he saw and heard what was familiar to him in Boston or New York. The same lovely proportions of houses and furniture caught his eye, richer perhaps and more ostentatious in decoration, but recognizably similar. He heard voiced the same discontents and the same aspirations. French-men and Britons talked to him of the tyranny of feudal privilege, of the glories of liberty, of the need for equality. He learned how they, too, felt their lives to be thwarted by kings and nobles and ancient traditional forms. He came to understand the strength of the age-old institutions by which European society was governed. Above all, he came to know that the fate of America was inextricably entwined with Europe, and that forces unleashed there would help to mould its destiny.

When George III succeeded to the English throne in 1760, the whole nation had become drunk with victory. The previous year, 'the year of miracles', London church bells had rung out day after day to celebrate fresh triumphs over France or Spain. Their colonies had dropped like ripe plums into the hands of marauding English admirals. Trade flourished, production soared. War, as William Pitt, London's hero, had forecast, brought wealth; wealth and empire as vast as his own wild dreams. This strange, lean, hawk-eyed statesman, sick in body and mind, felt called by destiny to lead England to an undreamed-of greatness. He believed that France had to be reduced to a second-rate power; Spain despoiled; his hero, Frederick of Prussia, could keep the rest of Europe in proper sub-jection. By 1760, this was no longer a dream but reality. In America, Canada, the West Indies, Africa and India, French power had been destroyed. British ships swept the seven seas, and the world lay at England's feet.

Neither the King nor Pitt's colleagues could bring themselves to accept so fabulous a prize. They feared, perhaps rightly, the jealousy of the defeated powers. And so, by the time peace was finally signed at Paris in 1763, Pitt had been cast out of the ministry and England's demands reduced. Nevertheless the gains proved enormous. Canada, Florida and all lands east of the Mississippi, were cleared of French-men and Spaniards; in India and the West Indies the gains were nearly as large; certainly sufficient to make the British Empire the greatest and the richest that the world had known since the fall of Rome; sufficient, too, to arouse that envy and hatred in Europe which George III and his advisers feared.

In the eyes of European monarchs, England was a wild upstart race, notable for its revolutions, and its almost pathological ad-herence to liberty; a people who kept its kings in subjection and rioted on the least provocation; a nation of hard-drinking, beef-eating shopkeepers with the instincts of pirates. Compared with their own rigid systems of government and law, Britain might appear unstable and anarchic. Yet no one could deny that she was rich, possessing an exceptionally buoyant financial system, growing trade and technological superiority. And these things mattered more than the power of despots.

Many contemporaries thought otherwise; to them the great European powers were stronger, richer, more cultured and more secure than Britain—absolute monarchies, blessed by God and stable to eternity. And the greatest of these was France, whose language had become the *lingua franca* of science, diplomacy and the arts.

The Earl of Pembroke insisted that his son must, cost what it might, have the best fencing and dancing masters in Paris. Russian, Swedish, German, Austrian, even Spanish and Italian aristocrats shared his sentiments. The French knew how to live as no one else did. The nobility of Europe talked French, wore French clothes, sat on French furniture, bought French pictures, collected French porcelain, read French books and pretended to believe in French philosophy. No one was educated until he had lived in Paris, visited Versailles, and listened to the gossip of the famous *salons*. There they imbibed the ideas of Bayle, D'Alembert, Condorcet, Diderot, Quesnay and, above all, of Voltaire, the arch-priest of the fashionable cult of reason. These philosophers vaunted man's capacity to control his universe; insisted that law, government, religion could only be respected in so far as their principles could be justified on intellectual grounds; they derided tradition, superstition, revelation and mystery. They talked endlessly of justice, equality, reason. But the heart, too, needed its prophet and it found him in Jean-Jacques Rousseau. He detested privilege, injustice, inequality, man's brutality to man. Nature was his panacea; the primitive his ideal; all wrapped up in a golden haze of sentiment and hope. So duchesses built dairies; installed a cow in a rococo setting and, to universal applause, milked it into a *Sèvres* vase. No nobleman's park was worthy of the name without grottoes, gothick follies or lonely hermitages. Decrepit peasants could be hired cheaply to add reality to the ghostly scene. After a refreshing draft of nature, the salons shone more brightly, the witticisms crackled, and the sharp laughter blotted out the future. As Louis XV so wisely said, '*Après moi le deluge.*'

Wise, because for the earnest middle-class, the lawyers, doctors, merchants, these ideas of Voltaire and Rousseau were serious matters; dynamite not fireworks. They hated the feudal privileges which warped their lives and longed for a juster, freer world. And the smart, slick talk of Versailles and Fontainebleau became revolutionary fervour in Birmingham and Boston; everywhere there was a sense of a new, brighter, more hopeful world struggling to be born; even monarchs felt it. Frederick the Great, the autocrat of Prussia, patronized both Voltaire and Rousseau. So did Catherine of Russia. Both saw the need for efficient government, both hated the Church and its privileges; but both feared the liberating influence of the new philosophy and both quarrelled with Rousseau and Voltaire. As with monarchs, so with aristocrats; they were attracted and repelled. These smart, fashionable ideas corrupted their faith in themselves, and in the institutions upon which their power was based. Only an eccentric few could swallow the consequences of the new ideas—a world in which all men were free, equal and brothers.

France led the world not only in thought but in all that adorns the life of man. The court of Louis XV, and afterwards that of his grandson, Louis XVI, achieved a standard of luxury that Europe had not witnessed since the Augustan emperors. Architects, craftsmen, painters of superlative excellence, created a world of decadent beauty. The *fêtes champêtres* of Fragonard, the luxuriant nudes of Boucher, the soft-sentiment of Greuze and the harsh realism of Chardin dominated European painting. The *ébenistes* of Paris and Versailles produced masterpiece after masterpiece of cabinet-making that renders much of the vaunted work of Chippendale and Sheraton heavy and provincial.

Nor was such excellence confined merely to Paris and the Court. France was alive to its own greatness; alive to the riches which lay in its soil and in the hands of its craftsmen. The government created the finest transport system in Europe, the best roads, the best canals. New ideas in industrial techniques were eagerly sought and if need be stolen. Population, trade, industry grew with each passing year. In science Buffon, Lavoisier and Laplace were the acknowledged masters of Europe.

With such wealth, with such intellectual and artistic supremacy, the future, most Europeans felt, must belong to France in spite of her recent setbacks in the struggle with Britain for empire. No European country could rival her. Prussia, well disciplined as she was, lacked the proper sinews of great power—coal, steel, men, money. Russia lay like a spastic elephant across the threshold of Europe. The Austrian Empire, better governed and more closely knit under the rule of Maria Theresa and her son, Joseph II, seemed greater than she was. Lacking trade, industry and proper communications, the Empire had no future; the fabulous wealth enjoyed by the Court derived from the rich but recent conquests of the Turk, and was soon dissipated. Geography denied Austria greatness. If Austria had no future, Italy and Germany had no present. A fantastic conglomeration of principalities, electorates, bishoprics, grand duchies and the like, some well, some badly governed, some homes of enlightenment, some archaic and feudal, all were too small to play any part in Europe's destinies except to provide cheap cannon fodder for the armies of their richer neighbours. Beyond the core of Europe, Spain and Portugal drifted along, sometimes energized by an active statesman, but usually content to follow in the course of their senior allies; Portugal had tied herself to Britain; Spain was strictly joined to France by a family compact between their Bourbon rulers, signed in 1761. Nor was there any rival of France to the North. The Dutch, rich and thrifty, lay moribund under a system of government that was too rigid and too decentralized, an ossified federalism which bound its energies in chains, preventing those quick decisions and desperate gambles so necessary for success in a world of armed competitive states. Scandinavia and Poland lacked force, and became mere pawns in the diplomatic game; their aristocracies grew rich and corrupt on French, English and Russian gold.

France was indisputably master of Europe. And yet in her fight for an empire beyond Europe France had failed, and continued to fail. The trouble lay in her state-system. Privilege shackled her economic strength and the system of government functioned so efficiently that a privileged nobility and church could maintain themselves in all their feudal but anachronistic splendour. With each passing decade both the social structure and the financial organization of the state drew further away from the realities of social and economic life, thereby creating a desperate crisis which only the exceptional authority of the monarchy and the efficiency of its centralization could bridge. Worm-eaten with privilege, the French state in all its glory could not match in a trial of strength the brash, chaotic world of its neighbour, Britain.

2.

Britain, like France, possessed many contradictions; archaic institutions, dating from Saxon and Norman times, attempted to serve a

B

society rapidly evolving into a modern industrial state—and naturally with little success. Political power did not always coincide with economic wealth. Feudal concepts still littered law, government and education as well as social behaviour. And yet Britain remained a mobile society, freer far than any other society in Europe. The Duke of Newcastle might plaster his coach, plate and linen with his ducal coronet and never appear in public without his stars and ribbons but his brother had been plain Mr. Henry Pelham; his relations lived modestly as country-gentlemen; his second cousins were parsons, soldiers, sailors and city merchants. Most aristocratic families sported a Lord Mayor of London in their genealogies, not a few an actress. And money, if made in sufficient quantities, brought a place in society and government, perhaps not always in one, but certainly in three generations. And the current set both ways. Younger sons of peers and squires drifted down the social scale until they became absorbed amongst the parsons, yeomen-farmers and tradesmen. Britain never became burdened with a vast, unemployable, poverty-stricken nobility. The demands of empire for soldiers, lawyers, engineers, administrators of all kinds made ever-growing demands on the ruling classes and India was soon to absorb all the sons that they could breed. This social mobility was a vital factor in England's strength. It made for opportunity. It took the edge from privilege for those born outside the governing class; at the same time younger sons were not frustrated in their ambitions to serve their country at a profit. Usually they could make enough money to maintain the style of life into which they had been born. The same mobility, the same opportunity stretched down into the lower classes. Small manufacturers, yeoman-farmers, craftsmen lived on terms of familiarity with their workers, servants and apprentices. London and the thriving towns of the West and North—Birmingham, Manchester, Sheffield, Liverpool, Leeds and Glasgow—offered chances of wealth and success to the quickwitted men and women of their neighbourhoods.

The unadventurous—and they were the majority—stayed in their isolated villages and hamlets, treading out the same pattern of life that their ancestors had laid down long, long ago. But unperceived by them, the new wealth that seeped into Britain like an estuarine tide, had sapped their ancient traditions. From 1760 England was in the throes of a social revolution that was to change the pattern of human life not only within its own shores but in the most distant corners of the world. Its concomitants were trade, invention, liberty, sound finance and weak-government. It is time to look closer at this strange land that could lose an empire and yet remain strong enough to withstand all the mighty force of the French Revolution and Napoleon.

3.

Britain in the third quarter of the eighteenth century was a strange mixture of privilege and liberty, elegance and filth, antiquated habits and new inventions; the new and the old were jostled uncomfortably together; fabulous riches mingled with dire poverty. The placid countryside and sleepy market towns witnessed rick-burnings, machine-smashing, hunger-riots. The starving poor were run down by the yeomanry, herded into jails, strung up on gibbets, transported to the colonies. No one cared. This was a part of life like the seasons, like the deep-drinking, meat-stuffing orgies of the good times and bumper harvests. The wheel turned, some were crushed, some favoured. Life was cheap enough. Boys were urged to fight. Dogs baited bulls and bears. Cocks slaughtered each other for trivial wagers. Bare-fisted boxers fought the clock round and maimed each other for a few guineas. Sailors and soldiers knew the lash and the savagery of their power-drunk officers. Each passing year saw the ferocity of the law grow greater. Death came so easily. A stolen penknife and a boy of ten was strung up at Norwich; a handkerchief, taken secretly by a girl of fourteen, brought her the noose. Every six weeks London gave itself up to a raucous fête as men and women were dragged to Tyburn to meet their end at the hangman's hands. The same violence, the same cruelty, the same wild aggressive spirit infused all ranks of society. At the great public schools boys were mercilessly flogged and bullied. Often they rebelled. Young aristocrats—the Macaronis—fantastically and extra-vagantly dressed, rip-roared through the town, tipping up night watchmen, beating up innocent men and women. Jails and work-houses resembled concentration camps; starvation and cruelty killed the sick, the poor and the guilty. This rough, savage life has been immortalized by Hogarth, Rowlandson and Gillray—so much truer to life than the delicate gentility of a Gainsborough or a Zoffany.

Vile slums in the overcrowded towns bred violent epidemics; typhoid, cholera, smallpox ravaged the land. And the cure of disease was as violent as the sickness itself. Young girls, given to hysterics, had their hair pulled out of their heads or they were thrown into an ice-cold well in the hope that the shock would cure them. Purges, emetics, vomits, artificial running sores; killing cures of mercury and arsenic; the surgeon's knife without anaesthetics, these things were the stock in trade of sickness. Children died like flies; most men got through two or three wives. Disease scourged the land and the stink of the common paupers' grave at Manchester grew too foul even for that tough age. The inhabitants of Acton pleaded for the removal from the gibbet of the rotting corpses that had become too high in the fierce summer sun. But the British were as tough and as callous as they were aggressive. Mainly they took these things in their stride, as part of life's vast gamble, a stimulant and a challenge. They grew to love risk. Betting provided an outlet. Raindrops running down a window pane, the fertility of a Dean's wife, as well as horse races, cricket matches, bear-baiting, dice and cards were fit subjects for a bet. Fortunes vanished overnight. When Lord Stavordale lost £12,000 in a single throw, he thanked God that he was not playing for high stakes. The Duchess of Devonshire bedevilled her marriage by losing nearly a million at cards. The lower classes aped their betters; cock-fighting ruined farmers; cricket bankrupted yeomen; pitch and toss and crown and anchor emptied the pockets of the labouring poor.

Yet these things provided an anodyne for the fierce, savage and uncertain life that they lived; likewise the hero-worship of highwaymen.[1] Dick Turpin, although he finished on the gallows, became a popular, romantic hero. And so did any general or admiral who took on fearsome odds in reckless circumstances. Clive at Arcot—a young man, almost a boy—gambled his life and puny army for the wealth of India. He became a national figure whereas the wise and cautious Admiral Byng was shot on his own quarter-deck for putting discretion and the safety of his ships before glory. Others found their emotional release in religion, in the violent, passionate call to salvation from a life of sin that Wesley and Whitefield preached with

---

[1] 3,000 people paid to see McLaren, the notorious highwayman, exhibited in his death cell.

such fervour. The tough miners of Bristol and Newcastle wept for the wickedness of their ways and found a new life in God. Religion, like gambling or robbery or war, became an opiate, a screen from the horrors of daily life; unlike them, it led, not to self-destruction, but to a new life of thrift and social service. Methodism reformed habits as effectively as it transformed the spirit.

Although life was hard and cruel, often violent, always shadowed by death, yet it was full, too, of light and laughter and wonder. For riches, no matter how unevenly distributed, were pouring into Britain, creating new standards of elegance and luxury for an ever-widening middle-class. And in the midst of the turbulence, the anarchy and the privilege, were groups of highly intelligent, strong-minded men and women, who possessed faith in man's capacity to order his world. Believers in science, in education, in industry, in invention, in good roads, new canals, lighting, paving, sanitation, clean jails, better laws, pure administration, social discipline, good housing, higher wages for better work, they were determined to create a richer, juster, more efficient society. They knew that the future belonged to Britain and to them their faith was derived from the evidence of their own eyes.

4.
'A vast change had taken place in English social life within two generations. View the navigation, the roads, the harbours and all other public works,' wrote Arthur Young. 'Take notice of the spirit with which manufactures are carried on. Move your eye which side you will, you behold nothing but great riches and yet greater resources.'

All he said was true. Brindley's canal, constructed in the 1760's, for the Duke of Bridgwater, demonstrated so amply the reduction of costs by water-transport that a mania for canal building swept the land, thereby widening markets and cheapening raw materials —coal, iron, wool and clay. And so, too, with roads; experiment was the order of the day and fast travel the conscious aim. Mile upon mile of new roads were being engineered, and along them were speeding a new race of men, 'commercial travellers', carrying in their bags the charming miniature samples of furniture, dresses, pottery, silver—now prized antiques. They were harbingers of a more luxuriant life for the professional classes and their advent in the little market towns caused a flutter in the feminine heart. Speed widened markets; orders arrived more quickly and were more quickly dispatched; and the clumsy local crafts were replaced by metropolitan fashions. Yet nothing demonstrated England's wealth nor its origins so vigorously as her crowded seaports. London, Liverpool, Glasgow resounded to the hammer blows of thousands of workmen building the new docks to house a merchant fleet greater than the world had ever known.

British sails crowded the most distant seas. Even the Celestial Emperor in Peking, Chi'en Lung, had heard of this strange race of red marauding barbarians who were foolish enough to barter silver for tea. Little did he realize that their ideas would filter into his ancient world, bringing destruction and change to a civilization far, far older than their own. Wherever they sailed, the British sought profit rather than empire; and great wealth poured back to fertilize expanding industrial revolution.

Navigation, roads and harbours did not tell the whole story; change was just as visible in the way of life of the prospering classes. In villages, in market towns, above all in London and in the new fashionable spas, new spacious houses were being built with a sense of elegant proportion that has given them a pre-eminence for beauty to this day. Sometimes grouped in terraces, sometimes curved in a crescent, occasionally rounded in a circle or formed into a square, these Georgian houses gave a new loveliness to the urban scene. They were decorated with exceptional taste, for their architects—the Woods at Bath, the Adams at Edinburgh and London, the Carrs of York and Smith of Warwick—were familiar with the finest work of Italy and France. The new classicism, given such impetus by the discoveries at Pompeii, controlled their exuberant delight in ostentation with a sense of proportion as exact as a mathematical theorem. Within, plasterwork, marble fireplaces, gilded panelling displayed the same faultless taste. Furniture, provincial and very plain by French standards, reached an excellence never since excelled by English craftsmen.

Silverwork of the highest order adorned the tables of the rich. The new invention, Sheffield plate, enabled the middle-class to copy the aristocrats' silver at half the cost. Porcelain and ornamental pottery, both novelties to the nation at large, became manias for all who had a pound or a shilling to spare. The well-to-do bought the beautiful productions of Chelsea, Bow, Derby, Worcester or Wedgwood, the thrifty poor indulged themselves with the crude chimney ornaments of the Staffordshire potters. The huge production of useful as well as ornamental china betrayed the wealth of the nation. Clothes, too, although simpler than the exotic aristocratic fashions of earlier decades, were as rich and as ornate and as handsome as the houses and towns in which they were displayed. And the art of pleasure was cultivated with the same intensity as the art of decoration.

Balls and masquerades, plays and burlesques, concerts at which the new and lively compositions of Bach, Haydn and Mozart could be heard for the first time, took place in a setting as harmonious as the melodies themselves. Never before had the arts of social intercourse been so assiduously cultivated. And the shopkeepers and artisans were equally avid for their finery and frills. Sadlers Wells and Islington Spa provided them with tea gardens, harlequinades, rustic dancing and all the delights that their superiors enjoyed in greater elegance at Ranelagh or Vauxhall.

The aristocrats were richer, far richer than they had ever been. Rents mounted year by year; house property, coal, iron, new ventures added to their wealth and what they won so easily was often as prodigiously spent. Down went the old house and up went the new palace; Italy, France, even Germany were ransacked for treasures, pictures, sculptures, tapestries; all noblemen were connoisseurs. Whims and fancies could be indulged—private orchestras played to the musical; zoos entertained the naturalists; gardens, for which rivers were diverted and the Himalayas pillaged, delighted the botanists; private laboratories, rare libraries, hired philosophers, nourished the intellectuals. Whatever they desired, they bought. But from peer to pauper there is a gusto about life, a confidence, an ebullience and waste that argues a profound belief in their own destiny.[1]

Certainly they felt *gauche* before French fashions; admittedly they respected French art and French literature profoundly. None of

[1] The Duke of Bedford planted his park with thousands of trees that could only come to perfection after more than a century.

them believed themselves educated until they had spent some years on the Grand Tour in France and Italy.[1] Nevertheless they knew their government and their church to be the best in the world; the most jealous of liberty, the most conducive to prosperity. Nor did their respect for antiquity blind them to their own achievement. They worshipped Shakespeare, revered Isaac Newton and John Locke—as indeed did Voltaire—took pride in Gibbon, Hume and Blackstone, and delighted in the novels of Fielding, Smollet and Richardson and in the plays of Sheridan and Goldsmith. And they were as impressed by the pontifications of Dr. Johnson as by those of any *Encyclopedist*. They were pervaded not so much by a sense of inferiority as a desire to learn.

Yet the wonders of this new age, its greatness and its hope, belonged to the few and not to the many. Old habits still clung like burrs to the minds of the majority, and behind the luxury lay the pig-sty of the poor. A world was in transition though few realized it. Great inventions and new sources of power had begun to realize the strange cunning of men; they had brought into being a ferocious, expanding world in which greater wealth would sooner or later bring greater justice, more freedom, more leisure and the final destruction of those feudal privileges under which man had laboured through the long and bitter centuries.

5.

War, commerce and invention, these were the factors that were primarily responsible for setting the social life of Britain in violent motion. Britain had been more or less continuously at war, apart from Sir Robert Walpole's twenty years of rule, for more than a century. As a young man, Chatham, in a speech of fiery eloquence, told the Commons 'when trade is at stake, you must defend it or perish'. When he died, the City of London raised a monument to him at the Guildhall upon which these words of Edmund Burke were inscribed: 'A statesman by whom commerce was united with and made to flourish by war.'

And it was true. Marlborough's wars had reaped victory's harvest in the West Indies and the Spanish trade; Clive had wrested Bengal, worth £2,000,000 p.a., from the supine hands of the decadent

[1] See pp. 54–66.

Moguls; at the same time he cleared the French out of the Carnatic. And Chatham's genius had won the greatest gains of all—Canada, India, West Africa had all witnessed his conquests and not only witnessed but also paid for them out of increased trade. Tobacco, sugar, rice, furs, timber, fish, silk, cottons, tea poured into British ports, a torrent of liquid wealth that fertilized all that it touched. Yet war had won trade not empire. Chatham himself spurned Clive's offer of Bengal to the nation. He preferred to leave such desperate problems of government to the East India Company. Chatham saw empire in trade, in the possession of ports and strategic points, in the denial of advantages to the enemy, France, and not in the rule and subservience of millions of his fellow-men. Hence, although a passionate imperialist, he could sympathize with the tribulations of the Americans in their struggle with Britain.

War, however, brought greater benefits, although less realized than trade, greater even than the stimulus to the production of steel and cloth and shipping. The need for larger and larger forces on land and, more particularly, at sea created an intolerable strain in William III's day on the ramshackle machinery of central government. England came near to defeat, through lack of money and lack of logistic competence. Ruin was averted by the foundation of the Bank of England, the re-coinage, the introduction of the land tax, direct administration of taxes instead of tax-farming (the bane of France), improved accountancy and a better system of budgeting and appropriation. So Britain acquired what, hitherto, the Dutch alone had achieved; a buoyant, flexible and reasonably just financial system. Such excellence bred faith; government funds were eagerly sought; money and credit abounded; interest rates fell in London to 3 % and even in war rarely rose much above 5 %. So war not only increased trade, but also freed money and multiplied it.

Cheap money stimulated speculation, new enterprises, invention; a risk was cheap; the effect on the industrial revolution was profound. Plentiful money created demand—for goods, for food, for those small personal luxuries that are the symbols of affluence. And as is usual in times of economic prosperity, the population began to grow at first slowly but with ever mounting momentum until by 1780, Britain was rapidly becoming a nation dominated by youth —in itself a factor making for enterprise and expansion.

The need for labour had long been apparent, and at last, a conscious attempt to tackle problems of disease and sanitation had to be made. The wide use of inoculation against smallpox, the attention paid to midwifery, the creation of foundling hospitals for unwanted children, the increasing use of cotton (and washable) underclothing, the change from wooden platters to pottery (again washable), the encouragement of personal hygiene and the brilliant medical teaching of Smellie, Pringle and the Hunters, all contributed to keep more people alive for longer. Yet neither the improved social conditions nor the even more important economic stimulus to early marriage and parenthood, produced labour fast enough for the growing economy. This shortage of hands stimulated men's ingenuity. They broke down restrictive practices, bypassing those fearsome medieval guild regulations that were the curse of French industry.

Their attitude to the working class also changed. Instead of wanting to keep them poor to keep them working, they began to provide incentives—better wages, better housing, facilities for education and religious worship. With money to spend and goods to spend it on, the working class worked harder and spent more wisely. Again, industrialists began to pay great attention to methods of production. Division of labour became the slogan of efficiency. Instead of one craftsman making an object, each process in its manufacture became the work of one man, thereby increasing and speeding production and also enabling women and children to be employed. It is easier to teach a man to make a spring than a clock.

The factory system spread, for the factory led naturally to greater discipline and to evenly flowing production. At first workers hated it and manufacturers were forced to use women and child-labour, both more amenable to regular hours and repetitive tasks. Slowly the system spread, but in the last half of the eighteenth century it was still something of a novelty and visiting notables from Europe were always shown the great Soho works of Boulton and Watt or the new pottery works of Josiah Wedgwood at Etruria, first opened in 1769.

Yet these things were insufficient in themselves to bring about the industrial revolution. They increased production but never fast enough. All the great entrepreneurs of eighteenth-century England were also preoccupied with invention. 'Everything,' wrote Josiah Wedgwood, 'yields to experiment.' And his commonplace books are full of notes on science and technology. New materials, new machinery, new techniques, these things led to improvement and they knew it. In all industrial circles a search for invention intensified. Manufacturers joined the Royal Society—Wedgwood himself contributed a paper on the thermometer—and cultivated scientists. The close relationship between Boulton and James Watt is well known. Watt's invention of the steam engine in 1769, and more importantly, the development of an improved version with rotary motion in 1781, freed mankind for the first time from the natural sources of power, opening up the limitless vistas for industrial society. Joseph Priestley, one of the most remarkable men of his day—scientist, philosopher, reformer—numbered dozens of manufacturers amongst his close friends and admirers. In all manufacturing towns the same spirit of inquiry dominated men's minds. The result was a remarkable spate of inventions. In textiles, Arkwright's spinning frame (1769), Hargreaves's jenny (1770) and Crompton's mule (1779) revolutionized the production of yarn and turned the spinning wheel into an antique. The demand for iron, stimulated by war, led to the inventions and improvements of Smeaton, Gort and the Cranages; smelting by coal, invented earlier in the century and kept a jealous secret, spread through the industry. The great works of Carron in Scotland and Dowlais in Wales became the wonders of their age. To show his faith in iron, John Wilkinson, the great ironmaster, built iron bridges, iron boats, iron chapels and was buried in an iron coffin. Human ingenuity left no industrial art unimproved.

The same vigorous spirit spread throughout England's greatest industry—the land. Improvement in agriculture was already many generations old. The great publicist, Arthur Young, sang the praises of Norfolk—its enclosures, its marling, its clover, its turnips, its rotation of crops and its long leases. Yet these things all dated back to the seventeenth century, as did the fashion for large estates which allowed so much better management through greater capital resources. From 1750 the pace of change quickened; agriculture became the rage. Robert Bakewell's farm at Dishley became an object of pilgrimage, for he bred larger and fatter and woollier sheep than men had dreamed of. New machinery, better fertilizers, stronger horses, milkier cows, fleshier bullocks were displayed with pride at County shows. The Duke of Bedford graced sheep-shearing contests with his presence; George III was nicknamed 'Farmer George' because of his passion for agriculture. The huge, beef-eating, beer-drinking caricature of all Englishmen—John Bull—was a farmer. More mouths to feed, more money for food, brought a golden age of prosperity to the land and, ironically, strengthened those traditional forces in society that were most opposed to all change in politics and society—the country-gentlemen.

6.

Not so, the new men; they took delight in reform and improvement. Their willingness to experiment, to risk the new against the old, did not stop at industrial organization or agrarian management. The Arkwrights, Strutts, Wilkinsons, Wedgwoods and Cokes applied the same principles to society. They lost patience with traditional muddle. Old broken-down roads with puddles the size of ponds, in which men and horses floundered and drowned, were useless to them. Slums, pullulating with disease, were an affront to their intelligence as well as their humanity. Good houses spelt healthy workers and a better output in the factory or on the land. Paved streets, like good roads, meant lower costs. A plentiful water supply eased industrial problems, provided better sanitation and improved health. Ample street lighting permitted late shopping and so better time-keeping in the factories. Both social discipline and social opportunity seemed utterly desirable to the great *entrepreneurs* —Whitbread the Brewer, Wilkinson the Ironmaster, Wedgwood the Potter, Boulton the Engineer. They were to be found in the vanguard of philanthropic reform. At Liverpool, men of a like mind laid out the first public gardens; at Newcastle-on-Tyne they founded a literary and philosophic society. At Manchester they sponsored a privately organized police force. They swarmed in turnpike trusts and canal ventures. They acquired a host of private acts of parliament by which they provided their towns with rudimentary social amenities. They were active in all societies to reform the manners and habits of the working classes. The desperate insecurity of the life of the poor naturally bred a feckless attitude; wakes, fairs, church ales, riots and drunkenness took off the edge of bitterness for the labouring poor but they also destroyed regularity of work by creating absenteeism. They brought about destitution and disease. The suppression of these working class bacchanalias became an urgent social necessity. 'I wish,' wrote Wedgwood, 'to make such machines of my men as cannot err.' His fellow manufacturers concurred and sought to relieve their workers of anxiety, fear and despair. In consequence, they gave support to Friendly Societies which provided insurance against sickness in return for a small weekly contribution; they provided schools or supported them; they built better houses and provided shops for, above all, they wished to raise the standards of living to encourage men to work harder. They might believe that some men would always be poor but none of them wished to preserve poverty for its own sake as their forebears had done earlier in the century. These 'new men' lived, therefore, in the ethos of social reform and an unquestioning belief in progress was a part of the air they breathed.

And yet at every turn they met traditional obstacles. Often they lacked the social or political power to achieve the smallest reform. Any body of manufacturers wishing to cut a canal had to solicit, maybe for years, the country-gentlemen in whose hands effective power lay. England was still governed by a remarkable collection of ancient, unreformed institutions, the slow accretion of time and as strong as a coral reef. Often these could be circumvented but only by much effort. Hence these new men became ardent apostles of reform. Their leaders, Adam Smith, Jeremy Bentham, Joseph Priestley and Richard Price, directed their attention to reform on a national scale as well as local. In their own work, they had come to appreciate the value of a rational approach. It was easy for them to believe that reason would be equally effective if applied to human institutions. Liberty and equal rights became their watchwords; and democracy their aim. Naturally they identified themselves with the struggles of John Wilkes and of the American colonists.

Their political impotence bred despair for the future; as one of these new men wrote to his son:

'Through the folly and wickedness of the present, you of the rising generation have indeed a dark prospect before you. . . . Your best way will be to gather as fast as you can a good stock of the arts and sciences of this country; and if you find the night of despotism and wretchedness overwhelm this hemisphere, follow the course of the sun to that country (i.e. America) where freedom has already fixed her standard and is erecting her throne; where the sciences and arts, wealth and power will soon gather round her, and assist and strengthen her empire there.'

This black mood fell time and time again across their spirits. Opportunity they saw, and the promise of a larger future. But they lacked power. Society still revolved about its old gods—monarchy, established church, the nobility; little oligarchies of traditional reactionaries hogged political power in the countryside and corporate towns. Even Parliament whose struggle for liberty against the Crown had made their ancestors' days heroic had now become effete, unrepresentative, concerned only with its own privileges and indifferent to freedom and justice. So they felt. And naturally their sympathies swelled to all who cried out against oppression and privilege—Dissenters, Catholics, Irishmen, Americans. Powerless, they watched their country's empire break to pieces; they protested, they petitioned, they cursed George III, Lord North and the Constitution. Without avail for the traditional forces were still too strong; harbingers of a new world they might be; the old still held them in thrall.

7.

Commerce had enriched, but industry scarcely touched the traditional structure of English society. The new mushroom towns were ruled by the same officials in exactly the same way as in the days when they were villages. The Lord of the Manor remained a power in Manchester. Birmingham possessed the government of a village for it was a parish not a corporate town. Growing population, new industries, increased wealth, could create new problems of social organization but it was left to the citizens to solve them. The methods of government remained almost untouched.

The Glorious Revolution of 1689 had been an almost unanimous revolt by the property-owning classes against interference in their local rights of government. In consequence the word *freehold* acquired almost a mystical reverence to eighteenth-century Englishmen—a *freehold* was not merely a tenure of land. It could mean a benefice, a commission in the Army or Navy, the possession of an obsolete office or ancient privilege. A blind, paralytic, mad bishop could not be deprived of his office until he died because his office was his freehold. To advocate the abolition of such sinecures as the Tastership of the King's Wines in Dublin or the Clerkship of the Pells smacked of revolution for these were some man's freehold. Also the Revolution had given a chance to the landed classes and their dependents to batten on the state. The Church, the Army and the Navy, the Court and the Administration had become a vast racket that provided outdoor relief for needy younger sons or dependent cousins. Lord Pembroke bought his son a commission so that he could wear a decent uniform on his Grand Tour. He did not see his regiment for four years but naturally he drew his pay and rose in rank. Lord Barrington was Secretary-at-War; his brother entered the Church and his career ran as follows:

1760 Royal Chaplain

1761 Prebend's stall at Oxford

1762 Two further stalls at Hereford

1768 Prebend of St. Paul's: the highly prized *Consumpta per Mare*

1769 Bishop of Llandaff.

And then, with his brother out of office, his career flagged, but on his brother's return, the bishop began once more to move up the ladder of preferment.

1782 Bishop of Salisbury

1791 Bishop of Durham—one of the richest of all sees.

Any army or navy list in these years reads like Debrett. Ships or regiments, the natural assumption was that they were property, and property that belonged by divine hereditary right to the ruling classes. And the same was true of much of parliamentary representation. The Duke of Grafton, short of cash, sold his parliamentary borough of Gatton in Surrey and the auctioneer described the purchaser's joys in these terms:

'No tempestuous passions to ally, no tormenting claims of insolent electors to evade, no tinkers' wives to kiss, no impossible promises to make, none of the toilsome and not very clean paths of canvassing to drudge through; but his mind at ease and his conscience clear, with this elegant contingency in his pocket, the honours of state await his plucking and with its emoluments his purse will overflow.'

There was no mention of electors because they were so few that they lacked importance. Lord Egremont bought the parliamentary borough of Midhurst for £40,000; the Duke of Bedford sold Camelford for £32,000. And as Chatham said, these little tiny towns that sent representatives to Westminster, but could be bought or sold like a parcel of fields, were 'the rotten parts of the constitution', yet even he would not hear of their destruction. The sanctity of the Constitution, blessed by the Glorious Revolution, could not be invaded.

At the same time, men witnessed a growing arrogance on Parliament's part, a jealous sensitivity to its privileges. Wilkes, elected for the most populous constituency in the country, Middlesex, was declared—not once but four times—not to be a member of parliament because he had crossed his King and had been convicted on a trumped-up charge of libel. It was Parliament's privilege to decide the question of its own membership. As with great, so with small matters.

'On one occasion,' wrote Lord Mahon, 'it was voted a breach of privilege to have killed a great number of rabbits from the warren of Lord Galway, a member. Another time the fish of Mr. Joliffe was honoured by a like august protection. The same never failing shield of privilege was thrown before the trees of Mr. Hungerford, the coals of Mr. Ward and the lead of Sir Robert Grosvenor. The person of one member's porter and another's footman was held to be as sacred and as inviolable as the persons of the members themselves.'

Those that owned the land, owned the institutions of government, and ran them in their own interests. More and more crimes against property became capital offences; the game-laws approached the savagery of the old forest laws of medieval Kings; enclosures multiplied. More entrenched in power than they had ever been, they were also richer; rents soared, their investments grew, the state provided. Naturally many of them took a rosy view of the universe. It was the best of all possible worlds and to desire change was to fly in the face of providence. Wilkes, the radicals and the American colonists were not only stupid but wicked.

So it seemed for those excluded from the magic circle of government; they seized on the little acts of tyranny, the assumption of privileges and the minor corruption that was obvious to all and saw George III as a Stuart tyrant and Parliament as a complacent tool. For those within the situation was infinitely more complex, a bewildering world of duty that pressed heavily on privilege and profit.

Throughout the changing centuries Britain had been ruled by the owners of the land. They dominated her counties; they filled Parliament and all the professions. Sometimes a new family, grown rich in commerce or the law, would buy up an improvident's estate in order to acquire that gentility which was the hallmark of the establishment. But land-owning, great or small, carried social responsibilities. The farmers, even the smallholders, had duties hard to escape. Then ran their parishes, provided the Constables, Churchwardens, Overseers of the Highways and of the Poor, unpaid jobs all, and all onerous in that aggressive, litigious society. They kept order, collected taxes, shared out collective duties, provided for the sick and the destitute. Often they were harsh, rushing an expectant mother across the parish boundary so that their neighbours would have to provide for the unwanted mouth. Yet to their own kith and kin and to those whose roots in the parish went as deep as their own, they parcelled out a rough justice and engendered some human warmth. And although they frequently did themselves well out of the rates, most of them were honest after the fashion of their age. Usually they were owners of small properties—like Arnold of Kent, or Thomas Turner of Sussex, or Carrington of Hertfordshire whose diaries have been published—and they too were enjoying the rising prosperity of the land. Their attitude to life was to accept it as it was; if they were undisturbed, they were content for the gentlemen to rule.

Most of these little oligarchies of village rulers were linked by ancient friendship with the greater landowners—the nobility and country-gentlemen of long standing; often they were bound by economic ties by renting of land or supplying of services or materials to the 'great house'. The real rulers of the county were to be found amongst the squires and aristocrats and their ecclesiastical dependents. They provided the Justices of the Peace upon whose backs rested the whole burden of law and order. They also officered the militia, needed as much to suppress the rioting poor as to withstand the ever-expected invasion of the French. Many gentle families stretched back into remote antiquity and naturally enough their politics were

C

patriarchal. Their destiny was to govern. A dozen families or so in most counties acquired a certain pre-eminence through wealth or ability or both. Often feuds divided them; like that of the Hastings and Greys in Leicestershire, dating back to before the War of the Roses; and great national issues always found the same set of families at loggerheads with one another. Since the Revolution these groups had often gone under the name of whig or tory but counties could be divided whig against whig and tory against tory. Family feuds and alliances had come to mean more than politics. Bitter battles for the honour of representing counties in Parliament had so beggared many families that by the accession of George III most English counties preferred to compromise on candidates than risk the expense of an election; often one Knight of the Shire was drawn from the whiggish families, another from the tories. In 1761 there were only four contests in the forty English counties, so the most democratic of all constituencies had little opportunity to express a political opinion. Yet such members of Parliament were not free from political pressure. As the American revolt progressed, the rights and wrongs of it became issues even in county politics and Knights of the Shire felt the need to make their views known. For generations representation at Westminster had been settled with hardly a thought about politics. The American war changed that for ever, invigorated political discussion, and helped to bring about a rebirth of the party system.

The families of these Knights of the Shire read like a roll-call from Debrett. Cholmondeleys sat for Cheshire, Courtenays for Devon, Lambtons for Durham, Cokes for Norfolk and the same ancient names were to be found representing the small county-towns or seaports. Over the generations a family had established its patronage over a borough; almost time out of mind Rashleighs had represented Fowey, Burrards Lymington, A'Courts Heytesbury. Such men spent much of their time on local affairs, securing bills for workhouses, river-widening schemes, turnpike trusts and the like as well as attending to the manifold grievances of their constituents. Such men, like the Knights of the Shire, were self-electing, but neither bribery nor government influence got them into Parliament.[1] They might favour this political group or that, incline to

[1] Only 11 out of 80 Knights lacked parliamentary ancestry in 1761.

traditional whiggery or traditional toryism, but the security of tenure bred in them an attitude of such independence that all ministry needed to win the support of the majority of them if they were to survive. It was to their serried ranks on the back-benches that the oratory of the parliamentary leaders was directed. Although most of them called themselves whigs it was not the whiggery of their ancestors; tradition, the constitution as laid down in 1689, was their watchword rather than liberty. They believed in monarchy, in the established Church, in the subordination of Ireland and the Plantations. Most of them were suspicious of Wilkes, worried by Chatham, and content with George III and Lord North.

Although these men provided the background to politics they did not fill it. There were corrupt boroughs. Many belonged to borough patrons who detested Lord North and George III. They brought in their henchmen. A successful merchant with political leanings could usually pick up a seat if he wanted one; so could lawyers. And some boroughs with tiny electorates—like Bath—spurned patronage and worshipped furious independents. And there were boroughs with enormous electorates—open to any demagogue with a purse large enough to provide the gargantuan orgies of beer-drinking and beef-eating that all voters regarded as their rights. Naturally the Crown controlled many boroughs and found seats for its admirals, generals and civil servants and court officials but it would be quite wrong to think that George III or his ministers controlled very much of the membership of Parliament. Indeed it has been shown that royal influence at this time was steadily declining, that George III controlled less in 1780 than he had done in 1760; and that the winners, as might be expected, were either the *nouveaux riches* or the long established parliamentary families. These factors gave Parliament its life and spirit, and brought it nearer to a truly representative assembly than its critics have allowed. Yet men of great estates dominated at Westminster, and their attitude to life was bound to be, except for a few eccentrics, traditional and averse to change.

Such men had little comprehension of, or interest in, the grievances of remote colonists; in their minds, the Americans were linked with the Irish, a difficult and disagreeable people, best kept under.

The heart of politics lay in the Court, for Kings in eighteenth-century England were expected to rule as well as reign; ministers were their servants as well as being responsible to Parliament. Hence the personality of the King proved to be an important factor in politics. George III came to the throne at a very early age—but mentally he was younger still.[1] He had developed late—he could not read until he was ten. He lacked faith in his own abilities, and dreaded the burdens which the Almighty had placed on his shoulders. Yet his sense of duty was quite remarkable and his natural obstinacy monolithic. Burdens they might be, but they were a sacred duty. Puzzled, determined, ignorant, and not apt to learn, George III turned to Lord Bute for whom he developed a schoolboyish passion. Bute, a career politician, and friend, possibly lover, of the Princess of Wales, George III's mother, was eager to exploit the King's dependence. Together they set about getting rid of George II's ministers—Chatham, Newcastle, Hardwicke, Devonshire; jealousies between rival whigs proved easy to exploit, but the creation of a stable ministry, loyal to George III, Bute and their friends, proved impossible. George III was forced to turn from one group to another. He married, outgrew his dependence on Bute, and looked for other father figures amongst his politicians. They all failed him —his uncle, Cumberland; Chatham who went quite mad; Grafton whose nerve cracked under the lash of Junius's letters.

Constant changes, squabbling groups of ministers, deprived the country of any settled policy. Grenville started the crisis. A careful administrator, good at arithmetic; a man who would have made a good banker but lacked even a modicum of imagination, decided, logically enough, that the Americans should pay towards the expenses of the Seven Years War which had freed them from the French menace in Canada. The furor caused by the Stamp Act astounded the ministry; naturally enough the opposition whigs, led by Rockingham, were not slow to criticize and to make fine distinctions between direct and indirect taxation. Once in office they repealed the Stamp Act and appeased George III, who regarded the American colonists quite simply as rebels, by passing the Declaratory Act which asserted that Great Britain possessed a sovereign right to tax the colonies. The Rockinghams soon went. Chatham succeeded, but insisted on creating a ministry that would be above the strife of faction. Unfortunately he went mad and whilst the King waited for

[1] See pp. 31–45.

him to recover, Charles Townshend pushed America further towards rebellion by his imposition of duties on imports; and so the sorry tale went on. Blunder followed blunder as ministries came and went; conciliatory moves pressed hard on the heels of firm, authoritative action. No one realized until it was too late that America was in the throes of a social revolution, stronger far than the similar movement in England, and one less hampered by tradition.

By the time George III found Lord North, the situation in America had become almost hopeless. North and George III have become the villains of the struggle for independence. Both were men of limited intelligence, no vision and little commonsense. George III knew his duty. The Americans must be made to obey for it was his sacred trust to pass on his empire unchanged and undivided to his heirs. So his policy was simple. Suppress the revolt; use force; do not negotiate. North, an adroit politician, fine debater and skilful administrator, lacked this simplicity of approach. He was a warm-hearted man, naturally timid, deeply loyal, above all, loyal to his King. He hated the war; indeed he longed to give up a situation for which he felt he lacked the abilities. He constantly hoped something would turn up—a victory, a chance of compromise, a change of heart. What he could not do was to give all his undivided energy to waging a ruthless war. As the sick and dying Chatham had long ago forecast, France and Spain seized their opportunity for revenge. And from the height of greatness, Britain plunged from defeat to despair.

North, too, had been hamstrung, not only by his own indecision and incompetence, but also by the noisy sympathy with America in England and by the growing opposition in Parliament. He was saved from defeat only by the steady support of the independent back-benchers, the self-elected country-gentlemen, whose attitude to Americans sprang from their hatred of change and reverence for tradition. Also they feared for Ireland. They had with difficulty held down that older land through the centuries; weakness to America would lead to weakness to Ireland, the loss of America to the loss of Ireland—so they feared. Nor were these fears groundless. And the terrible spectres of a break-up of Great Britain haunted the King's mind and jeopardized his sanity. So the squires supported George III and North to the sad, bitter end.

The majority of politicians whether in or out of the ministry knew little or nothing of America. The West Indies rather than the Northern Colonies were looked upon as the richest jewels of the empire. Exceptionally valuable, if kept in proper economic subjection; excellent producers of raw materials, most of them thought that the Northern Colonies might easily be a danger if allowed freedom of commerce and manufacture. Socially and politically difficult everyone knew them to be. They had been, for more than a century, the home of the discontented. The poverty-stricken malcontents from Scotland and Ireland had drifted there in droves, leavened only by religious bigots and fanatics. In one thing the colonies had proved convenient; they were admirable dumping grounds for thieves, whores, bankrupts and ne'er-do-wells. Many philanthropists cherished the strange idea that the socially incompetent would flourish in a harder environment. Only a few politicians knew the true state of America. A few, very few, had been there and even fewer had taken the trouble to learn of its economic and social problems.

This ignorance was in a sense natural. And so was the colonists' ignorance of British problems. Most resented the mother country and cared little about her struggle with France or Spain. As yet the great achievements in art, science and technology carried little weight, and did nothing to counterbalance the sense of subjection and the resentment of an alien rule.

If ignorant of Britain, the colonists were aware of their own vast opportunities. The new lands to the west called for an independent spirit and bred a sense of freedom and democracy. But, by and large, those who drifted across the Alleghenies left government and constitutional problems behind. Their only importance was to create an attitude of mind. Like Wilkes they became a symbol of freedom and liberty in the minds of those that grappled with the problems of government in the long-established colonies. To them they gave a sense of the limitless possibilities of America's future. And so did their own economic wealth. The colonists were making money hand over fist, at least in Boston and New York. They built excellent ships and trade boomed. The antiquated navigation laws could be evaded or the fines paid and Europe, the West Indies, the great Spanish Empire needed American goods. Tobacco, fur, timber, fish,

rice, sugar founded the fortunes of the great New England merchants. And yet they could not order their own world. A weak
currency put their financial system at the mercy of London; many,
particularly the tobacco factors, carried a mountain of debt partly
due to shortage of currency and the weakness of the dollar. And
although the commercial regulations could be evaded the need for
evasion itself created vast annoyance. Yet there were deeper resent-
ments. The richest offices—governorships, judgeships, registrars of
customs and excise—went to Englishmen, to brothers and cousins
of peers and politicians. Whatever patronage could be squeezed out
of America went to feed the system of privilege in England. Many
States kept up running feuds with the royal officials, creating every
possible difficulty about payment of salaries or respecting the
Crown's rights. Furthermore, most Americans knew themselves to
be remote and provincial. Their manners were as plain as their
living; birth and breeding meant less than success or wealth. And
yet they were entangled in a web of ancient and traditional economic
and social practices. Old privileges, old laws, planted obstacles to
their future greatness. Many felt the need to break free though few
guessed to what freedom might lead.

If the new spirit of the American colonies was little appreciated in
England, even fewer colonists realized that many Englishmen's
difficulties were in some ways similar to their own, for in England,
too, a new world was struggling to be born; a new industrial society,
freer, less privileged, more just and more democratic was the ardent
aspiration of the most forward-looking sections of society. The
success of the American revolt and the wild outburst of the French
Revolution did much to thwart their ambitions, so that when the
new industrial society did emerge in England, it still remained
encrusted in privilege and dominated by ancient practice. Ignorance,
lack of communication, and a sense of separate destinies kept the two
movements apart, which, if combined, might have changed the
destiny of mankind.

Chatham told Parliament that America could never be conquered
and he was right. British troops were too few, too unused to guerilla
warfare; they could not be properly supported with ammunition,
food and reinforcements. Communications were too slow; distances
too great; the opposition of France and Spain too strong. Defeat

followed defeat; no ally, not even the Dutch, came to Britain's aid. England plunged from the height of greatness. 'I wish,' wrote the Earl of Pembroke to his son in 1779, 'I was a Laplander, or anything but a Briton.'

The treatment of Wilkes and the obvious injustice of Parliamentary representation had led many to cry for reform long before the American revolt but now the chorus swelled. This crisis impelled all men to think of politics and to take a side. The magnificent oratory of Burke, of Charles James Fox and, above all, of Chatham, rang through the land, calling not only for an end to the war but for a change in government. All institutions were brought into disrepute; only the reformers gained. The American revolt forged a new attitude to monarchy, even in the aristocratic world; the whigs, led by Rockingham and Fox, came to believe that Kings should reign but no longer rule; that ministers should be chosen by the dominant party, not by the King. In 1782 the reluctant George III hesitated between abdication and compliance. He complied, and then outwitted his enemies; nevertheless the future belonged to Fox and Burke. And the constitutional concepts of parliamentary democracy of nineteenth-century England emerged from the struggle to defeat George III and North.

Indeed, out of this tragic combat both sides gained; the failure of the Crown and of aristocratic society was so complete that they never recovered their old powers. Indeed it so destroyed their own faith in themselves that the abnegation of their power to the middle-class, to the new men of the Midlands and the North who had acclaimed America's victories, became a matter of time. America acquired freedom, Britain moved towards a less privileged society. Furthermore, for the first time she was made to realize that empire was more than trade and riches but a complex problem of duties as well as rights.

In 1783 Britain was humiliated and isolated, the shadow of its former greatness, but victories and defeats in war fade quickly; the steady dynamic power of economic expansion and technological supremacy cannot be destroyed by the loss of territory or defeat at a diplomats' conference. In spite of George III, Lord North or America, the immediate future still lay with Britain; and for another hundred years she led mankind in its triumphant march towards a richer and juster world.

1957

GEORGE III

POOR George III still gets a bad press. In their famous television talk in London, the Prime Minister of Great Britain suggested to the President of the United States that the kind of colonial policy associated with the name of George III still distorted the American view of the nature and function of the British Empire, and Mr. Eisenhower smilingly agreed. It is not surprising. Since Jefferson's great philippic in the Declaration of Independence, few historians, English or American, have had many good words to say for him. True, he has been excused direct responsibility for many items of the catalogue of enormities that Jefferson went on to lay at his door, but to the ordinary man he remains one of England's disastrous kings, like John or the two Jameses.

Actually, as we shall see later on, toward the end of his life and immediately after it, his reputation improved, and even the writers of American school textbooks did not at first hold him personally responsible for the disasters that led to Independence. It was after the publication of Horace Walpole's *Memoirs* in 1845 that George III began to be blamed. Walpole's gossip appeared to give substance to Burke's allegations that the King deliberately attempted to subvert the British constitution by packing ministries and Parliament with his personal party—the King's friends—a collection of corrupt politicians bought with place and with pension.

Later historians held that these Tory incompetents, bent on personal government for their master, pursued a ruinous policy that ended only with the break-up of the first British Empire and a return of the Whigs to power. Historians reminded themselves not only of the disasters in America, but of the failure of parliamentary reform in England, of the oppressions of the Irish, the Catholics, the Dissenters; they remembered the treatment of radicals at the time of the French Revolution; they recalled the merciless suppression of trade unions; and the violent opposition to the abolition of slavery. It all added up to a huge indictment of George III and a magnificent justification for Whig doctrine. Here and there a scholar urged caution, but was little heeded. What the great historians formulated, the textbook writers cribbed. When English historians found so much to condemn, why should Americans lag behind? In 1954, two American historians—Leon Canfield and Howard Wilder—could write:

> In 1760, George III mounted the throne. A young man of twenty-two, he was unwilling to accept the idea that the King's power should be limited. His mother had always said to him: 'George, be King!' When he became ruler this obstinate young man put his mother's advice into swift action. He set out to get his way not by ignoring Parliament but by building up a personal following. He made free use of bribes and appointments, and presently the King's friends were strong in Parliament.
>
> The increase in royal power drove the wedge of misunderstanding deeper between England and the colonies.

In 1959, an English historical journalist, Jack Lindsay, was still writing in much the same vein. These views, however, are no longer fashionable. The greatest English historian of the eighteenth century, Sir Lewis Namier, hammered at them for thirty years. His friend, Romney Sedgwick, with a more caustic pen, has subjected them to ridicule in review after review, sinking his verbal darts into reputations as skilfully as a savage with his blowpipe. Professor Herbert Butterfield has not only traced the origins of the myths of George III's tyranny but also has shown how the now-fashionable view of George III was held by historians and textbook writers long, long ago—in the early nineteenth century. So the wheel has come full circle. Will it turn again? Or will blame and justification give way simply to understanding? Shall we at last have a balanced portrait of America's last king?

On one thing historians are agreed. To understand the part played by George III in the great tragedy of his reign, one must begin with the King's own personality, and with the environment in which he was reared. David and Absalom provided the pattern for kingly fathers and princely sons in the eighteenth century, except that most of the monarchs were less controlled than David. Peter the Great of Russia had his son Alexis executed—slowly and painfully. The Elector of Prussia, Frederick William, insisted that his son, whom he had kept in close confinement, watch the death of his dearest friend for what only a madman could call treason. So it is not surprising that George III's grandmother wished that her son, Frederick, father of George III, were in the bottommost pit of hell or that she became hysterical on her deathbed when she thought he might inherit some of her personal possessions. The Lord Chancellor had to be sent for to lull her fears.

George II's opinion of his own lacklustre son matched his wife's. He quite simply hated him as he had hated his own father, who, at one time, had put him under house arrest and removed his children. (It had required all the persuasive powers of the Cabinet to get him released.) This fantastic antagonism between father and son that went on from generation to generation found a situation in English politics that fitted it like a glove. The House of Commons always harboured a number of disappointed politicians who were so hated by the ministers in power that they had few prospects of immediate advancement. But as Sir Robert Walpole bluntly phrased it: 'Everybody who could get no ready money had rather have a bad promissory note than nothing.' So they made their court to the heir, who found them jobs in his household, and plotted the political changes that they would make when Father died. So throughout the century a Prince of Wales as soon as he was grown up became the leader of the Opposition. At times the Opposition made such a nuisance of itself that the monarch and his ministry decided to buy it off by giving jobs to the leaders, and then the astonished heir-apparent often found his friends deserting him with alacrity. This happened both to George III and to his father. The politics of hatred and the politics of betrayal, therefore, became a part of the environment of the adolescence and early manhood of the Hanoverian kings.

It was in an atmosphere of faction that George III was born; an environment that might have taxed the most gifted of men. Unfortunately George III was as unlucky in his heredity as in his environment. Neither George II nor his Queen, Caroline, was devoid of character or without some gifts above the commonplace. Her intelligence and his memory were unusual in monarchs, and their hatred of their son was tinged with genuine disappointment. Frederick, George III's father, was known to posterity as 'Poor Fred', and the epithet was not unjust. He possessed a small talent for music, a mild interest in games, particularly cricket, and little else. The unsympathetic Lord Shelburne described his life as a 'tissue of childishness and falsehood'; and his friends as well as his enemies despised him. George II married his son to Princess Augusta of Saxe-Gotha simply because there was no one else. The other Protestant princesses of sufficiently high birth had madness in their families, and George II rejected them, for as he said, 'I did not think ingrafting my half-witted coxcomb upon a madwoman would mend the breed.' As it turned out, it could not have made matters much worse, for an astonishing number of Princess Augusta's children and grandchildren turned out to be congenital idiots, or subject to fits of insanity, or mentally unbalanced, or blind; the rest were odd or wicked or both.

In some ways George III can be described as the best of the bunch. He was very stupid, really stupid. Had he been born in different circumstances it is unlikely that he could have earned a living except as an unskilled manual labourer. He was ten before he could read, and he never mastered grammar or spelling or punctuation. He was lethargic, apathetic, childish, a clod of a boy whom no one could teach. His major response to life was a doting love for his brother Edward. In late adolescence he began to wake up, largely because of a passionate romantic attachment to Lord Bute, the close friend and confidant of his mother.[1] Somehow Bute made the young prince conscious not only of his destiny but also of his shortcomings. The Prince promised time and time again to throw off his lethargy so that he could accomplish great things for Bute's sake. Naturally the greatest of things was to get rid of his grandfather's evil ministers and to install Bute in a position of power. The ill-spelt, ungrammatical, childish, heartfelt notes that he sent to Bute make pathetic

---

[1] The public at large thought she was his mistress. Probably she was not. The slander deeply distressed George III and made his attachment to Bute firmer.

reading. They are charged with a sense of inadequacy, a feeling of hopelessness before the immensity of the burden which destiny had laid on his shoulders, and with an anxious need for help that is almost neurotic in its intensity.

Every year his reverence for the concept of kingship grew stronger; nothing illustrates his regard more than his behaviour over Lady Sarah Lennox. This charming girl of fifteen swept him off his feet just before he succeeded to the throne. He longed to marry her. Bute said no, and George III wrote that 'he (i.e., Bute) has thoroughly convinced me of the impropriety of marrying a country woman; the interest of my country ever shall be my first care, my own inclinations shall ever submit to it.' And submit he did and married a dull, plain, German Protestant princess who bore him the huge family that was to plague his days.

A sexually timid, if nonetheless passionate man, George may have found it easier to take Bute's advice than many have thought. Lady Sarah attracted lovers as a candle moths, and George, conscious of his faults and of his inadequacies, must have realized that he cut a poor figure amidst *her* brilliant courtiers. His Queen, Charlotte, attracted no one. And yet sacrifice there was, and George paid for it. Shortly after his marriage he experienced his first bout of insanity. Later in life these periods of madness grew longer. It was only during these attacks that his thoughts escaped from his strict concept of marriage, and rioted in adultery. Then, and then only, was it unsafe for a lady of his court to be alone with him.

During these years of delayed adolescence George III learned, too, that kings had to make other sacrifices. Men powerfully backed in the Lords and Commons, and with an experience of a lifetime's politics behind them, could not easily be dismissed. The great Whig families had ruled since the Hanoverian accession in 1714. They had filled the court of the first Georges, monopolized the great offices of state, controlled the Cabinet, dominated the House of Lords, managed the Commons, and run the war with France which had lasted more or less for twenty years. The Duke of Newcastle, George II's Secretary of State, had held an important position in government since he had reached his majority. The Dukes of Devonshire took their high offices as if they belonged to them by hereditary right. Even the Whig career politicians, such as the Lord Chancellor Hardwicke, had been in power for so long that they had come to regard themselves as practically irreplaceable.

These men were not to be easily swept away and replaced by Bute; they possessed too much cunning, too much political experience, too many followers, whom they had gratified with places, who doubted Bute's capacity to survive. Time, however, was on George III's side. The greatWhig leaders were old men; indeed their party was known as the Old Corps. And in their long lives they had made plenty of enemies. They had disappointed some members of Parliament, made others impatient, and many disapproved of their policy. Chatham, that hawk-eyed man of destiny who had been responsible more than any other man for the sweeping English victories in the Seven Years War, deplored their caution, ignored their advice, and treated them, as one of his colleagues grumbled, 'as inferior animals'. And behind Chatham was the restless brood of Grenvilles, his relations by marriage—difficult, disloyal, able and ambitious men. There was yet another powerful group, led by the immensely rich Duke of Bedford, who thought it high time for the old Whigs to retire, and let them enjoy the rich pastures of court patronage.

The King's intentions, of course, were known to all these groups in 1760. His aversion to Newcastle and to Chatham, whom he labelled 'the blackest of hearts', was common court gossip. And after all, he was a young king with old ministers; many time-serving politicians thought that it might be wise to trim their sails and wait for the new breeze, from whatever quarter it might blow. Of course the old Whigs, and even Chatham, realized they had to accept Bute and somehow or other please the King, if they were to survive. They soon had the measure of Bute. He lacked a personal following, felt unequal to the supreme task of ruling the country and running the war. His dependable allies in the House of Commons were few. He faltered; he hesitated; he failed to force a showdown and kick out the old Whigs. True, Chatham resigned in a huff because, knowing the King's pacific sentiments, the Cabinet refused to go along with him and declare war on Spain and seize her trade. Instead, as Chatham forecast, Spain declared war on England.

But Chatham gone did little to strengthen Bute. By the end of January, 1763, the consummate skill of those hoary old politicians Newcastle and Hardwicke had so undermined Bute's confidence that he was little better than a nervous wreck. He told George III that even the Angel Gabriel would find it difficult to govern England; that his own life was rendered intolerable by infamous scenes and blackened by ingratitude and that he felt himself on the brink of a precipice. George III was too young, too inept, too unpractised in the arts of politics to help Bute, and so Bute resigned. George III tried to keep him as a private and secret adviser; the politicians would not let him. They grumbled, they nagged, they bullied. The King had to face his future on his own.

He was most reluctant to do so. Although peace had been achieved in 1763—he had ardently desired this—he soon found himself in the thick of problems which he felt were too vast for his poor comprehension. Yet he knew that the fate of his people and his Empire was *his* responsibility to God. He felt so young, so hopeless, so desperately in need of the help of someone who thought as he did on men and affairs yet was strong enough to force his will on the warring political factions. Although the old Whig empire had broken up under the strain of Chatham's resignation and the Treaty of Paris, yet the King found no stability. The King's necessity drove him back to Chatham. Chatham prided himself on being above party. The King's need, the nation's need, said Chatham, required men of ability, not politicians; sentiments that thrilled George III. But unfortunately Chatham's mental health was far from good, and no sooner had he become Prime Minister than the strain of office sent him off his head. He shut himself up, would speak to no one, and had his meals served through a trap door. The King waited and waited for him to recover for two long years, during which a leaderless ministry drove his country nearer to ruin. Chatham recovered only to resign and became a passionate supporter of the American cause and so, once more, the object of George III's hate. The ministries that followed earned neither the country's confidence nor the King's.

Thus the first ten years of George III's reign passed in political chaos; slowly, however, he learned the devious ways of politics, the price of men, and above all the necessity for a man who could manage the Commons in *his* interest. In 1770 he discovered Lord North, the eldest son of the Earl of Guilford; North, whose association with the King was to prove so disastrous for England

and so fortunate for America, was an odd character. An excellent administrator, a witty and practised debater, full of good humour and charm, he always pleased and soothed the members of the Commons; nevertheless his soft, fat, rounded body and full, piglike face bespoke an indolence that bordered on disease, a physical incapacity that made his laborious days an intolerable burden on his spirit. Time and time again he begged the King to release him from office. The King would not, for North reverenced as he did the mystical power of monarchy and thought as he did on the two grave political problems which vexed his country—Wilkes and America.

Without North, he could see only ruin for himself and his people. The constantly changing ministries and the bitter factional strife of George III's first ten years had bedevilled both problems. John Wilkes, wit, libertine, master tactician, raised fundamental issues concerning the liberty of the British subject. None of the cases in which he was involved was clear-cut; in each the ministerial cause was handled with massive ineptitude. Wilkes divided the Whig groups in Parliament as effectively as he united the discontented in London. George hated 'that devil Wilkes', and let this hatred be known to all and sundry. Thus Wilkes's supporters could talk of royal despotism and get others to believe them. In America Wilkes's name became a byword for liberty and for resistance to royal tyranny from Boston down the seaboard to Charleston.

America proved a greater problem than Wilkes; and the effect of ministerial changes far worse. After the great war with France which, through the Treaty of Paris, deprived her of Canada, the majority of Englishmen, and, indeed, many colonists, felt that some of the expenses of the conflict should be borne by the Americans. Each ministry from 1760–70 differed in its views as to how this should be done, and each had a separate solution for assuaging the bitterness aroused in the Americans by the inept attempts to get revenue. Acts passed by one ministry were repealed by its successor, and party manoeuvre became more important than the fate of America. Nor was it a question of revenue alone that infuriated the colonists—the British constantly betrayed their ignorance of American needs and American aspirations. They tried to restrict settlement beyond the Allegheny Mountains, took Indian affairs into their own hands, attempted to suppress paper currency, renovated oppressive customs laws, and restricted trade with the West Indies. No Englishman realized that the American colonists were moving toward a rapid expansion in trade, wealth and power, just as no American could conceive of the huge expense of war that arose from Britain's vast imperial connections.

By the late 1760's, hope for compromise was probably a delusive dream of men of goodwill such as Chatham and Franklin. But whether it had a chance or not, there can be no doubt that the known attitude of the King made matters worse. George III revered, naturally enough, the concept of kingship. Kings were God's immediate servants. Their duties were clear—to pass on all the rights, obligations, powers, territories, undiminished, to their heirs. The constitution was sacrosanct and unchangeable. And so absolutely did George III identify himself with the English Crown that any criticism of monarchical powers, any suggestion of reform or change, he regarded as a personal affront.

The King was so stupid that he could not distinguish between himself as a person and his constitutional position as a ruler. Although he accepted the American policies—either of compromise or coercion—with which his ministers presented him, placing his signature first on the Stamp Act and then on its repeal, his heart was always with the physical-force party, and he moved with uttermost reluctance to the idea of compromise, which, he thought, would infuriate as well as ruin Britain.[1] Those politicians, therefore, who were prepared to bring the 'American rebels', as the King called them, to their senses were the recipients of his warmhearted loyalty and devotion. In the small world of English political society, the King's views did not go for nothing. He was the fountain of patronage, the ultimate executive authority, the man who could make and break ministers and ministries. In consequence, the King's

---

[1] As may be seen from his letter to North of January 31, 1776: 'You will remember that before the recess, I strongly advised you not to bind yourself to bring forward a proposition for restoring tranquillity to North America, not from any absurd ideas of unconditional submission my mind never harboured; but from foreseeing that whatever can be proposed, will be liable, not to bring America back to a sense of attachment to the Mother Country, yet to dissatisfy this Country, which has in the most handsome manner cheerfully carried on the contest, and therefore has a right to have the struggle continued, until convinced that it is in vain.'

D

attitude began to polarize new attitudes in politics. He became the symbol of conservatism and reaction; his opponents, the men who thought that the liberties for which Wilkes and the Americans fought were essential, too, for all Englishmen, began to take a more radical attitude not only to the Crown but also to the very structure of English society. Naturally, the first effect of this was to disrupt the old political alignments; Whiggery began to break up into two groups, a right and a left wing; the Tories, who had been in opposition since 1714, now felt that they could support George III body and soul. It took many years for these new forces to push their way through into public consciousness, redefined, but George III's own personality—his meddling interference and his blind, obstinate conservatism—sharpened many men's intention to reduce the powers of the Crown even further.

The first twenty years of George III's reign were a public and a personal failure. He had done his duty conscientiously. He had tried, according to his lights, to put the government in the hands of tried and able men. The ills which assailed his country, he sincerely believed, were not of his making. Scarcely a man pitied him; the majority thought he had only himself to blame when disaster came. Yorktown ended his hopes that the tide might turn, and finished North.

During the long years of British defeat, the heirs of the Old Corps of Whigs, now led by the Marquess of Rockingham, had developed a new view of the role of kingship; and their great publicist and philosopher, Edmund Burke, had persuasively pleaded for a new attitude to party and to politics. When, at last, the failures in America led the independent members of the Commons to desert North, and thereby compelled the King to send for Rockingham to take over the reins of government, George III found Rockingham's terms hard to accept: freedom for America, peace with France, and, hardest of all, no say in the appointment of his ministers, which he regarded as the darling prerogative of the Crown.

The King, despite himself, now had to accept what the Whigs offered him—a revolutionary action that cut at the root of royal power. He had been broken by forces that his poor brain could not understand. And, perhaps not without justice, he was held to blame for England's defeat in America by contemporaries in both countries, and by generations of historians, though justice would also demand that the shortsighted, quarrelsome, ignorant, power-seeking politicians who had made policy toward America as changeable as the British climate should be held equally responsible. We, at least, can feel pity for him—ignorant, stupid, conscientious, prejudiced, a victim of his own inadequate temperament. Had George III died or abdicated in 1782, his reign would have been one of the most wretched in English history and he one of the greatest failures to sit on the English throne.

Twenty years later, hatred had turned to admiration. His foibles were forgiven; his prejudices respected; his inadequacies tolerated. The reasons, as before, were partly personal, partly public. Once peace was achieved with America and France, the sense of crisis passed and the need to invade royal prerogatives became less urgent. And the Rockingham Whigs overplayed their hand. George III hated these men with all the stubborn obstinacy of his nature. He was determined to get rid of them, and he would grant them nothing in the way of favours and honours. Desperate, they attempted to remodel the government of India so that they, and not the King, could exploit its patronage, and so be able to gratify their friends without dependence on royal favour. Their rivals saw their chance. The King, who had learned the game of party politics, dismissed them. Now he took the bravest step of his life. He exercised his royal prerogative and sent for William Pitt, aged twenty-four, to be his Prime Minister—a breathtaking choice. Only a stupid, insensitive man could have taken such a risk.

Pitt proved a fabulously able politician—adroit, wise, cool. He ignored his initial defeats in the Commons, planned a general election with meticulous care so that every ounce of government and royal influence would be deployed to his maximum advantage, and goaded his opponents into such extravagant attitudes that they alienated not only men of goodwill but also the electorate. The election result was overwhelmingly in favour of Pitt. For the next sixteen years Pitt managed his king with ease and handled the House of Commons with brilliance. At last George III's long search was really over. He had found a Prime Minister whom he and the nation could safely trust.

No sooner was Pitt solidly established than the French Revolution plagued England with war for a generation, and the Crown became a symbol of unity and resistance. Tribulations, disasters, defeats, high taxation, starvation, repression, visited the land; but no one, not the most prejudiced radical, could hold George III responsible; age and sickness had lifted him beyond the day-to-day struggle of parliamentary politics. It was, however, the King's personal life that turned the hatred which the public felt for him in 1780, to pity if not love.

The King wobbled on the verge of madness. His rapid manner of speaking—a torrent of questions to which he rapidly supplied the answers[1]—and his extreme restlessness were the physical expressions of a deep-seated excitation. Fortunately he lived a quiet, domestic life, and his farming and love of music helped to calm his spirit. Apart from a short attack just after his marriage, he remained sane until 1788 when he got out of his coach in Windsor Park and addressed an oak tree as his talented cousin, Frederick the Great of Prussia. From this moment the King began to talk faster and faster. At one point he talked for twenty-four hours without stopping; sleep seemed impossible for him. The Prince of Wales was sent for. The King tried to throttle him. He was put in a strait jacket. His death was hourly expected. The Prince, fully dressed and wearing his decorations, awaited the moment of his accession for two days and nights.

The King did not, however, die. He then slowly recovered to the horrifying spectacle of his heir quarrelling with his ministers about who should control the prerogatives of the Crown. He was never the same; his eccentricities were more pronounced than ever. He talked more, listened less, and grew frenzied if a difficult political problem, such as emancipation of Roman Catholics from their civil disabilities, was mentioned to him. He regarded these restrictions on the faith of the Stuarts as a sacred trust and thought the Almighty

[1] This was brilliantly pilloried by Peter Pindar in the *Louisiad*:
> 'How, how? what, what?—what's that, what's that?' he cries
> With rapid accent and with staring eyes.
> 'Look there, look there—what's got into my house?
> A louse, God bless us! Louse, louse, louse, louse, louse.'

The occasion was a louse dropping from a page on to the King's dinner plate at Buckingham Palace.

would destroy him, his progeny and his country if he failed to maintain them. But he meddled less in affairs. He could not concentrate sufficiently on day-to-day business, and he was forced to give Pitt a far freer hand than he had ever allowed anyone in the past. The public knew this, and so the greatest obstacle to his popularity was removed. Also, it had found another scapegoat.

At the time of Wilkes and the war in America, George III was blamed for all the ills that beset his empire; now it was his son's turn. The Prince of Wales, afterwards George IV, was a handsome, florid, reckless, extravagant, self-indulgent man of uncertain taste in women and architecture. Alternatively pampered and cursed, he had been kept like a child without a separate income or establishment and subject to the cheese-paring dreariness of the royal household until he was twenty-one. Warmhearted, uninhibited and devoid of common sense, the Prince naturally erupted dramatically into social and political life the moment he found release. At once he consorted with the King's enemies, particularly Charles James Fox, a man who was generous to a fault, utterly dissolute, profoundly witty, obsessed with gambling, soaked in alcohol, and indestructibly radical. The Prince's and Fox's friendship ripened in 1783 when Fox was doing his best to strip the King of his most cherished prerogative—the personal choice of his servants. This, of course, intensified the King's grief and rage.

His agony was increased by the Prince's sexual behaviour. The King was a very prudish man and intensely moral. The Prince was seen in the arms of an actress—the beautiful Perdita Robinson. Worse horrors followed. The Prince fell overwhelmingly in love with a Roman Catholic widow—Mrs. Fitzherbert. He worshipped her and married her. Although the marriage might be valid in the eyes of God, it was an empty ceremony according to the law of the land, which Mrs. Fitzherbert well knew. No sooner accomplished, the act scared the Prince. He denied it to everyone including Fox but the rumour intensified and spread, and the King, to whom Roman Catholics were a frightening bogey, was driven nearly out of his few remaining wits.

The Prince was as much of a wanton with his money as with his love. He adored building and grew infatuated with interior decoration. At Brighton he began to create the fabulous Pavilion—a nightmare of a building that combined eighteenth-century elegance with oriental fantasy. His London home, Carlton House, swallowed tens of thousands of pounds with the ease of a vacuum cleaner. The King was an intensely frugal man; the Prince's debts grew astronomic; his creditors became frantic, and the infuriated King was forced to pay them. The Prince consorted with the Whig radicals, fornicated with Catholics, and spent money like water. And George III's other sons turned out no better than their brother—indeed most of them were worse, for America's last princes were a fabulous brood.

All but one of this royal crew—Cambridge—were warmhearted, honest, generous to a fault. And there their virtues ended. York, a good soldier, connived at his mistress—a demimondaine called Clarke—selling army commissions like a broker; his debts, considering his prospects, overtopped the Prince of Wales's. Clarence lived in ostentatious sin with Mrs. Jordan, a second-rate actress, who had to make tours of provincial theatres to keep the home together for the ten little FitzClarences. Kent caused a mutiny through his sadistic brutality, lived for twenty-seven years with his French-Canadian mistress, repudiated her, married, begot Queen Victoria, and became a socialist to irritate the royal family, who would not pay his debts. Sussex was given to absurd marriages; Cambridge was merely bleak, mean to the point of mania, and mildly eccentric in behaviour. Cumberland was the most unsavoury of them all. The public believed that his valet had attempted to murder him because of indecent assault, and that he had a child by his sister. Neither was true.

Some of these antics George III never heard about, but his last years of sanity, when he lived in a strange twilight world between reality and fantasy, were rendered pitiful and tragic—at least in the public's eyes—by the wanton behaviour of his children. And undoubtedly they added an intolerable strain to a mind that had weakened under the burdens which had proved too great for it.

In 1811, America's last king went irrevocably mad. For nine years he roamed his palace, a pathetic figure in his purple dressing gown, with wild white hair and beard, blind, deaf, a Lear-like figure playing to himself on his harpsichord and talking, talking, talking of men and women long since dead.

Yet the last twenty years had changed the nation's view of its

King—half sane or mad though he might be. The people realized that he had tried within the narrow limits of his capacity to discharge the duties and obligations of kingship; that his faults, which were grievous, sprang from the best of intentions. He had succeeded to wide dominions, which he held to be a sacred trust. In his simpleminded way he could not believe that any provocation could excuse the terrible treason of the Americans who tried to break up what God had so obviously joined together and put under his rule.

As it had been with America, so with Wilkes, so with Ireland, so with his children. His motives were honourable; he gave all of his pitifully small abilities to the defence of what he thought to be the vital interests and essential rights of the British nation. Had he been as wise as Solomon, Britain and America would have gone their separate ways. The forces that crushed him would have crushed greater men. As it is, he remained a pathetic figure of tragicomedy; and, as the years passed, he acquired even a certain grandeur. There had been many worse kings to exercise rule over America and Britain. If he is to be blamed, it must be not for what he did but for what he was—an unbalanced man of low intelligence. And if he is to be praised, it is because he attempted to discharge honourably tasks that were beyond his powers.

1960

A CONSCIENTIOUS BULL
IN A CHINA SHOP

HISTORIANS know that what is taught earliest is the most difficult to eradicate. Indeed the myths and legends learnt in the nursery seem to be indestructible. But that doesn't really matter very much. The stories of Canute and the waves or Raleigh and his cloak are not dangerous. They do not distort in any essential way our knowledge of the past. But there are distortions especially in political and diplomatic history which can be dangerous.

It is with one of the common distortions of the eighteenth century history with which I wish to deal—a misconception which is to be found in almost all textbooks, although academic historians have been attacking it for the last thirty years and replacing it by a subtler and more realistic picture. But although I shall be primarily concerned with the early years of George III's reign yet the principles involved are of great importance for rightly understanding British political history. For generations historians have regarded the two party system as one of the clues to the smooth and orderly progress of parliamentary government. They have argued that since the Civil War there has been a party in favour of rapid social and constitutional development—namely the Whigs who became the Liberals of the nineteenth century—and another, the Tories, who were primarily concerned to preserve the great traditions of English life which naturally made them favour a slower progress. And they think that the explanations of our constitutional and political history are to be found in the conflicts and compromises of these two parties.

1760 is a critical date for this theory. From 1715 the taint of Jacobitism had prevented the Tory party from playing its true part in politics. In fact there had been great danger in the reigns of the first two Georges of the development of a single party system of government. This danger was averted by the accession of George III —and now I am going to give the usual account which is to be found in textbooks and general histories. George III, they maintain, had been brought up on a diet of high Tory doctrine—principally Bolingbroke's *Patriot King*—and he was urged by his mother and her empty-headed Tory friend, Lord Bute, to reassume those royal prerogatives which had been in abeyance since the seventeenth century. George III, they say, followed this advice. Naturally he could not do this unaided. He needed friends and he found them amongst the Tories who were naturally sympathetic to the Crown and its prerogatives. Therefore the early years of his reign witnessed —and now I quote from a leading, widely used textbook—'the able attempt of George III to recover the powers of the Crown . . . to make the Prime Minister a mere instrument of royal will, and to reduce the cabinet to a group of King's servants in fact as well as in name'. And so by these means George III brought to an end the long rule of the Whig aristocracy and rebuilt the Tory party. But the Whigs, and principally their great philosopher Burke, were alive to the true principles of constitutional liberty and realized the menace of this revival of royal power. As the government tottered from disaster to disaster, from the follies of its handling of Wilkes's case to the graver follies of its policy towards the revolt of the American colonies, Parliament at last awoke to the sense of its own and the nation's peril and passed the famous motion of Dunning that 'the power of the Crown has increased, is increasing, and ought to be diminished'. The subsequent fall of Lord North, the manager of the King's friends, enabled Burke's patron, Rockingham, to lead the Whigs back into power. They reformed the Royal Household by curtailing its patronage and so put an end for ever to royal interference with the orderly development of parliamentary government. But although the King himself was checked, the revived Tory party continued to play its full part in political life and the dangers of an oligarchy based on a single party were averted. Indeed in the younger Pitt the Tory party produced a statesman of the first magnitude.

This conception of George III's early years is no parody—

every year sees it served up afresh yet the attack on it began as long as twenty-five years ago when Sir Lewis Namier produced his brilliant analysis of *The Structure of Politics at the Accession of George III*. Others in articles and monographs have helped to clear away the misrepresentation and confusions of earlier historians, but a work of major importance has recently been published by Namier and Professor Pares in which the new ideas about George III and his politics have been carefully worked out.

Namier's contribution is of exceptional importance. He goes straight to the heart of the matter, although he does not deal specifically with the accession of George III but with the broad structure of eighteenth century politics. Now the heart of the matter is this— what misled earlier historians was the attempt to make eighteenth century politics fit their pattern of a two party political system and see it as a struggle between the Whigs and Tories. If the Whigs in power controlled George II, then naturally the opposition principles which George III heard as a boy were Tory principles. Having turned out the Whigs after his accession, he naturally tried to replace them by Tories. So really the kernel of the old view which I outlined earlier is, as I said, this idea of a two party political system.

Now Namier showed quite conclusively that by 1760 the names Whig and Tory—at least at the centre of politics—had ceased to correspond to the reality of political groupings. 'In fact,' he wrote, 'by 1750 everyone at Court, in office, and in the centre arena was a Whig, while the name of Tories, by a process of natural selection, was left to the residuum who did not enter politics in pursuit of office, honours or profits, that is, the country gentleman and to the forerunners of the urban radicals.' But even these Tories did not behave as an opposition party—sometimes they supported ministries, sometimes they opposed them, often these independents were divided. In fact independents is a far better name for them than Tories, but one fact is clear about them, they were not the men amongst whom George III sought for his friends and ministers. Their influence on the politics of their time may be profound but they were never considered as having the weight or strength to provide a ministry. Ministries were drawn both before and after 1760 from the Whigs, an almost meaningless label which covered a medley of groups and factions; clusters of men associated by ties of blood, friendship, self-interest and occasionally ideas, who hunted together for office and place, usually under the leadership of a nobleman of great fortune and wide territorial power. Their quarry was office and power but the hunt was arduous and bitter and the heats and animosities which it engendered often divided them more absolutely than questions of public policy.

But from 1715 there were always more Whigs than places, there were Whigs 'in' place and Whigs 'out' of place and this is the true dichotomy of eighteenth century politics, for those who were out, knew from Robert Walpole's example in 1717, that their best chance of getting 'in' was to make the maximum nuisance of themselves. Either that, or to gather round the heir-apparent at Leicester House, spending their days in splenetic denunciation of those dark factions who kept George II a prisoner—for they always presumed that it was the malice of their enemies and not the King who kept them from office. Or they raised their hopes by drawing up a shadow cabinet. For such politicians out of office, Bolingbroke had written his *Patriot King*, full of felicitous platitudes to sustain the altruism of the dispossessed. Whether George III read this book or not is quite irrelevant, but certainly he grew up familiar with its orthodox opposition commonplaces. But these were no more Tory than the politicians who uttered them. Bute, the much maligned Bute, came from unimpeachable Whig stock. Oppositions as well as ministries were principally Whig. Whatever happened between 1760–80 it was not the replacement of Whigs by Tories; the structure of politics remained the same.

Under the attack of Namier and Pares the old two party explanation of eighteenth century politics has been destroyed. Having been found wanting in this period, naturally other historians have subjected the two party theory to a very close scrutiny. Everywhere it is being found less adequate—in the seventeenth as well as the nineteenth centuries; for historians now realize that political parties need a continuity of organization and discipline if they are to achieve coherence and stability. But party organization and party discipline are very recent inventions. In the less coherent politics of the past— loyalty to friends or relations, hopes of preferment, the pursuit of power, all acquired a larger significance and may have had a greater effect on political behaviour than a man's attitude to public policy. Certainly the new outlook on political history is both more realistic and more subtle than the older simplicities. But it has its dangers. Some men hold inflexibly to a social attitude—particularly those not subject to temptation. So that the further one gets away from the Court, or Parliament, the more valid the old conception of two parties seems to be.

But to return to George III. What of the Whig historians' contention that George III tried to increase the powers of the Crown? Did he try to dominate the Whig factions with whom he had to work in a way which would have seemed alien to his grandfather? To the first part of this question there is unanimous agreement that he did not. Pares, in this brilliant book of his,[1] analyses with infinite care the constitutional behaviour of the king, and he shows that his behaviour was consistent with what the majority of politicians believed to be the true practice of the Crown. If anyone held revolutionary constitutional opinions it was Edmund Burke and Charles Fox, not George III. This, of course, is a most radical change of view for Burke has always been regarded as the greatest exponent of traditional constitutional principles. But Pares's case is unanswerable. In the eighteenth century, unlike the late nineteenth, politicians expected the Crown to play an active part in administration. Pares however does stress that there was a difference between 1759 and 1760 and a fundamental one. In 1759 the King was seventy-seven. He was a tired old man who, even when young, had been easily overborne by his ministers. Whereas George III, young, naïve, ill-educated as he was when he came to the throne, rapidly developed into a man of formidable obstinacy with an appetite for the detail of political life. Nor was he afraid to let his ministers know just where he stood on the great issues in which his governments were soon involved. Because the activity of the King became more obvious, the charge of Burke and Fox of his unconstitutional behaviour acquired greater prominence and which, of course, has made it easier for subsequent generations to believe it. And because of this Pares writes: 'It is more profitable to argue that the constitutional doctrines of Fox and Burke were newer, and less well formed in history, than those of George III. Yet even here, one can

[1] R. Pares: *King George III and the Politicians* (Oxford, 1953).

see how the King came to be considered as the innovator. He may have claimed no right that his grandfather had not claimed, but he exercised, in his prime, rights which his grandfather had not exercised in old age. I do not see how anybody can believe that George III's relations with North were the same as George II's relations with the Pelhams. . . . The differences were personal, but the constitutional history of this country . . . is made up of personal differences.' So that is Pares's answer—no fundamental change in political structure, no break in constitutional development, no change from Whig to Tory, what difference there is between the 1750's and 1760's is, for him, in the nature of the monarch who ruled.

Now, I doubt whether Namier would go so far as this, and he would probably have the support of other scholars in taking the view that George II was not so malleable a character as Pares assumes; but it is a question of emphasis; obviously the nature of the two men must have counted in a system of politics which still allowed the monarch such freedom of action.

Little remains of the old view which I sketched at the beginning of this talk but it seems to me that the picture is still not complete. The change in the personality of the monarch cannot explain everything. In dealing with a closed system of politics it is so easy to forget the effects of great public events or to underestimate the influence of public opinion. Even the most rigid dictatorships are susceptible to these processes and the eighteenth century political system was far from rigid. Indeed within it there was an important body that was susceptible to public opinion and world events. When the independent country gentleman lost confidence in Lord North and his handling of the American problem his ministry came to an end.

These independents were always likely to be swayed by public opinion, but as yet we know little about them but we shall—for Namier has them very much on his mind.

Personally I feel that the influence of public opinion has been underestimated and that the new view of George III's reign as yet gives too little prominence to the policies pursued by his ministries and the great public hostility that they aroused. The 1750's and 1760's may have differed in the personality of their monarchs but there was also a greater difference. In the 1750's the country was waging a successful war; French commerce had been destroyed; the prospects for English wealth immeasurably increased. The 1760's witnessed what seemed to many a disastrous peace; and whether disastrous or not it certainly brought what peace is apt to bring—retrenchment, unemployment, discontent.

This discontent was fed, firstly by the inept handling by the government of the Wilkes crisis and secondly by the rapid worsening of relations with America. And the discontent was widespread. The Liverpool press is as full of Wilkes and his fight for liberty as that of London. In Great Yarmouth Sylas Neville and his friends discussed the virtues of a republic and refused to call George III King. Everywhere the institutions of government were falling into disrepute. Patronage and racketeering are tolerable in victory or prosperity, but defeat breeds a desire for political morality. And even the most place-conscious politician is sensitive to the mood of a people. He may deliberately ignore it, but he cannot be unaware of it. And the consciousness that they had wide public sympathy may have strengthened the resolution of some, even perhaps Burke or Fox, in their opposition to the Crown.

The subtle interactions of a closed system of politics based on patronage and the response of society to political issues remain to be explored. But the crisis which marked the reign of George III may yet be found to lie in events and the public response to them rather than in the constitution or the political system. But of one thing we can be certain—it is far remote from any royal conspiracy to increase the prerogative and dish the Whigs. And it certainly cannot be explained in simple terms of a struggle between Whig and Tory.

This problem of George III and the constitution has been closely scrutinized by a formidable number of exceptionally able scholars but that is not fortuitous. A correct appraisal of the political system of these years is essential for a proper understanding of the development of parliamentary government and constitutional monarchy. But it has an even wider context which I've kept to the end, and possesses a significance far greater than the narrowness of the subject would seem to imply.

We now know that Burke's denunciations of royal tyranny and royal corruption were false but many contemporaries believed them, particularly Americans. And Burke's dogmas were used to explain why the rift between the American colonies and the mother country became so wide and unbridgeable. The responsibility for the misunderstanding, indeed for the conflict itself, was explained by the arrogance and obstinacy of George III. True, he cannot be acquitted entirely of responsibility but unfortunately hatred of George III has been used to forward the theory that British imperialism is always reactionary, high-handed and essentially Tory. This theory you will find reiterated in countless American school textbooks. It has done much to foster suspicion of British motives, and often with most dangerous results, for as the editors of *History Today* have so wisely pointed out, 'It may be plausibly argued that the intense distrust of British imperialism, which animated President Roosevelt and some of his advisers, and contributed greatly to their desire to appease Russia in 1944–45—contrary to British advice— was founded on their memory of American school textbooks in which British "imperialism" had been the free world's principal enemy.' And all the false history of the last hundred years has helped to strengthen this fundamental misunderstanding, so that it is not surprising that in the world of modern diplomacy the ghost of the Tory tyrant, George III, still walks abroad.

That ghost is now well and truly laid, banished by brilliant academic scholarship which has re-created in its full human reality the political world in which George III lived and ruled. The academic work is nearly complete but its influence is only just beginning to undermine the dogmas of ancient prejudice.

1953

THE GRAND TOUR

BEFORE the end of the seventeenth century, education in England, as elsewhere in Europe, was confined to a narrow compass. At a very tender age gentlemen's sons were boarded out with a country parson to learn their letters, their numbers and the rudiments of Latin grammar—like Robert Walpole, the future Prime Minister of England, who was sent away from home at the age of four. Holidays were sparse—a few days at Christmas and a month at harvest time. At nine or ten the children left the vicarage for the grammar school in the neighbouring county town where they boarded with the master. There they rubbed shoulders with local tradesmen's sons. They dressed alike and spoke the same dialect; in those days a difference in social rank did not inhibit close social intercourse. At adolescence their ways tended to part: the shopkeeper's son went to his apprenticeship, the gentleman's son left for the university or the Inns of Court to acquire that extra knowledge of religion and law that his station required. After two or three years at Oxford and Cambridge (and if his home were distant, there he stayed without a holiday), he returned to help his father with his estate. Apart from a rare visit to London and a more frequent one to the local metropolis—York, Bristol, Norwich, Exeter—his travelling days were over. He lived and died in his neighbourhood. And this, with few variations, was the pattern of education throughout North-Western Europe; it differed only for a few aristocrats attached to courts. Sir Philip Sidney was granted a passport to complete his education abroad, to perfect his languages, and to familiarize himself with different nations and governments so that he might be trained to play a part in the affairs of state. Sometimes a likely youth, noticed by a statesman, would be sent to a foreign university to be trained for a career in public administration. But generally governments regarded foreign travel as dangerous: Protestant states feared the wiles of Romish priests might corrupt their young, Catholic ones dreaded the contact with heresy.

By 1700 all this had changed. The grammar schools and universities were no longer crowded with gentlemen's sons; indeed they were emptying fast (Christ's College, Cambridge, had only three freshmen in 1733, and many of its rooms were deserted). Shopkeepers preferred the new education provided by private enterprise, the schools and academies which taught book-keeping, languages, geography, navigation—the arts necessary for commercial life; gentlemen sent their sons abroad on a Grand Tour. By 1720, no Englishman or German pretending to a place in society could expect to be regarded as anything but a country bumpkin unless he had spent two or three years in France or Italy. The aristocracy of Scandinavia and Russia quickly followed suit. The effect was to give a remarkable homogeneity of manners and taste to the nobility of eighteenth-century Europe.

The reasons for this change are clear and simple. The ferocity of religious conflict had been assuaged by the growing sophistication of the educated classes. True, barbarities were still perpetuated in the name of God. States, however, had grown confident of their abilities to impose the religion of their choice upon their subjects and the seventeenth century witnessed an ending of religious strife which was also civil. The disruptive powers of religion were no longer acute. The spread of philosophy, the cult of a rational deity and rational universe which became at the same time fashionable amongst the upper classes, made parents fear less the dangers their sons' souls might encounter from a sojourn abroad. Furthermore, North-Western Europe was growing rich on the fat commercial profits which the New Worlds, East and West, had brought into being. Sugar, tobacco, slaves and spices made the guineas jingle in the pockets of nobleman and merchants from Bristol to Hamburg. Rich, they were also raw. Italians, and even Frenchmen, were aware of their magnificent heritage from the ancient world. Buildings of beauty still greeted them either in decay or in ruin. Scientists, philosophers, historians, poets all proclaimed the greatness of *their*

E

past. But the English, the Germans, the Russians, the Scandinavians possessed no ancient glory. A broken military wall, an arch here and there merely proclaimed their ancient slavery to Rome. Apart from these, they possessed only what their age professed to regard as barbarous—the great Gothic cathedrals and the vast castles of their immediate feudal past. Their nations had grown up outside the pale of culture; they belonged to Europe's remoter provinces, to its frontiers with the outer world. They knew themselves to be uncouth. And this had been made even more self-evident to them by the splendours of the court of Louis XIV.

At Versailles Louis had created a world of sophisticated, aristocratic grandeur. His palace was vaster than any that had been built since the days of Imperial Rome. His painters and his poets constantly harked back in their pictures and their dramas to the glories of the Roman Empire, hinting that in Louis and in France, Europe had at last found an equal to the magnificence of Augustus and his age. The classical world, either in its reflection in the Italian Renaissance or in its own right, entranced Europe. No gentleman worthy of the name could be unfamiliar with the writers of antiquity, and Latin tags were bandied about in the House of Commons, the Virginia Assembly, and the Polish Diet. And throughout Europe developed the feeling that at last the long centuries of barbarism were over, and that life could be lived with that elegance combined with dignity which was the hallmark of Roman gentility. Louis XIV had achieved far more than a mere imitation of imperial grandeur. He had developed the arts of war and diplomacy to an efficiency which no other kingdom could rival, although all desired to do so. Soldiers and ambassadors in embryo could learn their trades only in France. And it was the only place where a nobleman could learn to live according to his station; there he could discover how an aristocrat should eat, dress, dance, converse, love and fight. Yet France itself was not sufficient: taste could be properly formed only by a visit to the fountainhead of antiquity itself—Italy. Some even considered Italy superior to France in teaching the young nobleman how to make love.

To learn manners, to learn the only trades open to an aristocrat— war and diplomacy—to learn the culture of his class made a Grand Tour a necessity for the young English or German peer. Fortunately the new wealth that was seeping into Europe enabled him to afford what was the most expensive form of education ever devised by European society. The young nobleman resided abroad usually for three, but often for four, and at times even five years. More often than not he was accompanied by two tutors: one for bookish study, the other for riding, fencing, the arts of war. Often the former were men of distinction—Adam Smith, the economist, accompanied the Duke of Buccleuch; William Coxe, the historian, tutored Lord Herbert. Usually one personal servant was taken from England, the others hired as necessary. The grandest people shipped their own coaches, but the enterprising hotelier, Monsieur Dessin of Calais, ran a highly profitable coach-hire business and had a virtual monopoly of it.

Usually the Tour started very modestly with a stay in a French provincial town, preferably where the English were few, so that the boy was forced to speak French. Strasbourg, Dijon, Lyons were favoured because they afforded convenient places for short tours to Germany and Switzerland. Others preferred the towns in the Touraine because the purest French was spoken there. A boy's day was meticulously regulated. William Coxe was instructed to make 'a return of the occupations of every day in the week and at what hours' to the Earl of Pembroke. Both Coxe and Captain Floyd, young Lord Herbert's second tutor, and the boy himself had to give an account of themselves on the first, tenth and twentieth of every month. The young man's hours of riding, fencing, dancing, tennis and billiards were as keenly regulated as his mathematics, history and geography. He was ordered to a dentist twice a year, commanded to take a purge of camomile tea every morning before eating, and to have the tips of his hair trimmed on the second day of every new moon. This vigorous, almost remorseless system could be kept up only whilst the boy was young, the society in which he moved alien and strange, and the tutors still in awe of the noble father at home. Paris with its salons and sophistication usually proved irresistible and the tutors' resistance easily overcome.

Paris either entranced or disappointed; the incurable Anglophiles saw it as a meaner, shabbier London, but the majority were delighted by the clean streets, brilliant lighting and the lovely royal gardens designed by Le Nôtre; gardens made for elegant lounging and discreet flirtation. Here the young Englishmen, Germans and Russians came to gape at fashion and to grow accustomed to the new French clothes it was *de rigueur* to buy on arrival in Paris. Even Dr. Johnson, who made his Grand Tour very late in life, gave up his brown fustian and went into silk and lace the day he arrived. Naturally the wellborn were amply provided with introductions to aristocratic circles and usually they were presented at Court. Weeks of balls and parties followed, interspersed with sightseeing and buying luxurious gewgaws—gold snuffboxes, seals of carnelian and agate, the lovely porcelain of Sèvres; fine velvets, silks and damasks; screens, fans, *étuis*, clocks in ormulu and marble; watches framed in diamonds; daring terra cottas by Clodion and bronzes by Bouchardon. All were boxed, packed, insured, and dispatched against the day when the exile returned to his distant province. Before Paris endangered the morals or ruined the finances, the young nobleman's steps would be diverted towards Italy. Until 1780, the usual routes were either through Savoy and over the Mont Cenis to Turin or by boat down the Rhone and by felucca—a coastal sailing craft—from Antibes to Genoa. Both could be exciting. The Mont Cenis route necessitated taking the coach to pieces and carrying the traveller in a chair over the steepest part of the path, a formidable undertaking in winter when bad weather might endanger everyone's life. During his passage, Horace Walpole had his favourite lap dog seized from under his nose by a wolf. The danger of the other route lay in the treacherous nature of the swift-flowing Rhone, particularly at Pont-Saint-Esprit, and after that there was always the possibility that the felucca would be seized by the Barbary corsairs who roamed the Mediterranean: rich Christians fetched a good ransom. After 1750, however, mountains became fashionable and the sea route grew neglected. The marvels of nature—particularly glaciers and above all the *Mer de Glace* on Mont Blanc—began to be admired and no Grand Tour was complete without a mountaineering adventure. So, on the way to Italy, many stopped off at Chamonix. Armed with guides and loaded with barometers, tea kettles to boil water on the glacier and so determine heights, luncheon baskets, tents and servants (the Empress Josephine took sixty-eight guides in 1810!) they braved the mountainside. Sometimes even an artist was hired to render the scene immortal—Lord Palmerston took a famous water-colourist, William Pars; so did William Beckford, who had with him J. R. Cozens. Their drawings are some of the earliest we have of romantically viewed mountain scenery. Amidst the towering peaks of snow and ice all felt a proper sense of fear, of man's insignificance, of the majesty and indifference of Nature. More than twenty years after his visit, Dr. Howard of Baltimore, one of the early travellers to the *Mer de Glace*, said: 'I cannot even now think of some of the situations without a feeling of dread.' Earlier generations, like that of Addison and afterwards of Gibbon, had ignored these mountains and concentrated in Switzerland on a course of comparative constitutional study for which the multiplicity of states and free cities provided ample material. But it was of the nature of the Grand Tour to increase in entertainment and diminish in education as time passed; also romanticism, through Rousseau, was making the transition easier by insisting that the feelings needed education as much as the mind.

Italy was, perhaps, the most important part of any tour and a far longer time was usually spent in it. As Dr. Johnson said: 'A man who has not been in Italy is always conscious of an inferiority.'

Italy was the land of marvels, the antique shop of Europe. Speculators dug feverishly for Roman marbles and bronzes, and the discoveries of Herculaneum and Pompeii inflamed the imagination still further. All Englishmen were expected to return festooned with works of art and they became dilettantes overnight, talking with assurance of patina and of significant form. They ransacked palaces, abbeys and convents, employed spies and informers, and were easily, too easily, gulled by fakes. But throughout the century an ever-increasing stream of works of art—good, bad and indifferent—flowed into the country houses of England, Germany, Scandinavia and Russia. Italy, however, offered more than art. 'Indeed,' pontificated Dr. Johnson, 'if a young man is wild, and must run after women and bad company, it is better this should be done abroad, as, on his return, he can break off such connections and begin at home a new man.' Better an Italian countess, Catholic and married, than an English actress, marriageable but impossible. Furthermore the Italian countess was likely to improve his style not only in the arts of elegant flirtation but also in training him for the marriage bed. And the worldly-wise parents expected their young to lose their hearts in Italy; some, like Lord Pembroke, recommended their old flames to their sons and wrote sentimentally about their own past. Strenuous sight-seeing days followed by nights, equally strenuous, of amorous dalliance completed the education of the young nobleman abroad. But it was a leisurely finish—Turin, Milan, Rome (the Jacobite Court carefully avoided), Naples for the ruins and the opera, and then Vicenza for Palladio's sake, and Venice for its Carnival. The pictures of Longhi—suggestive, raffish, elegant—recall for us the dissolute nature of Venice's charm. Here the mask permitted licence.

After one or two years in Italy, the long voyage home began. The traveller had left England as a stripling unversed in the arts of life; he returned sophisticated, urbane and a *cognoscente*. His portrait painted by Batoni, Rosalba or Mengs; one or two pictures of the first rank, sometimes genuine, sometimes false; a collection of water colours, drawings and lithographs; the latest volumes on Pompeii from the royal press of Naples; marbles, bronzes, Genoa velvet and Capodimonte porcelain that would embellish his state rooms were packed in their great crates and sent home via a warship for safety's sake. On his return to Paris, the success of his Grand Tour could be measured by the ease with which he bore himself in the *salons*. Back at home, he joined a magic circle. By turning the conversation to stories of Madame du Deffand, or by mention of a picture in the Pitti, or the prices charged by Busiri, he could quickly get the measure of each new acquaintance and discover whether he belonged to his own aristocratic world. This prolonged, extravagant education was achieved only at great cost—a young nobleman abroad could easily run his father into three or four thousand pounds a year —in gold. Expensive though it might be, the Grand Tour drew more and more people into its orbit; indeed, not only the young and aristocratic but also the middle-aged and the middle class. The fascination of a European tour even began to intrigue the well-to-do in the American States and the West Indies. By the end of the century, English, Germans, Scandinavians, bourgeois as well as aristocrats, began to swarm to the warm south. Philip Thicknesse pioneered and popularized the idea of making the Grand Tour cheaply. In 1790 William Wordsworth, the poet, and his friend Robert Jones were perhaps the first undergraduates to make the tour on foot with their belongings strapped to their backs. As steamships

and railways replaced the sailing ship and the coach, the swarm
became a flood and finally submerged the Grand Tour. Under the
pressure of middle-class values, aristocratic standards of education
began to give way and the tutor and the Grand Tour were replaced
by the public school and university. Entertainment became the aim
of foreign travel rather than education and fine manners.

During its heyday, however, the Grand Tour had influenced
social life to a remarkable degree; it also created the basic structure
of foreign travel which later generations were to adopt and to
extend. Some of the diaries and journals, which all travellers tended
to keep, got into print; others stayed in the family archives to warn
and exhort and advise youngsters. As the eighteenth century progressed, descriptive literature gave way to practical guides. Thomas
Taylor's *The Gentleman's Pocket Companion for Traveling into Foreign
Parts*, which provided maps, advised on roads, and gave distances,
also printed tables of money and weights for conversion, listed a
huge variety of information, and gave as well simple dialogues in
Italian, French, German and Spanish. It quickly became every
traveller's *vade mecum* and spawned a vast brood of guides that have
never ceased to pour from publishing houses.

Nor were the journalists, publishers, amateur writers the only
men to see that money was to be made out of the passion for the
Grand Tour. Fencing masters, dancing masters, riding masters did
so excellent a trade in Paris that their professions became overcrowded. The least successful drifted to Moscow, Budapest, Edinburgh and Stockholm to take the education in manners to the *petite
bourgeoisie* who could not afford either the time or the money to
leave their native heath, but wanted their sons and daughters to ape
the airs of the aristocracy. Language masters often pioneered the
way, for it became a mark of gentility in all countries to be able to
interlard conversation with a few phrases in Italian or French.
Although moralists might denounce the corruption of native
manners that French and Italian airs always produced, there can be
little doubt that the rage for southern European culture softened the
barbarity and increased the civility of countries in the west, north
and east of Europe. Yet when carried to excess, as it was in some
German courts and amongst the aristocracy of Russia, it possessed
dangers. The noblemen of Russia spoke French, dressed in French

clothes, sat on French furniture, mostly employed French servants, and became alien to their own people and their problems; and the cleavage between classes in Russia was immeasurably widened. In Germany the nationalistically minded *bourgeoisie* turned under the influence of the *Aufklärung* from emulation to envy and hate, and cultivated Teutonic customs—crude, absurd, cloudy with bourgeois romance—as a sort of protest against the aristocratic attitude of international culture derived from Greece and Rome and kept alive in France and Italy, of which the Grand Tour was the symbol. Perhaps both these disruptive effects were natural responses to the greatest achievement of the Grand Tour. This was to give a homogeneity never achieved since by any class on such an international scale: James Boswell had no difficulty in slipping into the best aristocratic society in Utrecht, Berlin, Darmstadt, Geneva, Florence, Venice, Milan, Naples, Paris; yet he was, as Scottish gentlemen went, rather a raw youth of no great family distinction. Horace Walpole, a youth of twenty, fitted into the highest circles in France and Italy with instinctive ease: taste, knowledge, background and education were the same—whatever their race—for young men of his birth and breeding. Their early years had been spent in learning those arts of living which the Grand Tour brought to perfection. It made for ease not only in the transmission of taste but also of ideas. Voltaire, Rousseau, Diderot, Gibbon, Hume were read as quickly in St. Petersburg or Naples as in their native lands. Yet the Grand Tour probably had its most profound effect in two spheres—travel and taste. The rudimentary foundation upon which the huge structure of modern European travel has been erected came into being very largely to fulfill the needs of the young aristocrats setting out on their tours. Hotels, couriers, foreign exchange facilities, specialized transport to beauty spots—the whole paraphernalia by which the aristocrats were housed, fed and informed came into being in eighteenth-century Europe. By and large these early travellers found and fixed upon what were to become the playgrounds of Europe. They discovered the delights of the Alps and made Switzerland a tourist centre of Europe; they recommended the French and Italian Rivieras for their climate and cheapness. Before the end of the century the old and delicate from northern Europe were infesting Nice, Menton and San Remo; the unmarried aunts of the European peerage drifted into the resorts—throughout France and Italy—which their noble ancestors had discovered on their Grand Tours.

Yet the greatest influence of the Grand Tour was in art and taste. Every museum in northern Europe owes something to the wealth and skill of those young aristocrats who made the Grand Tour, and bought on the strength of their taste—or rather the taste of that small band of Anglo-Roman expatriates who devoted themselves to the British nobility's passion for sight-seeing and for art. Usually they were failed architects or artists like Colin Morrison, James Byres and John Parker. They usually could be found hanging about the English coffeehouse in the Piazza di Spagna, waiting for their custom. They gave good value. James Byres took the historian Edward Gibbon on a tour of Roman antiquities that lasted eighteen weeks without a day's intermission, and left Gibbon exhausted. Even the indefatigable Boswell, who in a fit of enthusiasm insisted that he and Morrison speak Latin as they visited the Forum, discovered that he lacked the stamina and the spirit to maintain a passionate interest as Morrison remorselessly plodded in the Roman heat up and down the hills and in and out of the ruins, leaving nothing undescribed. Usually these *cicerones*, as they were called, kept a close contact with Italian painters and art dealers, collecting a double commission from the patron and the patronized. Byres was responsible for the Portland Vase reaching England, and the sale of Poussin's *Seven Sacraments* was negotiated by him. Obviously the young noblemen felt much safer if buying through one of their own countrymen: a weakness which a shrewd Welshman, Thomas Jenkins, turned to his own great profit. He became the leading art dealer in Rome. Often the aristocrat could not raise the huge sums Jenkins demanded for his statues, so he lent money for the purchase and thus took a double profit. Jenkins's histrionic powers were highly developed: he wept with emotion at parting with an object on which he was making several thousand per cent. profit. His head, however, was equal to his heart and no one could match him in the technique of restoration; under his skilful hands a battered antique torso quickly achieved arms, legs and head with the finest nicotine staining to give them an age worthy of the price that he charged. Nor was he humble to his clients. He underlined their ignorance, paraded his own virtuosity, and plucked their pockets in the mood of humility so induced. And, of course, there were far less reputable sharks than Jenkins, eager to catch the gullible nobleman with a bargain at an exorbitant price. The standards of professional honesty were low and the skill in copying old masters high, and many a Raphael was born to blush when seen in the cold, critical, northern light.

No traveller came back empty-handed: pictures, statuary and bronzes, ranging from antique Greek marbles to fashionable Italians, were brought back in thousands to enable English, Dutch, Germans, Russians and Scandinavians to appreciate and enjoy the great aristocratic inheritance of Europe. The astonishing virtuosity of these young men can be seen from a recent exhibition held at Norwich which displayed works collected on the Grand Tour during the eighteenth century, principally by the leading Norfolk families. This not only contained old masters, but also illustrated the patronage they brought to eighteenth-century Italian artists. No Italian artist of real merit was absent and the quality of many of their works was exceptional; there were magnificent examples of Canaletto, Guardi, Piranesi, Zuccarelli, Batoni, Rosalba, Pannini, Busiri and the Riccis.

This passion for all things Italian, whether antique or modern, forced painters and architects to make their own pilgrimages to Rome, for they stood little chance of making a living in England unless they could parade a recognizable virtuosity to the returned tourists. So off they went: some, like Reynolds, by man-of-war, in the luxury of great patronage; others, like Thomas Patch, on foot in poverty. They reached Italy in droves; some died there, some stayed, most returned with improved techniques and many splendid canvases to stimulate the powers and imagination of those who stayed at home. Strangely few Italian artists attempted to exploit the English market in its homeland; the most outstanding of these was Canaletto whose pictures of London, Windsor and Alnwick Castle are amongst the finest topographical pictures of the eighteenth-century English scene.

Passionately preoccupied as tourists were with art, few developed a keen critical judgment or displayed much independence of mind. They were willing to pay huge prices for Veroneses and Titians, they prized Caravaggios and eagerly bought early Bolognese painters—Guido Reni, Guercino and the Caraccis—artists who are now regarded as far, far inferior to Tintoretto or Botticelli whom they consistently ignored. As in painting, so in architecture: they confined themselves strictly to the limits of the fashionable, thought St. Mark's at Venice barbarous, and kept their praise for Caserta by Vanvitelli or for Bernini's colonnades at St. Peter's. Their classical education, however, gave them a profound interest in the discoveries at Pompeii and Herculaneum. Sir William Hamilton with his lovely wife Emma, afterwards Nelson's mistress, acted as host to a whole generation of the British aristocracy and not only taught them the beauties of classical design, but often secured objects for them that were both authentic and beautiful. Indeed the pilgrimage to Pompeii strengthened considerably the adoption of classical motives in architecture and decoration which marks the last half of the eighteenth century. The wily Josiah Wedgwood was quick to exploit this acquired taste of returned aristocrats, and he manufactured for them huge quantities of pottery in Pompeiian shapes festooned with classical reliefs. Indeed, he called his factory 'Etruria'.

The ideas, the attitudes, the tastes fostered and extended by the Grand Tour imbued the aristocracy with more than sophistication. They regarded themselves as the true heirs of the Augustans. They came, in consequence, to believe passionately in the virtues of courage and stoicism. They thought nothing became them so well as heroic death in the service of their country, and in the wars against Napoleon they died as well as many a Roman. Furthermore they regarded an interest in classical literature and a capacity to judge the decorative arts as essential qualities of a gentleman. At least these were the standards in which they believed, even though many fell short of them; for all did not respond, as Adam Smith realized, to the educational values of the Grand Tour. He thought that the boy 'commonly returns home more conceited, more unprincipled, more dissipated and more incapable of any serious application, either to study or to business, than he could well have become in so short a time had he lived at home'. True of some, it was not the common experience. The country houses of England, its museums and galleries, the vast literature of travel, the increased urbanity and the growth of civility of English social life in the late eighteenth century, reflected in the correspondence of Horace Walpole, show that this fabulously extravagant education for a ruling class—more costly than any invented before or enjoyed since —paid fat dividends. The rich are not always remarkable for taste, wit or elegance, but the eighteenth-century aristocracy throughout Europe insisted on these virtues. Thanks to the Grand Tour, taste acquired in Italy, combined with the breeding acquired in France, brought sophistication to the remoter outposts of European society which had previously lived close to barbarism. It also gave to the Western world a love of ancient Europe and its artistic heritage that has long ceased to be confined to the aristocracy. What was once the unique privilege of a nobleman is now the common experience of the English-speaking peoples.

1959

THE NOBLE HOUSES
OF EIGHTEENTH-CENTURY ENGLAND

FROM the year 1200, slowly and not at all steadily, trade, the life-blood of civilization, began to flow through the veins of barbarized Europe. In spite of war, pestilence, famine, depression and recession, the volume grew. Setbacks there were in plenty: prosperous markets vanished; wild inflation and gluts of gold and silver brought the society of Europe to the brink of disaster; the deep-rooted institutions of its primitive past, jealous of power and privilege, frequently thwarted its rapid expansion. Yet gradually a tide of wealth swept over the old noble warrior society—the world of feudalism with its great stone fortresses and their mailed retainers, a world of steel and war and bleak virility in which wealth was locked in gold and silver plate, barbaric jewellery, and gem-encrusted reliquaries.

Not all was submerged, even if feudal institutions suffered a sea change. Nobility remained, and kingship and priesthood still worked their magic; these, as we shall see, gave their own strange twist to the wealth that each passing century brought to Europe's shores. By 1750 the Western world had captured a vast commerce unequalled in man's history. The riches derived from it, or from the stimulus that it brought to industry and to the land, enabled men of property to live in a sophisticated luxury, previously enjoyed only by the aristocracy of ancient Rome, the satraps of Oriental despotism, or the mandarins of China. Nowhere are the changes from barbarism to sophistication so clearly mirrored as in the houses, the furniture, the clothes and style of life of the rich.

Venice led the way. Safe within its lagoon, it knew neither feudal aristocracy nor the fortified dwelling, and its most ancient palaces, open to the sun and sky and built for comfort and not security, were an augury of the future. Wealth for Italy followed quickly; its tiny city-states bred a jealous competitive rivalry; the monuments of its ancient glory spurred ambition; finally, the contraction of economic opportunity due to the failure of Byzantium stopped up new outlets for investment and permitted an extravagant self-indulgence in competitive living. The fifteenth and early sixteenth centuries witnessed an astounding efflorescence of architecture, painting, sculpture, indeed of all the arts and crafts that adorn the life of man. It was a curious blend of noble and bourgeois which combined grandeur with comfort, display with domesticity; aristocratic extravagance gave a panache to the delights of middle-class existence. Above all, it created new standards of architecture for all who could afford to build in the grand manner. The baths and villas of Imperial Rome provided models for a series of brilliant architects from Brunelleschi, through Michelangelo, to Palladio, whose *I Quattro Libri dell' Architettura* most strongly influenced the aristocracy of eighteenth-century England.

In the series of splendid villas that Palladio built about Vicenza and Venice, he achieved a combination of proportion, magnificence and brilliant decoration of incomparable quality. These and the palaces of Rome, Florence, Venice, Genoa and Milan set a new standard for luxurious living hitherto unknown in Europe. The fashion quickly spread—indeed much more quickly than the technical knowledge or skill in craftsmanship—and great palaces, often overblown and barbarous in concept, were built in northern and western Europe long before a detailed knowledge of the new architecture had been assimilated. Some of these great houses, modified and purified by later generations, still exist; a few which responded, as it were, to the distant echoes of the new style captured a sense of proportion that adds distinction to their barbaric charm. Of these the great English Tudor houses of Hardwick Hall, Longleat and Burghley are the most famous.

§

The great age of building came to France in the sixteenth century, the time when many of the fabulous châteaux of the Loire were built, creating a tradition of palatial architecture which, modified and refined, lasted until the Revolution. England's turn followed a century later. What Inigo Jones started, Christopher Wren and the eighteenth century completed. Yet the great age of English domestic architecture is brief, stretching from 1660 to 1830. During that time, as in France, a mania for building seized all who could afford it.

'Every man now,' wrote an Englishman early in the eighteenth century, 'be his fortune what it will, is to be doing something at his place, as the fashionable phrase is, and you hardly meet anybody who, after the first compliments, does not inform you that he is in mortar and heaving of earth, the modest terms for building and gardening. One large room, a serpentine river and a wood are become the absolute necessities of life, without which a gentleman of the smallest fortune thinks he makes no figure in his country.'

Millions of pounds sterling were poured into bricks and mortar and plaster to give Britain the splendid architectural heritage that is forever associated with the Four Georges. In every town or village, the Georgian houses—so easily recognizable with their mellow red brick, sash windows, elegant white porticos and fanlights—demonstrate how aristocratic taste spread quickly down into middle-class society. And not only down. This taste for light, airy, well-proportioned, elegant rooms speedily leapt across the Atlantic to New England and to the southern states, to give the same gracious setting to their growing wealth.

These houses are still eagerly sought, still lived in and loved, but the great Palladian mansions that inspired them have fallen on harder times. As wealth ebbs in England, roofs are stripped of lead, marble chimney pieces are wrenched from their sockets, gilded panelling is torn out, and finally the hammer blows of demolition men echo across the deserted parks. Other buildings, more fortunate, are turned into schools, nunneries, homes for the sick and aged. Many are handed over to the National Trust for preservation. Most of those that are still lived in, open their doors to an eager public whose half-crowns help to patch the crumbling stone and keep the rot at bay. A few, locked securely in their vast parks, still witness the traditional life that has always been lived there; but each year the number diminishes, each year sees another fabulous home, replete with pictures, statues, furniture, culled from the far corners of the world, open to public display.

To most visitors it is a strange, unreal world that opens before their eyes, and questions crowd in. Were the 365 rooms at Knole in Kent really necessary even for a duke? Two hundred yards, or 606 feet, to be precise, seems excessive for the front of any house; the Marquess of Rockingham thought his dignity required it; and an entrance hall sixty feet square and forty feet high put his visitors in a suitably humble frame of mind. But did Mylord of Exeter require four huge billiard rooms in which to disport himself? It seems odd.

Parks were in proportion to houses. A series of landscape gardeners—Bridgeman, Kent, 'Capability' Brown—taught the English nobility to remodel the surrounding countryside. Rivers were diverted, lakes dug, so that the house might be reflected in a peaceful stretch of water, sometimes decorated with gilded barges from which a private orchestra could entertain the guests with the latest airs of Handel or Mozart. No one baulked at planting vast woods that could not possibly mature for two centuries. Fifty miles was not an unusual circumference for a park, and Sir Robert Walpole, King George I's Prime Minister, used fifty men, women and boys merely to weed his plantations. Doric temples, 'Gothick' follies, Chinese pagodas, often exquisitely decorated and furnished with the same luxury as the house, garnished a vista, or, carefully concealed, caused delight by surprise.

The Duchess of Bedford had been in Paris when Madame de Pompadour, Louis XV's mistress, started a rage for dairies—built exquisitely, of course, and often lined with Sèvres porcelain. In these the great ladies of the court could ape the dairymaid. Not to be outdone, the Duchess built her own dairy at Woburn—larger, finer, more exquisite still—red and black, very à la mode in its *chinoiserie*, and mirrored in its own lake. The same reckless expense, the same lavish use of the finest materials, the same sense of building for eternity pervade even the stables. Those at Woburn are the size of a small village, beautifully designed and planned, built regardless of cost. The stalls for the horses at Houghton are made of the finest oak, exquisitely carved with a crispness of detail that argues the highest standard of craftsmanship.

Within, of course, the houses showed the same prodigality. There can be found the best marbles of antiquity; masterpieces of art of all times and countries—Rembrandt, Holbein, Velazquez, and a hundred others; French furniture of a quality and distinction hard to find in France itself; porcelain that graced the palace of the Celestial Emperor cheek by jowl with the finest china of Meissen and Sèvres; illuminated manuscripts, plate of gold and silver, Renaissance bronzes and jewels, rock crystal; tapestries and carpets from Aubusson and the great factories of the East; books by the million and family portraits—Reynoldses, Gainsboroughs, Romneys—by the ton. As room follows room, blazing with gilt and shining with marble, the perceptive sight-seer asks himself time and time again: why such magnificence? why did any class of men feel the need for such a wanton and public display of their wealth?—for public it was.

The thousands who now troop through the salons and boudoirs of the great houses of England are treading in the footsteps of generations of sight-seers. From the moment they were built, the houses were open to visitors; they needed to be gentlefolk and they were expected to be generous to the housekeeper. In the eighteenth century the curious and the *cognoscenti* designed for themselves summer tours and took their fill—sometimes admiring, sometimes critical—of the grandeur of their times. Few would have comprehended Dr. Johnson's meaning when he said to Boswell when viewing Lord Scarsdale's great house at Kedleston: 'Nay, sir, all this excludes but one evil—poverty.' Few bothered to ask themselves the questions that spring so insistently to the mind of the modern visitors. Why was this necessary? How much did it cost? What number of servants were required? Just how did people live in palaces as vast as these?

Although commerce diversified and fructified the wealth of Europe, it may be likened to the yeast rather than the substance of riches. The solid basis of Europe's economy remained, right up to modern times, the land and its products—foodstuffs, wool, hides, timber, minerals—and, of course, the rents that men were willing to pay either to wring from it a wretched livelihood or to exploit it like any other commercial activity. But in whatever way the land was used, its ownership conferred, as the long centuries passed, more

F

than wealth. It conferred status—power—greatness. From the wide, harsh steppes of Russia to the wild, sea-lashed coast of Galway, men were measured by their acres. The law, the army, the Church, the service of the State, might confer gentility, even nobility, on those who were successful in the practice of these professions, but such short cuts to social greatness were comparatively rare. The political power in all European states—except for a few merchant oligarchies such as Venice, Genoa and Amsterdam—rested on land ownership.

England, at the time when the great country houses flourished, was covered with a network of landowning families, some aristocratic, most belonging to the gentry. Every fifteen or twenty miles in the south—and fifty or so in the north—there would be the great park belonging to a nobleman or to someone rich enough to vie with the nobility. Seeping into the interstices of the large estates were the manor houses of the lesser gentry. Many of these families stretched back to that first great expansion of agrarian wealth which took place in the twelfth and thirteenth centuries; few, even among the nobility, derived from the great baronial aristocracy of the Middle Ages who had battered themselves to death in the Wars of the Roses. Most families had risen slowly, by prudence, by lucky marriage, by ability in law, commerce, or the Church; a few by the luck of a sovereign's favour. Usually it was a matter for generations rather than individual men, so the roots of families went deep into their neighbourhoods: intermarriage so that estate could be joined to estate was exceptionally common. As families grew in wealth, so they grew in standing, and naturally enough the offices of local government fell into their hands. The same families in Norfolk— the Walpoles, the Cokes, the Townshends, Astleys, Pastons, Hollands —provided the deputy lieutenants, the justices of the peace, the colonels of militia, the members of Parliament, decade after decade, century after century.

Land equalled power: that simple equation was quickly grasped and men set about deliberately extending their acres. They looked for heiresses of wide lands; they stopped providing estates for their younger sons, turning them out into the professions (law, Church, army, navy, or, if need be, commerce); they devised strict legal settlements so that the heir to great territories became merely the tenant for life—for they hoped by these strict entails that their agglomerations of wealth and power might be protected from the dissolute, the incompetent, the mad. Naturally, the well-endowed succeeded at the expense of the lesser gentry. They had the resources or the credit to buy up what became available; they could make better bids for heiresses; they could afford more specialized advice, legal or practical, take risks and win profits from more experimental farming or indulge their fancy in more industrial enterprises. Coral-like, their wealth grew. Sometimes the disasters of life—lack of heirs, civil war, insanity not in one but several generations—pulled a great family down, but when it did it usually enriched the few that remained, or scattered opportunities to the lesser gentry. Furthermore, the greater the family and the wider its local social and political power, the more certain it could be of playing an important and lucrative part in national life; and from this came titles, honours, sinecures, pensions, the great offices of Church or State.

In 1711, young Thomas Pelham-Holles, aged eighteen, succeeded his relative the Duke of Newcastle in estates (although not in title) and became the possessor of thousands of acres in a dozen counties of England, enjoying a rent-roll of more than £30,000 a year (multiply by 12 for modern pounds; by 36 for dollars). At twenty-one he was made Viscount and Earl and Lord Lieutenant for two counties, a year later Marquess and Duke, two years later Lord Chamberlain and Privy Councillor, and a year after that Knight of the Garter, and so on and so forth. He could personally influence the election of a dozen members of Parliament. Nottinghamshire and Sussex knew him as their master. The great houses that he built or adorned—Nottingham Castle, completely remodelled, high on its cliff above the town; Haughton, his hunting lodge in The Dukeries; Claremont, his uncle's vast new Vanbrugh palace for which he redesigned the landscape; the old family mansions of his father, Halland and Bishopstone, both gutted and re-created—these were the necessary symbols of his territorial greatness. Like the gold plate that loaded his table and the hordes of servants that attended him on every journey, they were necessities of his social status. Vast palaces, extravagant living, profusion in every act of life were compulsive in a world that equated wealth with power.

Nor was the Duke of Newcastle exceptional. The Dukes of Bedford enjoyed an income equally large from the vast estates their ancestors had acquired from loot of the monasteries Henry VIII had destroyed. In addition, the Bedfords acquired by judicious marriage great areas of London, principally Covent Garden and Bloomsbury. Docks at Rotherhithe cradled their own fleet of East Indiamen. It is not surprising that magnates such as these should require three or four palaces (among them the huge house at Woburn that now draws hundreds of thousands of visitors a year and whose enormous park and chain of lakes comfortably absorb a great zoo and numerous pleasure grounds).

The Devonshires were richer still, and grew richer with each passing generation. Hardwick Hall, Chatsworth, Bolton Abbey, Holker Hall, Lismore Castle and Compton Place and Devonshire House—all vast, all costly, all crammed with pictures, statuary, furniture and teeming with servants—gave them security and comfort in their peregrinations. At one time the Dukes of Buccleuch rejoiced in eight country houses (five gigantic) and two London houses (both palaces).

In themselves, or rather in their titles, these men symbolized great accretions of social and political power as well as wealth. They were heads of great clans of families who had served them or depended on them or allied with them for generations. These were thickest where the estates lay; these clients they needed to visit, to entertain and to impress. The great palace, abbey or castle in which they passed a few weeks each year remained after their departure as a symbol of their greatness. Furthermore it provided work, hospitality and sometimes protection, for the estates of these men were the centres of great economic enterprises.

Hidden behind the great rooms of state were the offices of stewards and bailiffs, the meeting grounds of merchants, attorneys, agents who drew up the leases, bargained for the timber, farmed the land, let out the mineral rights, and in one of the Duke of Bedford's houses even sold cloth at the back door. A host of upper servants—stewards of the household, housekeepers, keepers of the chamber, clerks of the kitchens, chaplains, librarians, tutors, governesses, personal servants—all required a host of minor servants to attend to their wants. Many a noble household required five or six great tables to feed the servants; three was quite normal.

Labour was plentiful and in general cheap in England from the sixteenth to the twentieth century. Sixty, seventy, or even a hundred indoor and outdoor servants were nothing unusual on one estate; if the owner had a passion for gardens and hothouses the number might be doubled. For such hordes not even Blenheim nor Castle Howard nor the stupendous pile of Wentworth Woodhouse were big enough, and the attics were as crowded with servants as the dormitories of army camps. This profusion of servants, like the enormity of the house, was a part of the necessary display, a piece of conspicuous consumption that proclaimed the wealth of the owner. And as grandeur bred grandeur, so servants bred servants. Tasks were fabulously differentiated: one man and one man alone might fill the oil lamps or replenish the candles; even the clocks had their own winder. The servants' hall became as hieratic as an Oriental despotism, as finely graded in precedence as a state banquet. In order therefore to keep the estate working and to provide the domestic setting that society thought requisite, the servants' quarters and offices in a noble house doubled the size required for show.

Diverse as were the economic enterprises and huge as the domestic staffs came to be, yet these things do not explain entirely why men built such vast palaces. The need to maintain their social and political status by the prestige won through ostentation lies nearer to the truth. This certainly is why many a nobleman built beyond his means—as the Suffolks beggared themselves in creating the monstrous pile of Audley End. Yet there was a more subtle factor involved. The British aristocracy, like the Kwakiutl Indians of the West Coast of Canada, found their egos, the whole idea of themselves as a class and as persons, involved in wanton display: the greater the man, the more absolute his disregard for thrift. Whims, moods, any mania, whatever the cost, could be indulged without guilt, without remorse, without any sense of betrayal of the standards of a class, even if it ended in bankruptcy and ruin. And it was the combination of these factors—political, social, economic, and one might almost say anthropological—which led to the profuse extravagance of aristocratic life over three centuries of English history. Yet it gave to Britain an exceptional artistic heritage.

As one walks through the great rooms of state one can sense some of the symbolism of these vast houses. Such rooms, of course, were not lived in; they were rooms for reception either on formal or semi-formal occasions, rooms to be strolled through to the more intimate private apartments where daily life was lived. In the seventeenth century this was usually the bedroom (frequently the bed was fenced off by a rail), but by the eighteenth century smaller, cosier sitting rooms, cabinets, or boudoirs became at first the fashion, then the rage. The great state rooms usually consisted of a vast hall (one of the most spectacular is at Holkham, derived by William Kent from designs by Palladio), one or two salons and drawing rooms (those at Wilton, the famous 'double-cube' room, and at Petworth, remarkable for its Grinling Gibbons carvings, are exceptional), a state dining room and at least one state bedroom, used only by visitors of extraordinary distinction.

For these rooms no expense was spared. The finest plaster workers were brought in from Italy; tons of mahogany and other rare woods were imported from the East and West Indies; gold leaf was squandered (at Chatsworth the window frames are gold-leafed *outside* as well as within); and Europe was ransacked for paintings and sculpture, furniture and marble. The cost is rarely known. Sir Robert Walpole at Houghton spent £1,219 3s. 11d. on the trimmings alone of his fabulous green velvet state bed, especially designed for him by William Kent (multiply by 12 for modern pounds; by 36 for dollars). This bed alone cannot have cost far short of a hundred thousand dollars, at present rates. The cost of Blenheim, without furniture or pictures, was rather more than a quarter of a million pounds. Eastbury, also by Vanbrugh, which only existed for twenty-five years, cost £125,000. Houses that were very modest by these standards, such as the delightful one at Ombersley, built by the first Lord Sandys, quickly devoured £30,000 or £40,000 (gold). Yet so essential to greatness were these houses that men would load themselves and their descendants with debt rather than deprive themselves of the glory of ownership. Lord Sandys, a man of moderate means but inordinate ambition, mortgaged his estate to the tune of £23,220 in order, doubtless, to impress the citizens of Worcester whom he represented in Parliament. By the middle of the eighteenth century such monuments to a family's importance were *de rigueur* —cost what it might.

And, of course, the contents needs must match the scale of building and the sumptuosity of its decoration. To form his great picture collection (now, because his bankrupt grandson sold it to Catherine of Russia, housed in the Hermitage at Leningrad—save for those pictures that a bankrupt Soviet Government in turn sold to Mellon or Gulbenkian), Sir Robert Walpole employed not only the ambassadors of the Crown to scour the dealers but also spies and secret agents to discover what might be extracted from the houses of the European nobility. Naturally prices soared; Sir Robert himself frequently broke his own records, like a Greek shipowner today after a Renoir or a Gauguin. Usually this hardheaded statesman, to whom suspicion was as natural as breathing, bought well; but many vain, arrogant young noblemen became easy dupes for the fakes and copyists. Yet even so, the artistic collections of the English nobility, even after the enforced sales of the last fifty years, remain of exceptional quality and worthy of the most distinguished museums of Europe.

As with paintings, so it was with all that was rare, exotic and costly: nobleman vied with nobleman over jewels, pictures, books, plants, animals. The world was ransacked to give distinction to an English house and garden. Here are a few exotics that poured into the household of the 'Princely Duke of Chandos': Captain Massey of Carolina sent him rice, kidney beans, pineapples, a Mexican squash, or little beavers and flamingoes; Chiswell of Virginia sent mockingbirds; Stephens of Cape Coast, a tiger that mauled a servant; Ashley of Barbados, pineapples, cinnamon, coffee trees, avocado pears; from Jamaica, pawpaws, star apples, custard apples, guavas, tamarinds; Harriman of Leghorn, broccoli seed, fennel, *agro di cedro*, orange-flower water, capers, *muscatello di Castello* vinegar, preserved citron, anchovies, Lucca oil, olives and evergreen-oak acorns; Oporto provided Lamiego hams; Lisbon, sugar, raisins of the sun, Malaga raisins, currants, lemons, oranges, musk and water-melon seeds. By 1739 Chandos boasted of the finest and largest collection of fruit in Europe. And his rare birds were equal to his fruit. They poured in from the four quarters of the globe: storks from Rotterdam, wild geese from Barbados, whistling ducks from Antigua, redbirds from the Gold Coast, blue macaws, Muscovy ducks, parakeets, a crown bird, ostriches, an eagle—all grotesquely expensive.

Chandos also loved music; so he created an orchestra of about thirty instrumentalists and vocalists, conducted by the famous Dr. Pepusch. 'His concert,' as he called it, lived in his house and provided background music to his dinners. It cost him nearly £1,000 a year in wages, but this was less than his wine bill, which ran at about £1,500 a year, roughly the same as Sir Robert Walpole's, whose household in 1733 returned 540 dozen empties.

For those who did not relish artists or menageries, furniture or gardens, there were the hounds and the horses, the women and the gaming tables. Lord Stavordale, scarcely beyond adolescence, lost eleven thousand guineas at cards only to regain them the next evening in a single bid when he cursed himself for not playing for really high stakes! Even generosity could grow as wanton as a weed. Lord Egremont, the owner of Petworth, disdained to pay his servants wages. If they greatly pleased him, he would give them £1,000 or at times £2,000 worth of stock; for little kindnesses they got £50 in the local savings bank. Guests at Petworth were always welcome; they stayed weeks, months, even years. He celebrated special occasions—victories, coronations, royal birthdays and, of course, his own—with vast public entertainments that amazed even his own age. Here is a description of the feast he gave when he reached his eighty-third year:

'A fine sight it was; fifty-four tables, each fifty feet long, were placed in a vast semi-circle on the lawn before the house. Nothing could be more amusing than to look at the preparations. The tables were all spread with cloths and plates and dishes. Two great tents were erected in the middle to receive the provisions which were conveyed in carts like ammunition. Plum puddings and loaves were piled like cannon balls and innumerable joints of boiled and roast beef were spread out, while hot joints were prepared in the kitchen and sent forth as soon as the firing of a gun announced the hour of the feast. . . . They think 6,000 were fed.'

Yet, lavish as this life was, it had its curious shortcomings, its little weaknesses and even its darker side. The plumbing in these great mansions was almost non-existent. Houses that had a bathroom, like Chatsworth, were famed for them. One lavatory was thought to be sufficient for the huge house at Harewood. And we find Chandos writing urgently to Jamaica for bitterwood in order to line his daughter's cradle to keep out the bugs. The absence of drains and the presence of parasites bred diseases. Chandos himself buried two wives and eight of his children. In all great households death was a constant visitor, and perhaps this gave a keener edge to their appetite for life; and perhaps in their need to build on a scale fit for eternity, we can discern their sense of life's transience, a hint of tragedy and a challenge to death. That is as may be.

Of what there is no doubt is that this life was wasteful, extravagant, ostentatious—an appalling contrast, as Dr. Johnson noted, to the human wretchedness of rural or urban slums; yet it was saved both by its humanity and by its taste. The houses, the pictures, the furniture, above all the landscaped gardens in which nature had been so gently subdued, are its permanent memorial and a part of the European tradition. They give style and grandeur to what might have been merely a gross and vulgar self-indulgence. These boastful, splendiferous men created enduring beauty.

There have been far richer men, before and since their time, greater connoisseurs, greater patrons of the arts, even greater eccentrics, but in the British aristocracy of the eighteenth century there met two hostile but fertilizing traditions that gave it its curious splendour. In it the feudal world was still alive in its arrogance, its fierce disregard of consequence, its personal sense of destiny, but it operated in the new world of bourgeois delights. Secure in its own greatness, the aristocracy could parade its great wealth without guilt and with a total disregard of the envy of the multitude. The noblemen's way of life was based not on wealth alone but on a sense of caste. Their blood and power stretched back into antiquity and looked forward to eternity. Greatness was all. Unawares, the great wave of democratic industrialization engulfed them; inexorably the end came. Yet the houses remain, and their parks that time has perfected. The paths thread through the ancient oaks and scented limes, disclosing across the calm lakes the Palladian grace of mellowing brick and stone.

1958

THE BRIGHTON PAVILION

TODAY, Brighton is Britain's Miami—brash, extravagant, a curious mixture of vulgarity and elegance, sophistication and naïveté in which literary lions, juvenile delinquents, successful *nouveaux riches* (mainly Jewish) and proletarian cockneys out on the spree, jostle in a lively garish world that possesses one of the most remarkable architectural settings of any seaside resort in Europe. Throughout the length and breadth of Brighton there are squares, terraces, crescents of exquisitely classical proportions, rivalled in England only by Bath and in Europe by Nancy. About these buildings, there is no whimsy; the only exoticism is an occasional decoration in the neo-classic style of the late eighteenth and early nineteenth century. They recall an age of leisured elegance, at once social and urban, an age of certainty and uniformity in taste. And then lying in the very heart of this formal beauty, close to the sea shore but set back from it, is the fantasy of the Prince Regent's Pavilion—with its domes and minarets, its fret-work tracery and lace-like embattlements: underneath this oriental masquerade, the fine proportions of Henry Holland's classical villa, the first Pavilion, can still be discerned, as Georgian and as classical as any house in Brighton. Like the prince, the eldest son of George III, who built it, the Pavilion grew more monstrous, more extraordinary, more dream-like with the years. But first, why Brighton?

Two hundred and fifty years ago Brighton scarcely existed—a few fishermen's hovels, a shingle beach, and right to the shore, smooth undulating grasslands that rose within a mile or two to the sharp escarpment of the Downs. It was excellent country for the horse, for riding it, racing it, or driving it. And that, later, was one of the reasons for Brighton's popularity, for many of the Prince's friends were crazed about horses as only the English aristocracy can be. But Brighton first grew to fame and fashion through the salesmanship of a successful doctor. He sold sea-water. Its virtues, said Dr. Russell, whether applied externally or internally, were boundless. A cold dip, it seemed, proved peculiarly efficacious to that feminine frailty of the age of elegance—the vapours, so long as it was taken at hideously inappropriate times: Fanny Burney, the novelist, bathed in *November*, before dawn; a very good time, the doctors thought. It also, as might be expected, encouraged fertility in young matrons, 'better even,' said its advocates, 'than the mud of the river Nile.' Nor were its virtues confined to women: male weaknesses—gout, rheumatism and the like—were banished by it and, not surprisingly in a village that was to grow to England's most exotic and erotic watering place, it restored male vigour to—so it was claimed—an adolescent capacity.

A surprising number of men and women of eighteenth-century England's upper and middle class were unhealthy in life as they were ambitious in love. An ill-balanced diet, an excess of hard liquor, a serious shortage of water in the home (even if it were a palace), bad ventilation, worse sanitation, heavy clothing and pullulating slums in town and countryside provided hothouse conditions in which bacteria and viruses rioted unchecked. Gout, fevers, malaria, tuberculosis, a regiment of skin diseases hung about society like gnats over a pond. Almost everyone had an excuse—a good medical excuse—for spending a month or two at Bath or Tunbridge Wells or Scarborough and Brighton as the mysterious properties of the new elixir—sea-water—became a fashionable talking point. And it was illness—either enlarged glands or scrofula—that first brought George, America's last Prince of Wales, to Brighton in the summer of 1784; the visit which confirmed the Prince's inclination for the bright, raffish town which had begun to build itself on the merits of Dr. Russell's sea-water.

The Prince's first visit—a short one—had taken place the year before at the invitation of his uncle, the Duke of Cumberland, whom the Prince's father, George III, regarded with such horror that he had forbidden his son to visit him. As soon as the Prince was twenty-one, with his own establishment, and free to please himself, he had accepted Cumberland's invitation with alacrity. Naturally Brighton went *en fête*. 'His Royal Highness's arrival,' reported the *Sussex Weekly Advertiser*, 'was announced by the ringing of bells and a royal salute at the battery, where, unhappily, through some indiscretion in reloading one of the pieces, it went off and wounded the under-gunner mortally. His body was blown off the battery to some distance on to a bank.' A tragedy in the midst of delight, an experience that was to be frequent in the Prince's life but, brushed aside as this was brushed aside: with conscience eased by the gift of a few guineas to the dead man's dependants, the Prince appeared for the evening, resplendent in embroidered silk, laced hat and French buttons at the most brilliant ball that Brighton had ever witnessed. The visit proved hugely successful and Brighton seemed to offer all that the Prince needed. It teemed with friends like Tommy Onslow, who was utterly crazed about horses and gambling. (Onslow immediately lifted twenty-five guineas from the Prince by winning a difficult but horsey bet. He drove his phaeton and four through two narrow gateways twenty-five times at a gallop without touching.) The Prince found Brighton gay, intimate, discreet. It was still too far from London for crowds to gather there: his own set could, and did, take over the place.

So Brighton became the Prince's playground. He and his friends were fond of vulgar and noisy practical jokes on their neighbours. Who could stop them in Brighton? They raced their horses and drove their phaetons in mad races across the wide lawns that bordered the sea. No one was likely to complain. They sat at their telescopes and watched old Martha Gunn dip their favourite girls into the sea: after all, the girls were there for adventure, too: occasionally they even sat in the ice-cold water themselves when they thought their health demanded it. They gambled endlessly: gazed at plays: danced: listened with respect to the Prince's fine baritone as he regaled them with ballads: drank furiously: ate gigantically: and wenched interminably. And they dressed. The Prince possessed a handsome, florid face, a splendid, if slightly plump, figure and first-class legs of which he was inordinately proud. He was even prouder of his taste in clothes, formed and guided by his friend, Beau Brummell, who had revolutionized an Englishman's dress by insisting on subdued colours, perfect cut and

exquisite linen as the marks of elegance. Only in the evening, on
full dress occasions, were princes and nobles permitted to dress like
peacocks. But clothes and the wearing of them was a matter for
daily concern and long discussion.

But princes and their friends, after setting on a place like a cloud
of butterflies, often gorge themselves on its nectar, and then flutter
away to stimulate their appetites in fresh pastures. But this time
fate riveted the Prince to Brighton. He fell in love. Of course, he
had been in love before: 'Perdita' Robinson, his first girl, lived
crippled but still 'protected' at Brighton: her life and her lovers'
made a little more comfortable by the Prince's pension. But this
time, his whole personality was captivated, and stayed captivated
until youth was left behind. The object of his admiration was a
dangerously unusual widow—Mrs. Fitzherbert. Mrs. Fitzherbert
was a Roman Catholic; pious, virtuous, very comely. She neither
welcomed the Prince's attentions nor responded to his ardour. She
preferred to be left alone. The Prince's siege grew hectic: he swore,
he cajoled, he promised: presents rained on her, letters pursued her,
finally marriage trapped her. Conducted in utmost secrecy, it was,
of course, illegal. No prince of the British royal family could marry
without the Sovereign's consent; no consent could ever have been
forthcoming from George III for a marriage of his heir-apparent to
a Roman Catholic widow. On the Prince's part the ceremony was
utter, meaningless folly, on hers the necessary religious sanction to
her bedding with the Prince. In Mrs. Fitzherbert's eyes, and in the
eyes of her Church and of her fellow believers, the Prince was for
all time her husband. In English law, she could be nothing but his
mistress. The Prince, of course, flaunted his conquest, but strenuously denied, even to a friend as close as Charles James Fox, the
method by which he had achieved it. Nevertheless, rumours rever-
berated: and George III, never a man of easy temper, regarded his
son with so prejudiced an eye that he left him to stew in his debts.
During his frantic courtship the Prince, according to Lord Holland,
had rolled in his grief on Charles James Fox's floor crying by the
hour and 'swearing that he would abandon the country, forgo the
crown, sell his jewels and scrape together a competence to fly with
her to America'. Instead of which, once wed, he drove off in ostentatious austerity to Brighton: and installed Mrs. Fitzherbert con-

veniently near to the house which he had begun to regard as his own.

As soon as Parliament had accepted the denials of his friends about his marriage, persuaded his father to grant him £10,000 a year more, and settled his debts, he began to devote himself to love, architecture and interior decoration, which, with food, drink and music were to be the abiding obsessions of his life. For more than forty years he pursued all of them at the Pavilion which he built himself at Brighton; or rather, that he went on building at Brighton, for like all compulsive builders and decorators the Prince was never finished. Indeed, when the Pavilion was at last completed, the Prince, by then King George IV, lost interest in it and gave his attention to Windsor, where, with both the Castle and the Royal Lodge on his hands, he could occupy fully both his old age and his regal income.

In 1785 when the Prince first took Mrs. Fitzherbert to Brighton to spend the summer in what they thought of as 'abject poverty', he rented a small, neat farmhouse from Thomas Kemp, who afterwards built the splendid Georgian terraces of Kemptown. The Prince could not live in any building without his imagination beginning to work on it. Already, his palace in London—Carlton House—had been more responsible than any other extravagance for his monumental debts. So in the intervals of his amorous delights and when he was too tired for the crude practical jokes in which he took such schoolboyish delight, he paced about his farmhouse.

In his mind's eye, he knocked down walls, threw out bow windows, transforming it into a charming marine Pavilion, suitable for a Prince wallowing in amorous bliss. Within eighteen months, one hundred and fifty workmen, directed by the Prince's architect, Henry Holland, had turned dream into reality. For some mysterious reason, the Prince's cook bought out Thomas Kemp and then gave his master a twenty-one year lease at the huge rent of £1,000 a year (paid, however, irregularly). Holland's Pavilion possessed the simplicity and elegance that Georgian architects achieved so effortlessly. Its central feature was a circular salon which was flanked by two wings with bow windows. The building veered towards austerity and the only whimsy which it contained was the Prince's bedroom where a vast mirror enabled the Prince, and presumably Mrs. Fitzherbert, to lie in bed and not only watch the sea but their friends strolling up and down the Steine, as the wide grass lawn of Brighton was called—a quaint, but no doubt restful pastime.

For the next eight years the Prince became a regular visitor to Brighton and these were probably the gayest, most light-hearted years of his life. After all he was a prince, likely one day to be King of a land in which the rich were getting richer year by year. He belonged to a world of confidence and ebullience, an age when men planned gardens for the enjoyment of their great-great-great grandchildren. He possessed a mistress: a little odd perhaps and somewhat ponderous, ample, cosy, middle-aged before her time, but for him —insecure as he was sexually—deeply satisfying. And about him, there was an intimate, smart, adoring audience, willing to be amused by him, anxious to entertain him. Already florid, and beginning to run to fat, the Prince, nevertheless, was an impressively handsome figure and wore his impeccably cut clothes with exceptional style. He loved parades, horses, gambling and coarse practical jokes: Brighton gave him exceptional opportunities to indulge most of his inclinations. Nor was the Prince without wit and intelligence. A good, if greedy conversationalist, he was also a superb mimic and a resonant baritone with that passion for music which had distinguished his family. And his interest in literature was sincere and sensible. In his small private apartments in the Pavilion half of the wall space is given over to books. Of course, he was vain, something of an exhibitionist, rather treacherous to his friends and, as princes tend to be, grossly self-indulgent. And it should be remembered that his ostentatious extravagance took place against a background of war and misery that brought near starvation to the labouring masses. Overweight, he could not resist gargantuan meals and he got drunk easily and frequently: and naturally the cartoonists seized on these weaknesses with righteous savagery. He could be touchy, and he enjoyed his rages. Once a friendship was broken, malice quickly obliterated ancient affection. The quickness of his temper, the speed with which he seized on an imagined slight, gave a certain edge to the Prince's circle, and strewed his life with broken friendships.

His friends were a quaint bunch: some, like Beau Brummell, lived for clothes, and spent the entire day dressing, parading, undressing and parading again: as fastidious and as pure in his private life as in the cut of his coat. Others, like Lord Barrymore, never washed. His fame and his brother's fame rested partly on their practical jokes— propping up coffins in doorways, then ringing the doorbell, was a favourite—and partly on their wild extravagance, due mainly to excessive gambling and extravagant theatricals. And then there was Letty Lade: anyone particularly foul mouthed the Prince would describe as swearing 'like Letty Lade'. She had lost her virtue to 'Sixteen String Jack', a highwayman hanged at Tyburn in 1774, enjoyed for a short time the bed of the Prince's brother, the Duke of York, and finally married Sir John Lade whom Dr. Johnson had advised, when asked if he should marry, 'I would advise no man to marry who is not likely to propagate understanding.' Sir John picked up his wife in a brothel on one of the rare occasions when he left his stables, for the dominating passion of his life was horse-flesh. He rode supremely well, handled the reins of a phaeton to every-one's admiration, and finished life supremely happy as a public coachman on the London-Brighton run. His wife proved as good with horses as her husband and the Prince delighted in them both. They lived utterly for themselves, provided a constant fund of incredible anecdote, and were one of the sights of Brighton with which he could regale his guests. Many of the Prince's friends were odd, obsessed, ingrown characters. Great wealth and absolute social security combined to create a hot-house atmosphere in which human characters could flower like monstrous orchids—vivid, splotched, nightmarish, haunting. Brighton, their own town, was for them a paradise, where for months on end they could forget the real world of lawyers, tradesmen, stewards, politicians and, above all, first the threats and then the horrors of war. Of course, not all of the Prince's friends were so eccentric as Lade, Onslow and the Barrymores. Thurlow, the Lord Chancellor, self-made, tough, intelligent, supremely worldly, was a frequent visitor; Sheridan, the liveliest and brightest butterfly of the English stage and politics, fluttered in and out of the Prince's circle and scattered wit and sense and good fellowship. Charles James Fox, the most generous of men and wiser far than the times he lived in, continued to be drawn to the warm springs of the Prince's nature, undeterred by his silliness and self-regard. The first Pavilion, built with an elegance and restraint that harmonized with the growing squares and crescents of the town, witnessed the most brilliant, and the happiest period of the Prince's life. The sole shadow was cast by the Revolution in France that brought boatloads of refugees to Brighton's shingle beach, and regiments in training to the Downs above the town. No one believed in the first few months that the war could last long, and the exiles, foolish with hope, expected soon to be returning to their *châteaux*. Before that hope died, disaster had overwhelmed the Prince; a disaster which broke his life in half, and opened the second chapter in the Pavilion's history which was to transform it into a fantasy of form and colour.

The Prince and Mrs Fitzherbert had begun their life in Brighton determined to live sparely. That resolution quickly vanished. The Prince transformed the farmhouse into his Pavilion, filled it with elegant and expensive French furniture and lived in it with the lavish generosity to which he was accustomed. But Brighton was a trifle compared with Carlton House where he spent most of the year. And, of course, he loved clothes and jewels as much as dinners and concerts: he always preferred to be the host rather than guest. So his debts mounted: by 1795, they were well over half a million —in gold. Furthermore, there was no immediate heir to the throne. All his brothers either lived in sin or contracted, like himself, marriages that no one would recognize, and although George III had plenty of bastard grandchildren the direct succession of his house seemed to be in jeopardy. And the Prince's love for Mrs. Fitzherbert had withered to habit and habit itself had grown brittle.

The solution to his financial difficulties was to marry a German princess, breed an heir, and for a grateful country to discharge his debts and increase his income. The alternative was a personal crisis of extravagant proportions of uncertain outcome: what could be certain was that the result would be exceptionally unpleasant for the Prince, and a sharp contraction in his style of living. He was far too middle-aged to face that or the uncertainty. And Lady Jersey, his new mistress, a sprightly grandmother with a husband still alive, had no qualms about the Prince marrying for money. So he married. He loathed his strange bride and only got through the marriage ceremony fortified with brandy. His wife was dotty: a hoydenish, blowsy, free-speaking German wench who dressed in outrageously bad taste, swore like an ostler and smelt like a farmyard. Or so the Prince and his friends said: at least it gave an excuse for the vile way he treated her. He managed, however, to get his Princess pregnant and, duty done, and the daughter born, he turned the Princess out of his house but not out of his life. She careered round Europe in vulgar ostentation as much to embarrass the Prince as to enjoy herself. And when he succeeded in 1820 she returned to claim her rights as Queen, plunged the country in turmoil and shattered what little popularity her husband retained with his subjects. Certainly the Prince's legal marriage was the most disastrous act of his life.

Once he had extricated himself from this horror, naturally he wished to re-create the years with Mrs. Fitzherbert which now glowed in his imagination, for his infatuation with Lady Jersey had been as brief as his marriage. So, with Lady Jersey and the Princess banished, he once more besieged Mrs. Fitzherbert. Her pride bruised, she showed her former indifference which naturally fanned the Prince's ardour to fever-heat. There was nothing like denial to raise the Prince's passion. After a becoming interval, Mrs. Fitzherbert sent off Father Nassau to Rome for advice. It was apt— return to your husband. She did and both returned to Brighton.

Not only did Mrs. Fitzherbert make the Prince supremely happy, she also made him creative. Naturally he began to play about with the Pavilion. In 1802, the gift of some Chinese wallpaper, made no doubt because he had created a Chinese room at Carlton House in 1801 (Mrs. Fitzherbert returned in 1800), gave him the idea of making not only a Chinese gallery at the Pavilion but a room with walls of painted glass which gave the impression of being inside a Chinese lantern. For the next few years, shortage of money and the need to complete the stables (they cost £54,000: no horses, nor grooms for that matter, had been more splendidly housed) limited the Prince's ambitions, but the Pavilion was enlarged a little and the interior decoration made more and more what the English thought to be Chinese. But the Prince was not satisfied, and he decided, some time about 1805, to reconstruct the Pavilion, to turn it from a princely cottage to a miniature palace: small, sumptuous, informal yet rich, fabulous, oriental. Not a Chinese pagoda, the Prince was moving away from Chinese towards what he conceived to be an Indian style. Already, at Sezincote in Gloucestershire, a nabob, returned

with a huge fortune from India, had built himself an oriental palace:
fortunately for him, his brother was an excellent architect—S. P.
Cockerell—and he took his task very seriously, carefully using
water colour drawings of actual Indian buildings. The result was
strange but pleasing. William Porden, who built the stables at
Brighton, had worked for Cockerell, and he used this exceptionally
original style of decoration at Brighton. This entranced the Prince.
In 1805, he commissioned Humphrey Repton to plan an Aladdin-
like transformation of his classical marine villa into an Indian palace.
The Prince praised the drawings but did not build. Once more, he
was broke. And possibly he had his doubts about Repton's scheme
which conformed very strictly to Indian models. Highly disciplined
and rather dry in tone, it lacked, perhaps, the personal accent for
which the Prince's imagination was searching. He hesitated for
another six years, until, indeed, the final madness of his father made
him King in all but name.

He enjoyed, however, as Prince Regent a nearly regal income
and so he began to build as no English king had ever built before.
The encouragement he gave to John Nash, his Surveyor-General
whom he personally appointed in 1815, made the Regent as responsible as anyone for the most beautiful domestic architecture London
possesses: the great terraces of Regent's Park. Nash's Pavilion at
Brighton, however, was due as much to the effect of time and
experience on the Prince's character as to Nash's architectural genius.
It is the final expression of his life fulfilled.

By 1815, too, youth had past: Mrs. Fitzherbert had been rejected
a second time. Indeed, another reason for his delay in reconstructing
the Pavilion was the change in direction in his amorous life which
kept him away from Brighton for a year or two. Mrs. Fitzherbert's
successor was another large, matronly grandmother—Lady Hertford: she was nearly as huge as the Prince himself. The amorous
attitudes of these two human whales provided the most savage
cartoonists England has ever known with limitless fodder for their
cruel and insatiable imaginations.

Life and age had battered the Prince. He had long ceased to be
handsome: for he had run to fat and he often found solace in drink;
and many nights saw him reeling drunk. Gross eating of a high
protein diet produced rheumatism and gout. Always quickly

alarmed by the first symptoms of ill-health, he had become a confirmed hypochondriac. He believed passionately in the necessity to keep his rooms at steam-heat and to be bled copiously and frequently; often he sent secretly for a second doctor so that he could be bled twice. The Prince had never been able to distinguish very clearly between fact and fiction, between desire and performance and frequently he told long circumstantial stories of feats that he had never performed, a habit that was to grow until, without the slightest hesitation, the Regent could describe the important, indeed crucial, part he had played in the battle of Salamanca to, of all people, the Duke of Wellington. Gross in body, somewhat wandering in mind, prone to invalidism, the Prince was driven further into his private dream world by the antics of his wife and the hatred of his subjects. At the visit of the crowned heads of the European alliance to London in 1815, his wife had returned to London and insisted on undertaking what she considered to be her rightful duties. The Regent was outraged and, this time supported by his mother, refused to countenance what he considered infamous behaviour. The radical politicians and the London mob took the Princess to their hearts. The politicians denounced the Prince, the mob pelted him when he appeared in public so that he became afraid to go out of doors. He knew himself to be a figure of contempt. He realized the contrast that he made to the handsome, debonair, immensely attractive and popular Tsar of Russia. Although the Prince got rid of his wife, she went on plaguing him by making him ridiculous in Europe. Age, and the sense of decay, he could only banish by shutting himself in a private world: a world of eating, drinking, singing, building and decorating, shared with a few dependable friends and ruled by a matriarch; the first was Lady Hertford, the second Lady Conyngham: two enormous, elderly women, much older than himself, who could treat him as he wished to be treated, as a lonely, loveless, foolish boy to be scolded and pampered and bullied and always forgiven. The Prince, throughout his life, had searched for security and affection rather than sexual excitement, and as he retreated more and more into his private world, the craving grew stronger and his last two attachments showed clearly enough the weaknesses of his nature.

Yet, bloated, corrupt, phosphorescent with decay as he was, the

Prince still possessed a saving grace. He needed, to see him through his life, to express himself, to create, to allow his imagination to roam. His nature, as his life showed, was deeply fissured with anxieties, frustrations, weaknesses that were hard to face. In fantasy, he could be soothed: so pretence with him easily became reality. Whether he was singing a ballad, dressing in regimentals or telling an anecdote, he was embroidering his life, living intensely at second hand, becoming creatively alive as he forgot himself. He was a man of romantic imagination, with the impulse of an artist and some of the temperament of an actor. And his strange nature secured its most effective, if not its most satisfactory, fulfilment in building and decorating; and the two architectural fantasies of his broken old age —the final Brighton Pavilion and the restoration and rebuilding of Windsor Castle—are both in their way romantic masterpieces. Windsor, with its stupendous Round Tower, is central to the tradition created by the Gothic Revival but Brighton in its completed state had neither past nor future: it belongs to the Prince as few buildings belong to one man.

Outside Indian and Moorish mingled with eighteenth-century elegance of sash and bow windows to create a unique building that baffled the understanding as much as it stimulated the imagination. William Cobbett, the home-spun radical, described it as 'a little Kremlin'; for William Hazlitt, the literary critic and essayist, it was a rare collection of stone pumpkins and pepper boxes; naturally an anonymous journalist was more vituperative, calling it 'a madhouse or a house run mad' but, as might be expected, the best quip came from the greatest wit of the age—the Reverend Sidney Smith—who dismissed the Pavilion in one sentence, 'The Dome of St. Paul's went down to Brighton and pupped.' Thousands of visitors to Brighton's seaside, generation after generation of them, stare at it uncomprehendingly and make it the butt of their witticisms. Aesthetes, connoisseurs, men and women, randy for whimsy, gush over it. Few accept it for what it is—a fantasy in bricks and plaster of a sad, ageing, self-indulgent, very rich king who possessed taste but little judgement, vivid imagination and no control. What control there was came from the standards of his age and the instinctive practice of his architects. The Pavilion is a dream, belonging neither to Russia nor India nor China nor Mongolia nor to Moorish

Spain, although it has affinities to the architecture of all of them, but to the Prince's longing for a smart originality that would astound his friends. The inside, like the outside, is a strange pastiche; at times, with its strong reds and yellows and blues, almost vulgar, yet it never is. On first viewing, it is overpowering, and slightly repellent: the huge lotus-like chandeliers, the dragons writhing down the walls: the imitation blue skies, palm trees in cast iron, banana trees in bronze, seats pretending to be dolphins, and everywhere bamboo chairs, bamboo beds, bamboo bookcases, bamboo seats (but, of course, imitation painted bamboo—even bamboo in iron). The Pavilion shocks as few other buildings do: it creates immediately the atmosphere of a life: the true setting for the man who made it. It is easy to imagine these rooms grossly overheated, to see again the vast kitchen teeming with gargantuan piles of food and noisy with sweating cooks and scullions, orchestrated by Carême, one of the greatest of French chefs, to provide excitement for the palates of the twenty or so old roués with their wives or mistresses who sat with the Prince in his Banqueting Room. This room and the Music Room are the two most extravagant and extraordinary rooms not only in the Pavilion but in Great Britain.

The Banqueting Room is dominated by its central chandelier—a vast structure, in 1818 immensely modern because it was lit by gas not candles.[1] It weighs a ton and consists of a bronze-leaved plantain tree from which hangs a large silver dragon who holds in his claws an enormous glass bowl, and around its rim are six smaller dragons with lotus flowers in their mouths. The cost—£5,613 9s. (multiply by 8 for present prices in pounds sterling and by 24 for dollars). The Prince loved light as well as heat. So, besides this huge chandelier, there are four other enormous water-lilies and eight ten-foot high standard lamps—a pedestal of gilt dolphins, a huge, deep blue Spode vase topped by a lotus flower of tinted glass (cost £5,322 4s.). The room itself is painted with Chinese scenes: the decoration is crimson, gold and blue. The decorative work cost £8,339 11s. and the furniture £9,710 16s. 1d. The total cost of this one room was about the equivalent of a million dollars.

[1] The Prince incorporated all the technical achievements of his time: the Pavilion is the first house to use cast iron pillars both for structure and decoration.

Certainly Carême's meals were worthy of it. The richness of the dishes was only matched by their number. At a dinner of no particular importance the Prince, greedier than ever, offered the guests the choice of one hundred and sixteen dishes in nine courses. He adored the table, but not only for the food and wine, for while he remained at table, his audience was captive and the Prince had become a compulsive raconteur with whom fiction had replaced fact. Time and time again he told a bored, sceptical, but subserviently attentive table-full of guests how he had fought a Brighton butcher with his bare hands and thrashed the man within an inch of his life. There, amongst the silver and the glass and the hissing gaslight, in a room that might have been Sam Goldwyn's idea of the Summer Palace at Pekin, he retailed such conquests—told of the battles he had never fought, of the women he had never possessed, of the triumphs that he had never known. There he was, a huge mass of flesh, corseted, bedecked, corrupted by his life and nature, yet retaining, even in decay, originality and something of the singularity of the artist. His outrageous stories were so vivid that his audience—softened by good food and excessive drink—could at least *pretend* without difficulty to believe them. When on top of his form or reckless with drink, he took to mimicry. Then he entered so wholeheartedly into the subject of his satire that his huge face and vast body seemed to transform themselves, even into the lean figure and hatchet face of a Wellington or the austere, arrogant good looks of his minister, Sir Robert Peel. When tired, at last, of the table, the Prince withdrew with his guests into the three small drawing rooms which had been the heart of Holland's villa. Here as in the Great Corridor the decoration, whether oriental or classical, is restrained and restful. The decorations of these rooms were repeatedly changed but the oriental motive was never powerful or dominant—the saloon was for many years (and is once again) hung with the real Chinese wallpaper, the gift of which, perhaps, started the Prince on his oriental theme for the Pavilion. But beyond this suite of drawing rooms lies the second wonder of the Pavilion—the Music Room. It was of this room that Princess de Lieven wrote, 'I do not believe that since the days of Heliogabalus, there has been such magnificence and such luxury. There is something effeminate in it which is disgusting. One spends the evening half-lying on cushions: the lights are dazzling: there are perfumes, music, liqueurs.'[1]

The room seemed to recall Marco Polo's description of the great tent of Genghis Khan. As in that, serpents writhed head first down the columns which divided the great panels of red lacquer painted with Chinese scenes in gold. The recesses of the great convex ceilings have roofs of beribboned bamboos. The central ceiling is a vast dome, decorated with diminishing scales. Flying dragons abound and the central chandelier is a vast Chinese water-lily. Again the cost was prodigious, and the result fabulous. Here in this room the Prince held his formal concerts at which Rossini and Kelby sang. Here, too, the Prince rendered his ballads in his firm baritone, now a little uncertain with age and drink, yet performed with *brio*.

Some of the most beautiful though far less impressive rooms of the Pavilion are the private apartments of the King, the rooms used by the Duke of Clarence, who afterwards succeeded him as William IV, and those of the Prince's ill-fated daughter, the Princess Charlotte, who, much to the Prince's grief, had died in childbirth in 1817. In these the scale is domestic, the colours delicate, and the Chinese and oriental motives give a gaiety and a difference to rooms that are essentially in the English Regency style. They illustrate, as the public rooms do, the exceptionally fine sense of colour that the Prince possessed for he had them painted time and time again until he achieved the perfection he sought.[2]

Although architecturally the Pavilion escaped into fantasy, it never extricated itself from the heart of Brighton. The Prince had bought land and houses at outrageous prices to make room for his stables and to give himself some privacy, but his gardens remained small, the front lawns scarcely bigger than those of a large villa. And even as the Pavilion was achieving its final form, Brighton was rapidly changing. The preoccupation, in the days of his youth, of his friends with horses had been a symptom of the age. Roads, carriages, even horses themselves, had undergone as rapid an improvement as the early motor-car was to undergo. By 1810, a day's visit to Brighton from London was not in the least difficult and frequently

---

[1] As might be expected, the Prince loved perfumes and cases of quart bottles were constantly being sent to Brighton.

[2] The total cost of the Pavilion was about £500,000 in gold: the equivalent of about £3,000,000 or $9,000,000.

performed. Families of rich merchants began to spend the summer there with father visiting them at the week-ends. By the Regency, Brighton had become the marine resort of London; speculative builders were running up a large town and the Pavilion was being swamped by this urban growth. The intimate privacy which the Prince had enjoyed with Mrs. Fitzherbert belonged to the remote past. And naturally as Brighton became more middle-class, the aristocracy began to look elsewhere for its playgrounds. The end of the Napoleonic war had opened up Europe once again. Fast coaches, and with a couple of decades the railway, made a villa in Italy or Southern France little less convenient than a house in Brighton or Bath had been for their grandparents.

Before, however, royalty and aristocracy finally left Brighton, it enjoyed a very quaint Indian summer. After 1822, the Prince's visits grew less, he was more and more addicted to the privacy which only the vast park at Windsor could give him. Windsor, too, had begun to absorb what creative energies were left in the mouldering hulk of his body. After his death in 1830, he was succeeded by his brother, William IV, the most outspoken, simple, eccentric monarch of modern times. William IV had been bred a sailor and he loved Brighton, loved to strut up and down the Pier as if it were his own quarter-deck, loved even better having his own cronies in to dinner at the Pavilion, utterly oblivious to the oriental magnificence that surrounded him. His Queen Adelaide was as homely as her husband, sitting patiently at her embroidery and worrying so much about the weight of the chandeliers that the King finally ordered the one in the Banqueting Room to be taken down. The gap in the ceiling did not worry them. However, times were not easier for royal guests. They might be bored by the tedium of royal domesticity but they needed to be prepared for shocks, as when one evening, when the band struck up a country dance to celebrate the New Year, the King seized Lord Amelius Beauclerk, a retired Admiral of the Fleet, and cavorted with him, hand in hand, down the Music Room. And then there was the even more electrifying occasion when the King stood up and said 'Now, ladies and gentlemen, I wish you a good night. I will not detain you any longer from your amusements, and shall go to my own which is to go to bed. So come along my Queen.'

And as for the growing crowds at Brighton, the King loved them. He enjoyed his people: loved stopping and talking to them, the more the merrier. And the quaint little pot-bellied, pear-headed monarch became immensely popular. His reign was brief and with it went Brighton's royal glory. Queen Victoria and her husband tried the Pavilion once or twice. They said they hated the staring crowds peering through the railings almost into the drawing-room. Probably they hated even more the atmosphere of the place which, unlike William IV, they were too sensitive to ignore. George IV and his brothers were not regarded by Albert the Good as respectable. So off Victoria and her husband went to Osborne in the Isle of Wight to build themselves their own marine villa where the furniture, instead of being in imitation bamboo, was in real stag horn.

The Pavilion itself hung on the brink of disaster. The best bits of furniture and the finer and less ornate chimney pieces and mirrors were packed off to Buckingham Palace that was being enlarged for Victoria's growing family. And it seemed inevitable that the demolition men would take it over. Messrs. Cubitt of London, the speculative builders of the day, already had their eye on it. But Brighton had a mayor of imagination: and he moved heaven and earth and the bankers to raise enough money to buy it for the town. So the fabric was saved and the Pavilion entered on a long mouldering old-age: the furnishings had been removed and sold and the original painting and decoration was swamped in institutional browns and maroons and greys. The rooms were used for dances, flower-shows, public meetings of all kinds. During World War I it was touched by fantasy again when it became an army hospital—for Indian troops! And then it was reborn. From 1920 onwards more and more men and women began to realize that Britain had inherited a priceless architectural heritage from the eighteenth and early nineteenth centuries and that Brighton's Pavilion as well as Brighton itself was one of the most original parts of it. Fortunately the late Queen Mary took an interest in the rehabilitation of the Pavilion. Slowly and steadily the old colours were discovered and revived; attics and cellars were searched at Windsor Castle and Buckingham Palace for furniture bearing the Pavilion and the Regent's mark. Some has been given, some returned on loan by the Royal Family, a few that escaped from the Royal collection bought. The process continues; each year sees the return of more; each year sees the Pavilion nearer to the dream that the Regent made a reality. Such a private and sumptuous place demands total restoration: china and silver and furniture are still needed but enough has been done to restore the Pavilion to its proper heritage. As with Versailles and with Neuschwanstein, the Pavilion at Brighton is the outward expression of a strange King's character in all its extravagance, oddity and poetry.

1962

CHATSWORTH
AND THE DEVONSHIRES

STRIPPED of works of art, worth many hundreds of thousands of pounds, will Chatsworth still be the same? For Chatsworth I have a special affection. As a small grubby boy, I made my first cycle journey of 100 miles in a day to gape at its riot of gilt and crimson and to wander, disconsolate and not without envy, in the wild grandeur of its park.

Since that first visit, I have returned time and time again to study in its archives as the Devonshires threaded themselves into my work on the history of the seventeenth and eighteenth centuries. More vivid than the letters or accounts was the house itself, and its works of art, a tribute both to the taste and wealth of generations of Cavendishes that have lived there.

Always one looked for the Rembrandt, Memlinc's triptych, the astonishing Apollo and the lesser delights such as the silver-gilt toilet service that gleamed like burnished gold in the Sabine Room: all now gone for ever. And yet so rich is Chatsworth that the loss hardly matters; there is still more than enough to fill the percipient visitor with wonder and to arouse his curiosity about a family that could afford to live and to collect on a scale as vast as this.

Yet neither architecture nor the contents of the house are the most moving things about Chatsworth. Few houses in England can rival its setting—the dark, dramatic woods that tumble down the precipitous hills, the sweeping, rippling river, and the terraced green of fine pasture broken by rock and oak—a setting one feels as immemorial as time itself. But quite wrongly!

Every aspect that feeds the eye is man-made, as artificial as the great cascade of water that graces the garden: all, save that, is the work of England's outstanding landscape artist—Capability Brown, who, in the eighteenth century, rendered picturesque the barren and forbidding Derwent valley.

To do this required courage as well as taste and wealth, for the west front of the house was, until the middle of the eighteenth century, the site of kitchens, stables and the elaborate formal gardens, replete with artificial ponds and ingenious water-works. The fourth Duke swept them away at a cost of 40,000 golden guineas. To see whether it was worth it, walk down, whether wet or fine, to the beautiful bridge James Paine built for him and contemplate the lovely vista of the west front—'as delicate as wrought plate', as Horace Walpole thought. This is one of the most beautiful views of a house that exists in England and alone worth a visit.

The Devonshires—quaintly named, as they have never possessed an acre in Devonshire itself—owe more than this vista to the fourth Duke. In him they produced their one Prime Minister and his political ability was higher than that of many great noblemen who held office in eighteenth-century England. Yet far more important than his politics—at least for Chatsworth—was his marriage. He married very wisely—Lord Burlington's only daughter and sole heiress. Burlington, fabulously rich, was the early eighteenth century's arbiter of taste, and doubtless gave his son-in-law a great deal of advice. Much of the fine eighteenth-century furniture may have come from him—particularly the superb gilt tables in the dining room by William Kent, whose patron he was.

Marriage, of course, is the answer, as far as an answer can be given in one word, to the question which becomes insistent as soon as one enters the main gate and moves towards the house itself. How could any family afford a house like this?

And remember this is but one of the Devonshire houses. There is, or was, Hardwick, twenty miles or so away, the most beautiful of all Elizabethan houses and well worth combining with a visit to Chatsworth; Compton Place, on whose estate Eastbourne was built; Bolton Abbey (this from the fourth Duke's wife); Holker Hall in Lancashire; Lismore Castle over in Ireland; and Devonshire House, a palace in Piccadilly, to say nothing of the magnificent villa at Chiswick; all belonged to them.

By 1883 they had acquired 198,667 acres which brought in a rental of £180,750 a year. Add to this mineral rights and income from investments, and then there is no surprise that forty or fifty sat down for dinner in the great dining room at Chatsworth, that 140 servants slept in the house and attended to their wants; that the sixth Duke could build the huge block that you pass on entry, with its strange Italianate loggia, to house his private theatre, or that he could indulge his mania for coins to the tune of £50,000 (sold for £7,000); or build a conservatory almost as big as the Crystal Palace (and by the same architect), alas now destroyed, or squander £50,000 on his embassy to the Tsar.

By judicious marriage that piled estate on estate the Devonshires could even afford the famous Georgiana and her equally reckless husband—the fifth Duke. She was the loveliest of all the Duchesses and the most feckless. Her picture by Reynolds, one of his most famous, may easily be missed. It is in the Sculpture Gallery on the left-hand side: look carefully, for there is nothing in the guide to show you where it is.

This lovely woman, friend of Charles James Fox and the Prince Regent, became famous for trading kisses for votes in the Westminster election of 1784. Less well known was her passion for gambling which is said to have cost her husband a million; maybe this mania was an anodyne for the strange private life that she was forced to live. Her husband, a dull lethargic man, kept his mistress in the same house and legitimate or illegitimate children shared a common nursery.

Perhaps she did not care at all, for her own life was far from blameless. Such was her gaiety and charm that all her faults were speedily forgiven; her beauty and vivacity captivated the world of fashion and made Devonshire House the centre of society as long as she lived.

After her death, the reputation of her beauty and her fame gave rise to one of the most remarkable stories in the world of art dealing. A supposed portrait of her by Gainsborough was sold at Christie's in 1841 for £46; in 1876 Agnews bought it for 10,000 guineas; three weeks later it was stolen from them. Twenty-five years later it was discovered in the false bottom of a trunk in America; in America it stayed, for Pierpoint Morgan paid £30,000 for it. It was as much

Georgiana's as Gainsborough's reputation that raised the price so astronomically.

Chatsworth, however, owes little either to her or her husband; its greatness rests squarely on the shoulders of two men—Sir William Cavendish, who came from Suffolk to be the husband of Bess of Hardwick, the builder of Hardwick Hall and a fabulous heiress, and the first Duke. Nothing of Sir William's Elizabethan house remains but the Hunting Tower high up in the wooded hillside, but the core of the estate was formed and the Cavendishes of the next generation were rich enough to buy an Earldom for £10,000.

As knowledge of Italian architecture and French taste spread among the Stuart aristocracy, Chatsworth became too old-fashioned for the Devonshires. The first Duke (he got his title free for helping William of Orange obtain the throne) devoted the last twenty years of his life to building the house which stands today; modifications and additions were carried out principally in the nineteenth century.

But essentially Chatsworth is the first great house of the Whig oligarchy that ruled England after the Revolution of 1688. Its superb proportions were the work of William Talman, the Duke himself and his amateur architect friend, Thomas Archer, for in those days architecture was as much a gentleman's pursuit as a professional's.

The inside lives up to the magnificence of the exterior. It possesses rooms of an almost riotous opulence, stuffed with splendid furniture, pictures, porcelain and statuary. The eye is immediately absorbed, perhaps too absorbed, by the rich painted ceilings—largely the work of a French artist, Laguerre, although the best to my mind is that by Sir James Thornhill in the Sabine Room.

The great state rooms, beautifully adorned and decorated, deserve more than a cursory glance. Stop in the Chapel for at least five or ten minutes. A scent of cedar wood pervades it; high above the altar hangs a picture by Verrio; the marble statuary is partly Cibber, partly Watson, whose lovely carving in wood and stone is one of the glories of Chatsworth. (Note his splendidly crisp armorial trophies on the East Wall of the inner courtyard.) Aesthetically this provides the deepest satisfaction of any part of Chatsworth.

Mostly these great rooms are adequately described in the brochure which one can buy, but it is also worth asking about special features, particularly in the state music room, where a violin on the door deceives the sharpest eye—is it real or painted? Ask the custodian, who will tell you the story of it.

It is the smaller objects or less obvious sights that everyone tends to miss on a first visit. Driving back recently from Chatsworth, I asked myself what I remembered most vividly, excluding the obvious visual delights of the great state rooms. The first thing I recalled was the outside from the inside.

Most visitors are so absorbed by painted ceilings and crimson furniture that they never look from the great windows that frame wonderful panoramic views of the park or elegant vistas of the formal garden with its playing fountains. When looking through the windows, notice their outer frames; these are not painted but gilded with gold leaf!

And within. First, the exquisite ormulu candelabra in the Sabine Room; by contrast the black wrought iron by Tijou on the main stairs—the finest French craftsmanship of its day; the two marquetry chests in the South Sketch Gallery, wholly satisfying in the simplicity of their proportions, and again by contrast the extravagantly realistic carving of a bird by Grinling Gibbons on the sideboard in the dining room; the baby carriage designed by William Kent in 1730, and placed at the top of the Great Stairs (on the right). He used his favourite double shell motif, and the baby Cavendish must have been as snug as a winkle.

In the ante-library is an unforgettable Rembrandt, a sharp reminder that in all the rooms and corridors through which one has passed there are pictures of the finest quality, if none quite so memorable as this. Equally unforgettable, but not for excellence, are the sickly, cloying, sentimental marble nudes—angels, Venuses, Endymions—in the Sculpture Gallery. These are so bad, so daintily refined, that it is difficult to check a tendency to rush out through the orangery into the fresh air—a great mistake, for at the end of the gallery are some truly excellent pictures by Poussin, Claude and Caravaggio, and a china cabinet, easily missed, which contains one of the most beautiful Vincennes basins and ewers in *gros-bleu* that I have ever seen.

Out in the formal garden, get away from the crowds by climbing up to the Cascade House, or find a seat in the rose garden or the

Temple of Flora that no one seems to use; sitting there, the years will drop away, the past be recaptured.

The realization grows that this is, or was, more than a rich man's house. In the gold and crimson, the profusion and ostentation, lurks the ghost of a different age; of the days of the mailed knight of the iron keep, of lord and retainer. The wealth of the last three centuries transformed that harsh chrysalis into the brilliant, extravagant display which in its arrogance still recalls its feudal origins and makes Chatsworth a symbol as well as a home.

In Chatsworth, in the great rooms of state, the power and the riches of the Devonshires was there for all men of Derbyshire to see. Knights of the Shire, Justices of the Peace, Deputy-Lieutenants, Mayors and Aldermen came for the Duke's favour which alone could ensure their success. And this territorial greatness gave the Devonshires a voice in the affairs of the nation as of right. That age has passed, yet Chatsworth remains, a work of art, in which splendour is all.

1958

BATH

BATH lies in a cup of the Cotswold Hills—a lovely, golden, stone-built city. Its elegant terraces have an air of secure prosperity. They recall an age of leisure when men and women, freer far than ourselves from the world's anxieties, could cultivate the art of living. But this is partly a mirage conjured up by the ordered beauty of the city's buildings, for Bath has its roots in the ugliness of life, in sickness and in pain. Fear of death and the hope of life have been more powerful than any other factors in the growth of Bath. Its Abbey is a vast lumber-room of the wealthy dead. The urbane memorials upon its walls read like the pages of Debrett—Seymours, Howards, Stanleys, Beauforts, Windhams, and the rest, came here to die. The knowledge of this endless chain of suffering, the sense of the brief transience of life, which these memorials breed, gives to the beauty of Bath a tragic quality.

From time out of mind, and still today, men and women have pinned their faith on the hot springs which well up by the side of the Avon. It was natural that man's imagination should have endowed them with magical qualities for there are no other springs like them in Great Britain. In very ancient times they were probably worshipped as holy, life-giving waters. The Romans built the first baths around the springs and much still remains of their work. After they had gone Bath decayed, but its warm radio-active springs continued to draw people for they were found to give relief to 'Scabbes and Great Aches' and barren women pinned their faith on them. Bath grew steadily in popularity and the King's Bath, the Queen's Bath and the Cross Bath were all well established by the end of the reign of James I. The visits of Catherine of Braganza and Mary of

Modena in the hope of children made them more fashionable. In the seventeenth century medical men began to popularize the internal application of waters containing salts or sulphur, and the development of Bath at this time is paralleled with other spas, as they came to be called after the Belgian town which had set the fashion. Spas nearer London, Tunbridge, Epsom and Islington, were more popular than Bath. But Bath had many natural advantages which soon began to tell. It was centrally situated for the South, West and Midlands; it was reasonably close to London yet far enough away, unlike Epsom or Tunbridge, to make for a real 'change of air' in which the doctors also believed.

Advice to go to a spa in earlier centuries would not have led to the growth of towns because few people, even the richest, had sufficient leisure to spend three weeks or a month taking an expensive cure. By the end of the seventeenth century, however, English society was more prosperous and its upper class more numerous, but it was no more healthy. One of the greatest revolutions in modern times, and the least publicized, is the revolution in health. Until recently the correspondence of men and women, their journals and diaries, were full of their aches and pains. And there was little but death to relieve them of their sufferings. So anyone who could afford it sought health at the spas. And it was not only the sick who came to Bath, but also those who thought that taking the waters would preserve the health which they enjoyed. The sick needed distraction, the healthy entertainment and the card-sharpers and ladies of the town soon followed in their wake.

Bath became a boisterous town, so boisterous that it might have suffered a decline but for the appearance of Richard Nash as Master of Ceremonies in Queen Anne's reign. 'Beau' Nash was a powerful personality and quickly brought the city to heel. He enforced his rules with equal impartiality on the Duchess or the farmer's wife and he made Bath an agreeable city to live in. He introduced music, turned dances into balls, abolished swords, riding boots and aprons, cleaned up the pump room, made special privileges for invalids, secured decency and good order, yet he preserved considerable freedom. Gambling and intrigue still flourished but discreetly and subject to convention. Nash's success was immense. Bath became 'the summer colony of the *beau monde*: the resort of the leaders of fashion, wit and public affairs'. Through the energy of Nash's friend Ralph Allen, old Bath was torn down and replaced by a gracious city of incomparable buildings. In the two Woods Bath found architects of genius. The Circus, Queen's Square and the Royal Crescent are in the great tradition of classical architecture.

Until the middle of the nineteenth century Bath retained its pre-eminence as the fashionable health and pleasure resort; and the list of the eminent men and women who have lived there is too long to record. But it appealed strongly to writers, for there was no other city save London where the weaknesses, follies and eccentricities of mankind were more amply demonstrated. Smollett, Sheridan, Jane Austen, all exercised their wit and malice at Bath's expense, but by the time Mr. Pickwick paid his visit the glory of Bath was fading.

Its comfortable life had drawn to it half-pay officers, retired parsons, spinsters with small legacies—the twilight world of gentility which gave rise to a harsher morality. Gambling ceased; intrigue was frowned upon. Bath became sedate and dull. The fashionable world departed for Monte Carlo or Baden Baden where stakes were still high and girls plentiful. Bath was left once more to the sick and aged. But its prosperity did not cease; industry replaced fashion and new suburbs, regrettably ugly, grew around the majestic core of the eighteenth-century city.

Once more the tide has turned. The last thirty years has witnessed a renewed interest in Georgian architecture and a greater appreciation of the eighteenth-century attitude to life—its charm, its wit, its stoicism, and its never-ending delight in the physical world. Now in summer time the tourists flock and stare.

There are few cities in Western Europe which reflect an age so completely as Bath, and none is so redolent of Time. Nostalgia pervades its streets and memories cling like moss to its squares and terraces, but not only memories of ordinary men and women bent on the pleasures of life but also faced with the difficult art of dying.

1954

THE EARL OF CHATHAM

THE central problem of foreign policy in eighteenth-century England was this: should Britain be content with a moderate prosperity or risk poverty in a gamble for the trade of the world? The answer was easy to men whose wealth was in land. They wanted peace and a low land-tax. To the enterprising merchant, with a fortune still to win, the answer was equally simple—war and a share in a privateer. But most men's wealth was neither in land nor in trade, but in a mixture of both. The Duke of Bedford, one of the greatest landowners, possessed East Indiamen that unloaded at his own docks in Rotherhithe. On the other hand, the great East Anglian merchants, the Turners of Lynn, invested their profits from the wine trade in estates in Norfolk. And for such men of mixed property the answer to the question was far from simple. Their cupidity was riven with doubt: either war or peace might bring them the greater gain.

Eighteenth-century parliaments have been considered quixotic because, although primarily composed of landowners, they embarked on aggressive commercial wars and voted for large increases in the land-tax. This paradox has been explained by endowing eighteenth-century politicians with a capacity to put national needs above private gain. A wiser interpretation would be that many Members of Parliament were incapable of determining their true self-interest. Indeed, it was because of this very uncertainty that Chatham became so powerful a figure in English life.

Chatham himself had no doubts. He believed that England's moral duty was to capture the trade of the world, if need be, by war. It is probable that this conviction was derived from his grandfather, 'Diamond' Pitt, a buccaneering East India merchant who began life as an interloper in the Indian trade and finished as the Governor of Fort St. George at Madras. His wealth and success were the result of risks resolutely and aggressively taken. A hard-headed, hard-fisted pioneer of trade, he knew that in the East enormous fortunes were to be won, and could be won easily, if English merchants were backed by force from home. He was also aware that Englishmen were not alone in this race for trade and wealth. The French were our rivals, and the prize was so great there could be no compromise. War alone could decide. These were to be the deepest convictions of Chatham's life. This preoccupation with questions of trade is the key to his policy; but equally important for an understanding of his career is an appreciation of the strangeness of his character.

From time to time throughout his later life, Chatham was insane. He suffered acutely from manic-depression. Periods of intense exhilaration, almost of ecstasy, combined with an immense sense of power, would be followed by prolonged fits of abject despair in which contact with other human beings would be intolerable to him. During these times all work was impossible. He isolated himself in his room, and his meals were pushed through a hatch. But such an affliction was not all loss; it often gave a frenzy, an urgency, a sense of destiny to his utterances which had an hypnotic effect on his audiences. Apart from his madness, Chatham was a difficult character. Except within his own family circle, he lacked all *bonhomie*. He was stilted, affected, given to gestures of irritating ostentation, as when he rode about London in a one-horse chaise to mark his poverty, after being dismissed by Walpole from his army commission. He was all that the convivial, intimate political world of the eighteenth century found difficult to assimilate. The Grenvilles were glad to use him as a bogey with which to threaten George II and Newcastle; but even they never relished working with him. Yet his very defects in the private world of politics were virtues in the eyes of the public. The ostentatious purity of his public life—he refused the usual perquisites of Paymaster-General of the Forces—combined as it was with a theatrical truculence and independence, endeared him to the hearts of those who felt that English politics were corrupt and despicable. The idol of the middle-class, the 'Great Commoner', as he was called, he was the first politician who both demanded and used the approbation of the public to further his own political ends. This public notoriety and esteem allowed him a freedom of action and expression which would have been denied him had his power rested solely on a parliamentary faction. His position was further strengthened because, although *nouveau riche*, he was not a *parvenu* like Wilkes or Canning; he was an accepted member of aristocratic society, tied to it by marriage and by blood, and could not easily be excluded from the authority that his talents and social standing demanded.

Chatham entered the House of Commons in 1735 for the family rotten borough of Old Sarum which Governor Pitt had bought with his diamond. At once Pitt went into opposition, furious opposition, in which the King's Hanoverian interests were denounced with a venom, startling even in an age used to unbridled invective. Walpole's policy of peace was ripped to shreds in words which burnt themselves into the memory: 'When Trade is at stake it is your last Retrenchment, you must defend it or perish.' 'Sir, Spain knows the consequences of a war in America. Whoever gains it must prove fatal to her.' Such an open avowal bred its own elation for a war of plunder—a war, as Burke afterwards described it, that was to be attended with something more solid than glory. In the end London got its war, but Chatham stayed in the wilderness. George II regarded his remarks on Hanover as unpardonable.

Chatham spent his spare time investigating the comparative commercial statistics of France and England, and in cultivating the merchants of the City against the moment when events should force an entry to the royal closet. But he had to wait nearly twenty years before he obtained the direction of affairs—twenty years spent in and out of office. His early career was a curious mixture of threats and apologetics; for, ironically enough, he was called on now and then to defend the King's Hanoverian interests. It was a career that had gone off at half-cock, ruined partly by illness, partly by the desire to please: the promise of his volcanic eruption into politics seemed to have come to nothing. After a series of intrigues and manoeuvres, curiously at variance with the stark integrity of purpose that both Chatham and the public liked to assume was his chief characteristic, he obtained supreme office in 1757, in alliance with the Duke of Newcastle, who was to provide both the parliamentary majority and the cash to pay for the war, of which Chatham was to have the sole direction. For the next four years, British arms enjoyed a series of victories unprecedented since the days of Marlborough. By 1761, the French had been routed in Canada, India and the West Indies and a monopoly of the world's trade was within our grasp. No Prime Minister, until very recent times, has achieved so much in so short a time. His success has been variously explained by inspiration, by his gift of selecting courageous and resourceful men, by revolutionary strategy. Certainly, Chatham inspired Wolfe and the others who merited his regard; but his strategy was far from revolutionary, except in its range and the thoroughness of its application.

Throughout the eighteenth century, a school of thought, largely Tory, had considered that England should avoid using large armies in Europe, but should subsidize her allies, and confine her military activity to small-scale continental raids. It was argued that her main force should be concentrated in the navy, to be used to deny her enemy overseas trade. This policy had tremendous advantages for England. She had little or no surplus manpower to draw on for military purposes and by European standards her army was weak and inefficient, whereas her vast shipping resources could be readily utilized in naval warfare. But the argument which attracted most support for his policy was that the capture of the enemy's trade could be made to pay for the war and to show a profit. Of that Chatham was convinced. For years he had studied this question in consultation with his city friends, Cumming, Beckford, Vaughan and others. As soon as he was in power he put this policy into force. In 1746, he had come to the conclusion that the capture of Quebec would mean the capture of the valuable fur and fish trade from France.[1] In 1759 Wolfe's expedition proved him right. Similarly he mounted attacks on Dakar (Goree) in order to wrest the gum trade from France, and, as soon as it was won, ordered explorations of the interior, and promptly set up a Committee of the Board of Trade to determine whether the retention of Senegal would be

[1] This, too, had been realized long before. Robert Walpole, as Secretary-at-War, had worked out the logistics for such an expedition in 1709. See J. H. Plumb, *Sir Robert Walpole* (1956), I, p. 133.

commercially profitable. But his greatest *coup* was the capture of the
sugar islands of Martinique and Guadeloupe. The attacks on these
islands made some of his city friends apprehensive, for fear that their
possession would lead to a sugar glut and a fall in price. Pitt thought
a glut impossible. He was right. Within two years of its capture
Guadeloupe was producing twice as much sugar; the expedition
had been paid for and a handsome profit shown. As his Guildhall
monument proudly boasts, Chatham increased the wealth of his
country 'by commerce, for the first time, united with and made to
flourish by war'. This was the true aim of the 'blue water policy'—
maritime strength translated into trade and wealth and power. It
was no part of his policy to acquire an Empire in the sense of vast
colonial possessions; islands and forts at strategic focal points of
trade were desirable but not more, unless necessity compelled it, as
in Canada.

Chatham's war was a triumph which intoxicated, leading him to
call for the destruction of Spain as well as France. London was with
him, but the government refused to follow. George III had no love
for his grandfather's ministers or for their policy. He secured half-
hearted support from Newcastle who hated the mounting cost of
war and was haunted by the growing fear, particularly amongst the
landowners, that such fabulous triumphs must inevitably unite the
whole of Europe against Britain. That Chatham could have viewed
with equanimity, but few others shared his faith or his vision. He
was obliged to resign. All the arguments of common sense were
against him: any peace would bring down taxes; a reasonable treaty,
with large returns of captured property, might bring a lasting peace
and years of plenty and security. This was a siren's song that gained
eager attention, for England had suffered more than twenty years of
war. Chatham knew it was a dream, an illusion: that France, even
generously treated, would still scheme to regain her empire and her
trade. In December 1762, in the most forceful speech of his career,
he damned the Treaty of Paris which George III and his ministers
were eager to sign. All, or nearly all, that he had won was returned.
'We retain nothing,' cried Chatham, 'although we have conquered
everything,' and in words which afterwards seemed prophetic he
phrased the principles which had guided his policy. 'France is chiefly,
if not solely, to be dreaded by us in the light of a maritime and

commercial power and therefore by restoring to her all the valuable West Indian islands, and by our concessions in the Newfoundland fishery, we have given her the means of recovering her prodigious losses and of becoming once more formidable to us at sea.' Of course, he was right; as soon as we were in difficulties with the American colonies, France attacked.

From 1761 onwards, Chatham was the most formidable statesman in opposition to the Crown, for his popularity in the City bordered on idolatry which even the disastrous premiership of 1766 and his elevation to the peerage could not destroy. Fortunately for the government, his health grew steadily worse; he was mad during nearly the whole of his second period of office. Yet when national tribulation or folly called him out of his retreat, he never failed to make his appearance in Parliament. Then, sick and wasted as he was, his utterances acquired supernatural force and an oracular wisdom. His most important interventions were in the great causes of Wilkes and America. It was Wilkes's truculent denunication of the Treaty of Paris in No. 45 of the *North Briton* that led to his quarrel over general warrants with the government and subsequently with Parliament over the Middlesex election. Although Wilkes could in some ways be regarded as a martyr of Chatham's own cause, and although he had the complete support of the City of London, Chatham was nevertheless circumspect in his attitude; for he had the highest regard for the sovereignty of the Crown in Parliament. He thought the actions of the Commons inexpedient, but he did not regard them as illegal. It was only when the Commons ordered the deletion of a judicial decision of a court of record of the City of London that Chatham's fury was fully unleashed. This act he denounced as the act of a mob, not a parliament; and his withering criticism helped to put an end to the persecution of Wilkes.

It was the cause of America which called forth his greatest efforts. The same principles upon which he had formed his attitude to affairs throughout his career are apparent in his American policy. He recognized at once that the fundamental issue was commercial and not constitutional. America, he said, 'was the fountain of our wealth, the source of our strength, the nursery and basis of our naval power' and 'she has been the great support of this country; she has produced millions; she afforded soldiers and sailors; she has given our manufacturers employment and enriched our merchants'. In order to preserve this fountain of wealth Chatham was prepared to go to any lengths of compromise, short of independent sovereignty. He conceded that Britain had every right to regulate America's trade and commerce, but he knew that to do so was folly and he was prepared to make any concession and even allow America to tax itself, so long as she remained a part of the empire. He dreaded independence and hated the war.

'The colonies,' he told the Lords in 1777, 'were too great an object to be grasped but in the arms of affection.' And he saw that victory would be meaningless. 'If you conquer them, what then? You cannot make them respect you; you cannot make them buy your cloth.' Yet the prospect of defeat was a nightmare which haunted his dying days, for American independence must, he thought, enrich France. He believed America too poor, and too untrained in the arts of government, to escape the tutelage of a great power—and if not Britain's, then France's was inevitable. And such a contingency must ruin England commercially. Nor was Chatham's a lonely voice. All the great trading towns believed as he believed and that is why there was so much reluctance to support the war. At the end of a great speech against the Stamp Act, the merchants of London trading to America removed the horses from his coach and dragged him home. They were not moved by the abstract principles of liberty, but by the prospect of economic ruin. Chatham might rise to great heights of moral fervour in his perorations, but the principles of his policy were based four-square on profit and loss.

And yet—herein lies his greatness—his attitude to empire was not entirely rapacious. There was too much darkness in his own life for him not to have sympathy with shame and humiliation. He detested the corrupt tyranny of the East India Company in Bengal and denounced it roundly. Wealth, success, victory had their obligations, their moral responsibilities; of this he was always conscious, and it gave a loftiness to his oratory which a call for mere aggression, no matter how fervid, could never have achieved. Similarly his support of Wilkes and of America had a moral quality. He believed in liberty, not in economic or social liberty, but in liberty for men, accepting the circumstances of their time, to have life on their own terms, free from the arbitrary interference of government. An attitude of heart and mind which always drew a quick response in eighteenth-century England.

His death was as dramatic and as theatrical as his life; for dying, and scarcely able to walk, he struggled to the House of Lords to protest against the government's American policy. The effort killed him, but it was a fitting end to the greatest orator Britain has known. Neither during his life nor afterwards was there question of the greatness of Chatham. Arrogant, affected, megalomaniac, he might be, his contemporaries nevertheless were aware of his genius; for he could create the sense in all who listened to him that he was the mouthpiece of destiny. And posterity, alas, has known it to be true.

1952

JOSIAH WEDGWOOD

JOSIAH WEDGWOOD was a pioneer of the Industrial Revolution! For many of us who were bred in the liberal tradition, such a phrase conjures up a picture of a square-jawed, steely-eyed grinder of the faces of the poor. You might expect him to be a man of inflexible character, narrow, philistine and possibly hypocritical: one whose interests were limited to profit and the accumulation of capital: and, perhaps, indifferent to poverty, squalor and human suffering: one of those men whose sole memorials are the mean streets of the dirty towns which erupt like boils across the Midland plain. Naturally there were such men—every rabid social change creates an opportunity for the tough and the heartless—but Josiah Wedgwood was not one of them. Certainly he was tough. You have only to look at the Reynolds portrait of him to realize that. His jaw was formidably square, almost brutal. And only a tough-minded man could have done some of the things that Wedgwood did for the sake of his business. He had a weak leg, the result of a serious illness in childhood: the slightest knock caused inflammation and pain, and knocks were unavoidable when riding through the deep muddy Midland lanes in winter. So to avoid the long periods of sickness and the interruption of business Wedgwood had the leg amputated. In those days there were no anaesthetics, no sterilization of instruments; each act of surgery was a gamble with death. The key to much of Wedgwood's success in life was his boldness and courage in decisions such as this. Although Wedgwood's square jaw immediately attracts the eye, no one can look at his picture without realizing that he was far from being a simple man. His eyes are wide, frank, enquiring, but his mouth perhaps is even more interesting than his eyes. It is soft, sensual, the one beautiful feature of that powerful, ugly face. The final impression of this portrait is of strength, intelligence and, oddly enough, compassion—a quality not often associated with a pioneer of industrial revolution but one borne out by the story of Wedgwood's life.

He was born in 1730 at Burslem—then the only 'town' in the Potteries and not a very prosperous one at that. His family was typical of a curiously English mixture of class. He was descended from a long line of small landowners; some had married well, others had drifted into trade, most eked out their inheritance with a small pottery business. But it was a family of wide connections and one which possessed a number of useful reserves of capital. Wedgwood tapped one of these when he married his cousin, Sarah, the daughter and heiress of a prosperous cheese factor in Cheshire. The origins of many of the great figures of the Industrial Revolution were similar to Wedgwood's. Few of them were born in absolute poverty; most of them came from families with a little money and a knowledge of trade.

As potters the Wedgwoods were well known and quite successful within the narrow limits of the Staffordshire trade. The invention of salt glaze in the 1690's and the proximity of the great Cheshire salt deposits gave the district a fillip in the early years of the eighteenth century. By the time, however, Wedgwood was growing to manhood in the late 1740's, the industry was losing ground. The naïvete of much of the salt glaze was beginning to bore the public. The gentry and aristocracy preferred Dutch pottery or German porcelain, or the even more costly porcelain imported at great cost from China. The English products were too heavy, too grossly decorated, too obviously peasant ware for the growing refinement of the wealthy classes.

The potters knew it and Wedgwood grew up in an atmosphere of experiment. From his earliest days he was determined to improve Staffordshire pottery. He was a man of enormous patience and resource and once set on a course, not easily deterred by failure. That square, obstinate chin was highly symbolic of his rugged determination. Before he perfected his famous Jasper ware—that blue or sage green pottery with white decoration which immediately springs to the mind when Wedgwood is mentioned—he made over ten thousand trial pieces. From the first he set his standards very high and that was one of the reasons for his success. He tried, and finally succeeded in making English pottery almost as fine as the best that Europe or China could offer. I say 'almost as fine' deliberately. It was never Wedgwood's intention to produce a few exquisite master-pieces. From the start he wanted to capture a world market; to make fine pottery cheap enough for the middle classes and beautiful enough for kings and princes. That is why from the first he con-centrated his attention on his 'useful' pottery, the white Queen's ware which quickly achieved an international reputation; Catherine of Russia ordered a magnificent dinner service of a thousand pieces; a generation later a service followed Napoleon to St. Helena. In the years between the use of Wedgwood had spread to the uttermost ends of the earth.

This astonishing achievement which poured a new invigorating wealth into the Midland counties was not easily brought about. Great difficulties needed to be overcome; and technical advance was not enough by itself. For one thing the human material was not very tractable. The Staffordshire potters were no more easy to discipline than most eighteenth-century craftsmen who liked doing their jobs in their own way and in their own time. They wandered from process to process as the mood seized them; worked hard and then drank hard. Everything was done by fits and starts. That was not Wedgwood's way and once they started to work for him, those habits had to change. In his factories hours were regular and processes methodical, so that production could be continuous. Exhortation, rewards, punishments and education—by these methods Wedgwood created a factory system capable of mass production of fine quality pottery. At the same time, he provided far more stable and profitable working conditions than the journeyman potters had ever known. Increased trade and population increased amenities—schools, musical festivals, literary and scientific institutes—all were encouraged by Wedgwood. They helped to dispel the mediaeval barbarity into which so many of the potters had been born. Living conditions improved greatly. It is hard for us to realize that. The mean, crumb-ling slums which we view with so much disgust represented in the eighteenth and early nineteenth centuries a triumph in working-class conditions, an advance on the mud and wattle rural slums of the earlier centuries.

Disciplined labour, systematic production, high technical achievement, even these were not enough to secure Wedgwood's success. In his early youth, coal for firing the potter's oven had frequently to be carried on the backs of men—no other beast of burden could struggle through the deep quagmires which the roads became in winter. Packhorses and the wagons of summer time were not much cheaper than men. The raw materials, salt, lead-ore, coal and the fine clays from Dorset, Devon and Cornwall, were all bulky, all expensive to move. Hence it is natural to find Wedgwood in the forefront of the battle for improved communications, and here luck was on his side. Liverpool, under the energetic inspiration of a small band of highly intelligent merchants, was growing fast. The Duke of Bridgwater and his engineer Brindley were beginning to solve some of the problems which its growth created by developing artificial waterways or canals. Liverpool was the natural port for Staffordshire and Wedgwood became the leading agitator for a Trent-Mersey canal which, however, involved far more difficult engineering problems than any previously tackled by Brindley. Of course there was much opposition but the tide of life was with Wedgwood and his friends. They got their canal and were splendidly justified—freight was reduced from 10d. to 1¼d. per ton per mile.

It needed, however, more than efficiency and cheap transport to capture a mass market; more even than fine technique. Wedgwood had to win and keep the approval of the fashionable world. During one of his visits to Liverpool Wedgwood was laid up for many weeks with that leg of his. He was introduced to a Liverpool merchant, Richard Bentley. They became devoted friends and lifelong partners. Bentley was a highly sophisticated and sensitive man with a wide knowledge of art, well known and respected in the literary and scientific circles of London. He brought Wedgwood into contact with ideas and attitudes which stimulated his imagination. It was through Bentley that Wedgwood obtained the services of Flaxman, one of the finest modellers of his day. Bentley conducted the firm's London showrooms with great skill and such profit that Wedgwood was able to indulge both his love of experiment and his ambition to repeat, if not surpass, the ceramic triumphs of the ancient world.

By middle age Wedgwood had transformed a peasant craft into

an industry with a world market, yet one whose products were acclaimed as works of art by informed opinion. Now Wedgwood believed that his success was due to scientific experiment, to the steady application of rational principles to all problems, and to riding roughshod over traditional attitudes and ancient prejudices. 'All things,' he wrote, 'yield to experiment.' Naturally, therefore, he was drawn to the society of men whose views on life were similar to his own; to men such as Priestley, Darwin, Franklin and their kind, men who believed in applying reason to the problems of politics and society. Bentley held similar views, and the two partners became stalwart supporters of that admirable liberal humanism of the late eighteenth century. They believed in parliamentary reform and universal suffrage. They denounced the slave trade; one of their finest cameos was of a slave kneeling in chains with the inscription: 'Am I not a man and a brother?' Wedgwood told Bentley that he blessed his stars and Lord North that America was free from the iron hand of tyranny. He refused to be scared into obscurantism by the spectre of the French Revolution. In spite of the loss of trade, he welcomed it. Wedgwood believed passionately that he and his friends were the harbingers of a new and better world from which prejudice and poverty would be banished and in which reason would triumph. A naïve attitude, perhaps, but one which mirrors the noble aspects of eighteenth-century life. His beliefs were very much of his time and place, as was his success, yet not entirely so. He possessed compassion and the ebullient, life-giving quality of genius. He would never prosecute a debtor; rich as he became he loathed accounts and ignored them; he paid no attention to the little men who pirated his works. 'So far from being afraid of other people getting our patterns,' he wrote to Bentley, 'we should glory in it. . . . There is nothing relating to business I so much wish for as being released from . . . those mean selfish fears of other people copying my works.' In that fine, expressive face which mirrored so accurately his complex nature, it was the fine eyes and sensitive mouth which in final analysis dominated the rugged jaw. In the largeness of his heart and the liberality of his mind he transcended the age in which he lived.

The seeds of creative genius settle and flower in curious places. In the fertile mind and active personality of Josiah Wedgwood they

I

found good soil. Amongst the arts and crafts that adorn the life of man, his works still have an enduring place, and remain unmistakably his. His personality, his individual genius make them as singular as a Dickens novel or a Bach fugue. Eighteenth-century England bred few men of finer quality.

1955

THE WALPOLES: FATHER AND SON

THE Walpole manuscripts from Houghton Hall consist mostly of foreign despatches, cabinet papers, parliamentary speeches and Treasury memoranda—the expected relics of a long ministerial career. But there was found amongst these papers a number of bundles of a more personal nature—private family letters, account books and household bills—documents which Archdeacon Coxe ignored when he came to write his official life of Sir Robert Walpole.[1] Unfortunately they are sadly incomplete. There are very few private letters after 1707; the accounts illuminate only an occasional decade; the bills relate to a year here or there. Yet these documents are very precious for they are the only source we have which throws any light on the way Sir Robert Walpole lived or on his family background and early education. Also some of his father's accounts survive, and it is possible to compare the daily life of a simple country gentleman of the seventeenth century with that of a great statesman of the eighteenth, a contrast which illuminates the class structure of the Augustan age, and reveals some of the causes of the political bitterness of that time.

The Walpoles had lived for many generations in North-West Norfolk. They had emerged, like so many gentle families, in the late thirteenth century, taking advantage of the great expansion

---

[1] This chapter is based on the Cholmondeley (Houghton) MSS., deposited at the University Library, Cambridge, by the Marquess of Cholmondeley, to whom I am deeply indebted for the permission to quote from them. The following account books are the major sources:—Nos. 9, 15/1, 20a, 22, 24; the bills too have been used, principally those for 1733, and detailed references to these sources have not been given. Anyone requiring them can find them in my *Sir Robert Walpole* (1956–61), 2 vols.

in agrarian prosperity. Possibly their success was due to their enterprise in taking into cultivation the arid and desolate heathland of
this corner of Norfolk. Thereafter generation had followed generation at Houghton; their lands increased little; their social position
remained what it had been for centuries. They belonged to the ruling
class of families, providing Justices of the Peace, Deputy Lieutenants,
Colonels of Militia—and, on rare occasions, a Member of Parliament. They were akin to scores of families which spread like a net
across the counties of England, giving them coherence and form
and government.[1] The Walpoles lived and died and were buried at
Houghton, the little village which nestled by the side of their
rambling house and which provided so many generations of its
servants. The pattern of life there scarcely changed as century
followed century—the great fields were tilled and cropped as they
had been time out of mind; the vast flocks of sheep grazed on the
brekes as they had done since Doomsday; the tenants paid their
rents in cash, in produce, and by boon work according to the
ancient manorial custom. More often than not they were in debt
to their lord. It mattered hardly at all, for little was needed which
the manors themselves did not provide.

Nathan Solden, the steward of Sir Robert Walpole's great-
grandfather, kept a careful account of his household expenditure in
a neat but angular hand—one book from 1647-49 survives. The
purchases which it records are of the simplest. Food is the most
important item—'a cupple of ducks'; teal occasionally; and a
regular purchase of two hundred oysters for two shillings every
week. Meat was entered in large quantities but this can only have
been a question of book-keeping between home and farm for no
Walpole can ever have needed to purchase mutton. 'Oringes and
lymons' were a different matter and these and a peck of turnips were
most probably bought at Lynn. But such fancy foods were rare. The
family diet was plain; the routine of meat and game was only
occasionally relieved by a 'dishe of udders'. Lumped in with the
food are other purchases—nails, matting, wire, new tiles, calico for
shirts, the mending of doublets, but even so the household expenditure was very small. Robert, an elderly widower, lived with his son,
Edward, and his wife who had five children, and a flock of indoor

[1] J. H. Round, *Family Origins and other Studies* (1930): 'The Origin of the Walpoles'.

servants, but only on occasion did the weekly bill, including the meat, rise above £10, usually it was about six or seven. There are no signs of any extravagance. Robert Walpole's income was about £750 a year. During the Civil War he behaved himself with great circumspection, thereby evading the compoundings and sequestrations which bore so heavily on many Norfolk families. And as Walpoles were wont to do he had married well, the daughter of a Lord Mayor of London, and so had his son whose wife, Susan Crane, the daughter of a Suffolk gentleman, brought a jointure of £132 a year. They were a prosperous family and Robert's son a rising man who had helped Townshend seize Lynn for Charles II in 1660. He became its Member of Parliament in the Cavalier Parliament—a tribute to his own as well as his family's standing in the county for he did not possess a settled interest in the borough. To add to his glory, Charles II made him Knight of the Bath, and in 1661 life must have seemed sweet to Sir Edward Walpole. He could look forward to a distinguished career, excellent marriages for his children, and a steady accumulation of wealth in land. But rich or poor in seventeenth-century England lived constantly in the shadow of death. Within a few years his father, his wife and himself were all buried. Sir Edward's bright hopes were gone, and Houghton was left to the care of his son, Robert; a boy of seventeen who had been born in 1650.

Robert inherited a good estate but many obligations. There were his aunts, his brothers, his young sisters, all had to be provided for, and soon there would be children of his own. We know very little of this Robert Walpole. Only a few of his letters remain and there is but one reference to him in contemporary memoirs. But his account books are extensive and they disclose the man. Later in life Robert Walpole became known as Colonel Walpole—his rank in the Norfolk militia—and it is simpler to call him by this title in order to distinguish him from his more famous son.

Colonel Walpole was a solid, well-integrated character. The steps which he took were those of a man who had measured carefully his opportunities. They were never hurried yet he was not an over-cautious man for he was quite capable of taking risks with the money which he garnered so carefully. He had temper and made it felt opportunely when his interests were endangered, but it was never wanton nor rash like his brother Horatio's. He was also a highly intelligent man; very well read in the classics, with an abiding passion for his library. Whenever he went off to the Norfolk fairs, he rarely came back to Houghton without a parcel of books strapped behind his servant's saddle. They still remain at Houghton —histories of Sweden, the Netherlands, Bohemia, in large folio: bound volumes of sermons including those of his old Trinity tutor, Dr. Barrow, for which he paid £1 14s. 6d. on January 26, 1684. He was interested in the new learning and Francis Bacon's works found a place on his shelves. This passion after knowledge gave him a reputation, according to Francis North, 'for study and learning extraordinary'.[1] He provides another illustration, if another were needed, of the falsity of Macaulay's picture of the illiterate rural squire of seventeenth-century England. Colonel Walpole was well read in history, geography, theology, law and the classics. Much of his time was to be spent in farming, in hunting, in drinking, in those rural pursuits which were natural to a country gentleman, but his love of books remained with him to the day of his death.

Perhaps his intelligence can best be seen at work in the way he managed the farming of his own estates. In the early seventeenth century the Flemings had developed new agricultural methods on dry sandy soils similar to those at Houghton. The contacts between King's Lynn and Flanders were very close, and the new husbandry must have been discussed by the gentlemen farmers and merchants when they met together at the fairs and markets, for there were very few of the great merchants of Lynn who were not almost as interested in land as in merchandise. By 1660 a certain publicity had been given to the improvements in Flanders by pamphleteers, but there is no evidence that Colonel Walpole had read their books. During his early years as a farmer he never once visited London, and his knowledge was most probably derived from the talk that he heard in Lynn or what he saw about him in Norfolk. He was certainly convinced of the wisdom of Flemish techniques and he became one of the pioneers of a new school of agriculture in which root crops and grasses played an important part. By 1673 turnips were being grown at Houghton in very considerable quantities; they were weeded regularly and double-hoed—payments for both

[1] *Lives of the Norths* (1826), III, p. 304.

processes occur regularly year after year in the account books. Colonel Walpole was interested in the new grass crops as well as turnips. On April 25, 1677, he paid 'Godfrey for 4 days sewing my clover seed, beside his board . . . o4s. od.'[1] He had bought the two hundred pounds of seed a fortnight before for £4. The next year he grew some of his own seed, but it was insufficient for his spring sowing in 1679, so he bought another three combs. The accounts also refer to 'The Great Clover Close'. Clover, along with turnips, had become a part of the established Houghton practice. He was also experimenting with wheat, a difficult crop on these dry sandy soils, on a modest but not insignificant scale, for he bought seven bushels of seed wheat in October 1679, at 13s. 6d. Marling and enclosing were long established processes which Colonel Walpole not only maintained but also extended. A hundred years later Arthur Young regarded these features of Norfolk husbandry as new and progressive: later centuries, following his lead, hailed their introduction into England as a part of the eighteenth-century agrarian revolution.

It is time that revolution was antedated by a century, for Colonel Walpole was not a lonely pioneer. He bought clover seed from his cousin, Ruding, a yeoman farmer of Rougham; from Mrs. Arminger, another small landowner at Burnham Thorpe; from Allen of Ingoldisthorpe, one of the lesser gentry, and from Kent, the steward of Lord Townshend at Raynham. So it would seem that landowners great and small were busily experimenting with Flemish methods in this corner of Norfolk. Nor was it only Flemish methods which Colonel Walpole adopted. The demands for food of the growing population of London had influenced the husbandry of southern and eastern England for many generations; the influence gradually spread in ever widening circles until it reached Scotland. In London Scotch beef became a luxury food, and it occurred to Colonel Walpole and probably to others that Scotch cattle could be fattened in Norfolk after their long trek south for the London market. In August 1676 he bought half a dozen steers, possibly as an experiment; they cost him £17 2s. od. Another famous point of Norfolk husbandry established long before the days of 'Turnip Townshend'

---

[1] Naomi Riches, *The Agricultural Revolution in Norfolk* (Chapel Hill, 1937); J. H. Plumb, 'Sir Robert Walpole and Norfolk Husbandry', *Ec. Hist. Rev.* (1952), pp. 86–9.

or Coke of Holkham! There can be no doubt that Colonel Walpole was an intelligent, adventurous man, quick to seize his opportunities, and free from many of the prejudices of tradition and custom.

And of course, he prospered, but this prosperity, derived purely from his farming, was not dissipated; few young men of seventeen with a large patrimony can have been so cautious or so level-headed. It was some seventeen years after his inheritance of Houghton before he ventured to London. Until then his journeys were confined to visits to the Norfolk fairs and Norwich assizes or to his Suffolk property where his father-in-law, Sir Jeffery Burwell, lived hard by at Rougham. A similar prudence can be discerned in his expenditure; there is no extravagance, not even at election times—a guinea and a half was all that he laid out at Norwich in 1679. There is no sign of self-indulgence, save perhaps for eight barrels of Colchester oysters for 19s. (but surely a bargain at that price!), and even then he had the excuse that doctors thought oysters essential for health. The accounts illustrate a life of utmost simplicity. The reason was not only the need for Colonel Walpole to accumulate capital to buy land, although that doubtless was important, but the extent of his family obligations also constrained him to a plain way of living, unless he were to risk burdening his estate with debt, for at seventeen he had inherited not only an estate but a nursery full of children. On February 22, 1671, he had married Mary Burwell, only a girl of sixteen, and their own children arrived with the regularity of the harvest.[1] During the early years of his marriage his sisters were boarded out, rather expensively, with Lady Crane; his brothers, Horatio and Edward, had to be maintained at school. This was costly enough, but the time would soon come when he would have to find his sisters' portions, together with the interest which had accumulated over the years. He could and did charge them for their maintenance, but even so he had difficulty in raising the money. In the end he persuaded his father-in-law to sell his estate to Sir Robert Davers who had made a fortune in the Barbados. Colonel Walpole, whose wife was to inherit his property in any case on her father's death, then paid Sir Jeffery Burwell an annuity, equivalent to 5 per cent. interest on the capital raised by the sale, and so by this ingenious method he avoided mortgaging his own property. This, at least,

[1] J. Foster, *London Marriage Licences* (1887), p. 1406.

was the kind of business transaction of which his own son might well have been proud. This deal, and the marriage of his sisters, eased considerably Colonel Walpole's circumstances and allowed him and his wife to live a little more expensively. At the end of June 1678 he made a brief trip up to London, visiting his Suffolk property on the way. It is very probable that the preliminary negotiations for the sale of Rougham to Sir Robert Davers made a visit necessary. He left his wife with her father and stayed with his cousin, Edward Mann, the linen-draper, in the Strand. He bought himself a watch 'of Jones make' for £6, a couple of wigs for £3 14s. 6d. and exchanged his sword for a better one, paying a guinea for the difference. He did not forget his wife, her modest present was a gown for £3, and he found a few trinkets for the children. He also took the opportunity to have his coach entirely refurbished —an expensive item, costing him £32. But even so his expenses for the whole trip did not amount to £50.

It was not until 1681 that Colonel Walpole permitted himself a long stay in London with his wife. They remained there for the whole of June and July. They spent £290 12s. 6d., a quite considerable sum and a clear indication of Colonel Walpole's growing prosperity. Most of this money went on the purchase of a new 'chariot' and Mrs. Walpole, in London for the first time since her marriage, seized her opportunities with both hands and ran through nearly a hundred pounds. The trip was not purely for pleasure; the long negotiations for the sale of Sir Jeffery Burwell's estate had at last been concluded and Colonel Walpole spent many days with his lawyers going over the final settlements. The sale of land was always a very protracted business at this time, for estates were rarely free from a multitude of obligations which had to be resolved before a sale could take place. The lawyers thrived on this complexity and Colonel Walpole had to pay out £69 8s. od. to Messrs. Cracherode and Mosier for their pains. It was four years before Mrs. Walpole saw London again, but her husband seems to have made a short visit every year until he became a Member of Parliament in 1689. In the early summer he would set off for Loughborough in Leicestershire where his favourite sister, Susan, was living with her husband, John Wilson. From there he made his way to London, spent a few days with his cousin Mann, then returned to Houghton via Suffolk, where he viewed his property and collected his rents. It was done with great frugality: the whole trip cost only £16 in 1684. Apart from her pregnancies which did not always fall conveniently for a summer jaunt to London, there was a good reason for Colonel Walpole keeping his wife in Norfolk, for we know that she was an extravagant woman. The entire correspondence with her son consists of demands for money, and whenever she did get to London, the entries in Colonel Walpole's account book increase rapidly. In 1685, she went with her husband for three weeks, taking her eldest girl with her, who was immediately placed with a writing master. She bought clothes for herself and the younger children and persuaded Colonel Walpole to spend quite extensively on the house—for the first time in her fourteen years of married life. In all this time nothing had been bought for Houghton except a few tin dishes at Lynn fair and a coffee-pot for a shilling. Now his wife persuaded him to buy six Dutch chairs and three dozen cane ones and to spend £32 18s. 6d. upon their upholstery. They were packed and sent to Houghton by sea. But Mrs. Walpole probably took the pendulum clock back with her in the coach, along with her picture which she had had painted—not by an artist of repute for the picture and its frame only came to £6 14s. 6d. It is probably the one which still hangs at Houghton—a dull, wooden-faced picture which betrays nothing of the sitter's character.

Such trips were rare, and in the main, Mrs. Walpole and her daughters had to rely for their finery on what they could pick up at the Norfolk fairs. She seems to have been a poor needlewoman. Her children's clothes and her husband's cravats were made up for her by local gentlewomen—Lady Barkham of Southacre made the girls' coats and the father's cravats; and a Mrs. Cremer was called in to do the shirts. Payments for stockings, shirts, neckerchiefs, even an Indian gown and a screw of black buttons are carefully listed in these meticulous accounts by Colonel Walpole, but they may be searched in vain for payments to a tailor for himself, or even for broadcloth for a suit. From 1671–89, Colonel Walpole probably made do either with the clothes that he had as a young man or those which he inherited from his father. He only bought one hat, and even then he sold his old one in part exchange.

Such a model of prudence did not waste his substance in riotous

living. Until the 'eighties there is very little mention of wine, and
it is not until the 'nineties that he began to buy in any quantity.
Until then half a hogshead of claret, a small barrel of rum, or a
couple of bottles of Rhenish sufficed to meet his needs. The same is
true of food—a cag of sturgeon, a barrel of oysters, oranges and
lemons, a few luxuries such as these make an occasional appearance
in the accounts but in general the household at Houghton lived
entirely on its own produce. The same economy was exercised in
relation to his children. Sir Robert Walpole's pocket money as a
boy was two shillings a year, paid half-yearly; his and his brothers'
only toys, unless made at home, were the 'Shittle Cocks and Battle-
dores' which cost their father half a crown. Their neckerchiefs were
bought from the 'tinker woman'; and their hats, in bulk—ten at a
time—at Lynn fair. What a contrast this makes with the way Sir
Robert Walpole's youngest son, Horace, was treated forty years
later. That pampered little boy received expensive toys, made by
Edward Beach, every few months. His French tailor, Nicolas Olivier,
charged as much for one small satin suit as his grandfather spent in
his lifetime on clothes; before he was ten he had a footman of his
own. His childhood was elegant, cushioned, metropolitan, and
when he left his private tutor for Eton—he took with him his fine
furniture and smart chintz curtains.

His father had a ruder childhood. At six he was packed off to
school with his two brothers. His master was Richard Ransome, the
parson at Great Dunham, which lay some twenty miles from
Houghton towards Swaffham. There he stayed most of the year,
coming back home only for two short holidays. When he was
thirteen, he rode with his father to Eton where he was entered in
College, prudently under a false age (twelve instead of thirteen) so
that he would be eligible for a scholarship. During this austere and
isolated boyhood he learned to love the simple pleasures of the
countryside, particularly hunting, in which his father had indulged
as soon as he felt that his wealth was capable of supporting a hunts-
man and hounds.

The picture which emerges from Colonel Walpole's account
book is one of prudence and careful husbandry; of growing riches
wisely invested in yet more land, that solid basis of his wealth. But
with Colonel Walpole prudence was allied with ambition. He rode

regularly to elections at Norwich; and he became a freeman of Lynn, no doubt in order to acquire a parliamentary vote there. He was appointed a Justice of the Peace; he was active in the Norfolk militia. He managed his political career with that same wise patience with which he conducted his private affairs, and it was not until 1689 that he stood for Parliament for the pocket borough of Castle Rising which belonged to the Howard family, partly to the Duke of Norfolk and partly to Thomas Howard of Ashted, the son of Sir Robert Howard, the dramatist. On whose interest Colonel Walpole first entered Parliament may only be guessed; his cousin, Cufaude, was the Receiver-General of the Duke of Norfolk's rents, and Robert Walpole's election bill of £20 was paid to him, so most probably he was brought in by the Norfolks. Once elected he began to create rapidly his own interest. With the help of his brother, Horatio, and his brother-in-law, James Hoste of Sandringham, he bought up enough cottages, which carried a vote, to secure the control of one seat, and this control was so firm that it lasted in his family until the Reform Bill. In this struggle Colonel Walpole was reckless of expense, spending as much as £300 for houses which had sold at £30.[1] For the next ten years he played the part of one of the leading men of his county, going up to London for the parliamentary session, sitting on the back bench, voting no doubt as his conscience dictated, but keeping, if his friendships are a guide to his views, to a Whiggish attitude. And when he died in 1700, at the early age of fifty, his life could be taken as typical of the most enterprising and effective members of his class—the country gentlemen.

He remained rustic. Rustic in his tastes, in his clothes, in his old house: rustic in his pleasures, in his devotion to the land. His life was simple in all its aspects but it was not uncultured. His farming was a model of efficiency and enterprise: his library was well stocked and well read: the wandering fiddlers from Thetford, Swaffham or Lynn were always sure of a warm welcome and a modest tip at Houghton. But it was a plain hard life that had its dark places. His children came and went like the swallows. 'Paid for digging my little girl's grave . . . 2s. 6d.';[2] so the accounts run, and the register at

[1] H. L. Bradfer-Lawrence, 'Castle Rising and the Walpoles', *Supplement to Blomefield's Norfolk* (1926–9), ed. C. Hussey.
[2] *Cholmondeley (Houghton) MSS.*, Letters from 1700–1.

Houghton records their frequent funerals. Usually they lived long enough—two, three, four or more years—for their deaths to be a deep sadness; on one occasion an epidemic with tragic suddenness emptied the nursery. At Houghton few years passed without dying of suffering, and Mrs. Walpole bought her powders to excite labour, vomits, electuaries, and 'hysterical cordeall water'; Colonel Walpole, never after 1690 a healthy man, needed his night pills and purges. 'Little miss' was given 'a Julap against the Rickets', and Master Charles, who did not last long, 'Hydropick Syrup'. The apothecaries and the doctors with their violent and repulsive cures were rarely absent. And this aspect of life, at least, did not change from father to son. Sir Robert Walpole's life was threaded with sickness, from his boyhood a recurrent fever, possibly malaria, and the stone attacked him year after year. His wife's bills tell the same story of sickness and misery. His children were bled and purged and vomited with the same gruesome regularity of his own childhood. But in every other way his daily life makes a remarkable and violent contrast to that of his father.

   Unlike his father, Sir Robert Walpole rejoiced in spending money whether he had it or not, and at the beginning of his career he certainly lacked it, for his father died at a most inopportune moment for the family fortunes. The creation of his parliamentary interest at Castle Rising had been very costly, and in 1697 Colonel Walpole raised a considerable sum of money to buy his Cousin Pell's estates at Dersingham and West Winch, worth £450 p.a., but this property carried two considerable life interests. These were burdens which the prudent Colonel could have borne, but his son was faced with paying off a number of his father's loans immediately. Furthermore, the payment of his mother's jointure and his sisters' annuities cut sharply into his income, for true to the tradition of the time they immediately left Houghton and became the paying guests of Lady Turner, Sir Robert's eldest sister, at Warham near Wells-on-Sea. His brother Horatio was at King's; his brother Galfridus at school. He himself had recently married Catherine Shorter, a woman of small fortune and extravagant tastes. Bad harvests or low prices dogged his early years and his tenants fell badly behind with their rents. Nevertheless he was determined to cut a figure. He touched everyone he could for a loan—shopkeepers at Lynn, his father's old friends, his uncles, his cousins—and all that he could lay hands on he spent. For the next forty years he went on spending all that he could get and, fortunately for Robert Walpole, he was destined to get hundreds of thousands. Yet extravagant as he was, there was a certain prudence, a sense of direction in his spending which prevented it from being merely wanton or reckless. Robert Walpole lived and spent as the great men of his day lived and spent, because from the very first he intended to live and die a great man.

As soon as he succeeded his father he was in a hurry. Even before the funeral he wrote to Thomas Howard of Ashtead telling him of his intention to stand for Castle Rising and, as soon as it was over, he set out for London without bothering to wait for his election. Yet before he left Houghton he had given extensive orders for the reconstruction of the old house—new sash windows, new fireplaces, new wainscotting. He never lived again permanently in Norfolk. He might parade the country gentleman, and after his enforced retirement he was prepared to extol the virtues of country life, but London, the Court, the Palace of Westminster—there was the atmosphere which he really loved to breathe. And when he quitted Norfolk in December 1700, he was never to return except for short periods, often reduced to two or three weeks in a year.

In London he had no intention of living like his father. He set up house with his wife's grandmother in Berkeley Street—modish and grand. A room over a linen-draper's in the Strand, at a pound a week board, had been good enough for Colonel Walpole, nor had he ever considered it desirable that his wife should keep him company. Her place had been at Houghton with her children and women. But Catherine Walpole had been born and bred in London, bred on the fringe of fashionable life, yet lacking either birth or sufficient wealth to give her a secure social position. Both her mother and her grandmother had used their husbands harshly, spending on extravagant living every penny that they could extort from them. Unfortunately it became a family habit, and Catherine Walpole was as determined as her husband to lead a gay life in London. She was a difficult wife, moody, hysterical, given to acts of cruelty, but Walpole's love for her can be judged by this one letter of his which survives:

'May I measure your heart by my own. O there I find that love that tendernesse for you that are there any failings in you they are still perfections to me and doth my Dearest doe or omit any thing that might seem better otherwise, I am blind, cannot, would not, see any thing in my deare self but what is most agreable.'[1]

She disliked Norfolk intensely and frequently stayed in London when Walpole had to go there for elections or the business of his estates. So from the very first he was compelled to maintain two households—an expense which bore very heavily on his already burdened estate.

Houghton was made to contribute all that it could. A wagon service had recently been started from Lynn via Swaffham, Brandon and Newmarket—a slow lumbering affair but a most necessary artery in Walpole's household economy in these years. Geese, turkeys, collars of brawn, barrels of oysters, jars of mushrooms, apples, hampers of home-brewed 'hogan' ale, flowed along it, for a wagon rarely left Lynn without two or three boxes for the Walpoles in Berkeley Street. And the steward, fat John Wrott, who was always so anxiety-ridden by his master's debts and the tenants' inability to pay, used to secrete the rents inside the geese—a simple countryman's dodge for avoiding the depredations of the highwaymen. Bulkier goods, particularly hay, went by sea by the regular coasting service from Wells to London. Without these supports from Norfolk, Walpole's debts would have been far greater. But within a few years Norfolk was full of gossip of the extravagant way the young Walpoles lived; a great stir was caused by a ball which they gave at Christmas in 1706 at which the Duke of Grafton was present. Uncle James Hoste of Sandringham disapproved and said so sharply to the Turners, Walpole's relatives, who lived at Lynn. Old Charles Turner wrote off to him in great distress, begging Walpole to send him some money to stop the mouths of his creditors who were making bitter remarks and doing his reputation great harm. Naturally the simple Lynn shopkeepers, who had lent him £20 or £50, could not realize that a young and ambitious politician had to cut a figure in the world.

But the Walpoles succeeded in cutting a figure and their social success may be measured, not only by the dukes who attended their ball, but also by the election of Walpole himself to the Kit-Cat Club

1 *Walpole MSS.*, Yale University, quoted by kind permission of Mr. W. S. Lewis.

—the most exclusive and fashionable of all the Whig clubs. In rotation each member acted as host, vying with other members in the production of exotic food and magnificent wines. When Walpole's turn came round he bewildered Wrott by his request for ruffs and reeves. These were netted for him by his cousin, Thomas Turner, in the marshlands of the Wash and sent to Houghton to be fattened. They reduced Wrott to a jelly of anxiety; his letters are full of concern about them and he longed to get them despatched to London. 'I think the Ruffs and Reefes,' he wrote, 'are now fat and I feel there will be danger of their dying if they be kept too long, therefore the sooner you have them up the better, and I know no safer way than to kill them and send them up by the Lyn coach.' And then with a touch of sly humour, he added: 'John Cornwall brought here a couple of young Shelducks which I shall send by the wagon.' Shelduck is said to be so rank that the bird is quite inedible even when skinned. It seems unlikely that these were served to the Kit-Cats.[1]

Houghton was a great support to the household living in Berkeley Street, and Walpole also relied upon Norfolk for the bulk of his wine and beer. His Turner cousins were wine-merchants and with them he could run up big bills for hogsheads of port, white Lisbon and claret. But he was able to supplement this, when he became a member of Prince George's Council, with a little smuggling. The Prince was Lord High Admiral, so Walpole's first job brought him in touch with Josiah Burchett, the Secretary of the Admiralty. Walpole and Burchett, by adroit use of an Admiralty barge to fox the Customs officers, managed to smuggle in a fair quantity of champagne and old burgundy, a welcome addition to the rather commonplace wines which he got from the Turners.[2] Smuggling, of course, was widespread. James Swanton, the Wells smuggler, called regularly at Houghton with his Dutch linens and Walpole's old mother at Warham recounts with glee how she had baffled the Customs officers and got a load in through the back door.[3] But, even so, for two highly placed officials in the Admiralty to engage in large-scale smuggling is, perhaps, somewhat brazen. No doubt it

[1] Pages 21–3 are based on *Cholmondeley (Houghton) MSS.*, Letters, 1703–6.
[2] *Ibid.*, 1706.
[3] *Walpole MSS.*, University of Chicago.

made a good joke at the Kit-Cat and led to many toasts.

His creditors remained unpaid; some of his lands were sold or mortgaged, yet Walpole prospered. He had his reversals, even a taste of the Tower, nevertheless office came his way, first Secretary of War, then Treasurer of the Navy. During these years of modest affluence he took a house in Dover Street and began to invest seriously in the funds. Then he lost office and hard times followed —his wife had to borrow half a crown from her maid to hire a hackney coach when visiting him in the Tower. (It was eighteen months before the maid got her money back.) But when Queen Anne died, Walpole came safely home to port. At first he enjoyed the extremely lucrative office of Paymaster-General which he left in 1716 to become Chancellor of the Exchequer. His career was interrupted by three years of opposition in which he and Townshend struggled with Sunderland and Stanhope for supreme power. This he captured in 1720. For a time he took the office of Paymaster again. 'He was lean,' he is reported to have said, 'and needed to get some fat on his bones.' But he fattened quickly and in the reshuffle of offices which followed the South Sea Bubble he became First Lord of the Treasury and Chancellor of the Exchequer, posts which he held until he was forced from office in 1742.

He made an enormous fortune. It cannot be calculated. He banked with so many bankers; involved with his own money were the government surpluses with which he was allowed to speculate; at times, especially in the boom months before the bursting of the South Sea Bubble, he was investing money for his relatives and friends in Norfolk. His salary was handsome: the fees which his offices brought him, princely. And yet none of these sources seems quite sufficient for the river of gold which flowed in and out of his coffers. Such bank-books of his which remain throw little light on the sources of his wealth. The entries are brief and laconic:

Reced of y^r Hon^r in Bank		500 0 0
Reced of D^o	D^o	500 0 0
Reced of y^r Hon^r		4000 0 0
Reced more		500 0 0

And so on and so on, with here and there the receipt of money from the sale of tallies or the interest from investments. Where the bank notes came from in such profusion no one will ever know and it is

K

idle to speculate. The standards of Augustan morality were not ours, and Walpole never claimed to be a saint. He loaded offices on his brothers and children; no Norfolk friend went without reward. The 'Robinocracy' became the butt of the Grub Street hacks but it was no myth. Having arrived at the summit of political power, Walpole was determined to make his family so rich that it would be immune to the natural disasters of time. He built for eternity. This ambition was not peculiar to Walpole; but his attitude was becoming a little old-fashioned, and he was one of the last of the King's servants to make a great fortune from politics. But in his day, apart from Charles II's bastards and their descendants, there was scarcely a noble family whose fortune had not been founded on or augmented by the loot of office. And Walpole saw that, no matter how many centuries had elapsed since their ancestors had served the state, these families had remained great and powerful in the land.

We may not know how Walpole acquired his wealth, and we can only surmise the causes of his voracity, but we know exactly how he spent his money—two important accounts survive—one with his banker, Robert Mann, from 1714-18, and more importantly the accounts of his London steward, Edward Jenkins, from 1714-26. In addition to these valuable sources there are several cubic yards of bills, perhaps almost complete for 1733. Finally, there is Houghton itself; apart from the pictures sold by his grandson to Catherine of Russia, it is as he left it. From this evidence it is possible to build up a detailed picture of the way 'The Great Man' lived. And what a contrast it makes with the simple homespun life of his father!

Let us begin with Houghton. The old house, mediaeval in origin, patched and added to by the succeeding generations, had been good enough for his father. At his inheritance, Walpole had spent a lot of money on its modernization; in 1716 he reconstructed it again, but by 1721 he had decided it was hopeless to attempt to turn it into a great house. So he razed it to the ground and from 1722 to 1735 the masons and carpenters and plasterers were at work. At the same time Bridgeman began to change the landscape for miles around. In 1729, the village which for centuries had clustered about the house was moved a mile away. The furnishing of the rooms went on for years; France and Italy were combed for pictures to adorn their walls, for Walpole was an avid collector who paid the highest price then known for a Poussin. Even amidst the anxieties of the political crises which preceded his fall, he could find time to negotiate for a Domenichino. Artari did the plaster work; Rysbrack the chimney-pieces and statuary; Kent the furniture and decorations. Genoa velvet, the best silks and damasks from France adorned its walls. The state bed, a magnificent creation by Kent, blazed with gold thread. Everything that was used was of the finest; the craftsmanship the best which money and discerning taste could buy. The house was built to outlast time. Those of Walpole's contemporaries who did not hate him regarded Houghton as the finest house of its kind in England, and that remains true today. Architecture, furniture, land-scape, harmonize like notes in music, for Walpole who exercised complete control over every detail was a man of superb taste.[1] No one will ever know what it cost Walpole to transform Houghton from a country-gentleman's house to a nobleman's palace. But with the furniture and pictures it must have run into tens upon tens of thousands.

Yet he rarely lived there. During the twenty-one years while he was the King's first servant he visited Norfolk only twice a year—for about a fortnight at the end of parliamentary session, which normally ended in May or early June, and for about a month in November when he held what the satirists called his 'Norfolk Congress'. Then Houghton was filled with the most important men of affairs. They hunted; they ate gargantuan meals and drank ferociously, but hunting, drinking or eating, they talked politics. In the charming library which Walpole built for himself (lined with his father's and grandfather's books, for his own editions were largely confined to his College books and the Statutes of the Realm), he settled the business of the next session with his most intimate

---

[1] For anyone who doubts Walpole's detailed interest in his building there is Hervey's testimony that he alone was responsible, against all advice, for the stone cupolas (Ilchester, *Lord Hervey and his Friends* (1950), p. 71). The second Earl of Oxford, it is true, said that Gibbs was responsible for them (*H. M. C. Portland*, vi, p. 160), but Hervey was Walpole's friend, Oxford a casual visitor to the house. There is also a rather bawdy joke in the plasterwork of the ceiling of the Stone Hall which can only have been Walpole's idea. The dado is festooned with *putti* but one, hidden in a corner, is quite blatantly a little girl. Artari is most unlikely to have done this on his own initiative. Walpole liked a coarse joke and I suspect this gave rise to a great deal of fun at the Norfolk Congresses and to many wagers. But it does show how closely he was in touch with the work.

advisers—Newcastle, his brother Horatio, Henry Pelham and Hard-wicke.

There was an extravagance, a grandeur about his hospitality, a wantonness in its profusion which argues that it was the expression of a deep-seated need of Walpole's nature. Had he resented bitterly his confined and parsimonious childhood; a younger son with no prospect but the Church and Bircham parsonage? Or had he hated the plain homespun and the cheap neckerchiefs bought from the tinker's wife? Or did his ostentation spring from a lack of security that went deeper than the insecurity of class or family origins? Was there in this great man of whom the world went in awe the need to please, the need to compel both admiration and gratitude? Whatever the cause the hospitality was unique of its kind and became the gossip of society and the butt of satirists.[1]

The same profusion, the same reckless expenditure, marked the whole of Walpole's life. Houghton was not the only house on which he allowed his imagination full play; in many ways he was more devoted to his Chelsea home—Orford House—from which he was to take his title. He went to live there when he was Paymaster-General and later he managed to secure a long lease from the Crown. It was a part of Chelsea Hospital, but Walpole spent large sums adapting it to his needs. Sir John Vanbrugh was responsible for the alterations but Walpole was, it seems, keenly critical of his plans.

'I have conceiv'd about your Room,' Vanbrugh wrote to him in 1716, 'and will bring it to you (I think) on Tuesday morning. 'Tis an expedient between the two so perhaps you'll like it.'[2]

One of the major additions to the house was the orangery which Walpole intended to use as a picture-gallery, for his pictures at Chelsea were as fine as those at Houghton. He bought adjacent land for enlarging his garden; built a river-wall by the Thames, creating a large terrace walk adorned at one end with an elegant octagonal summer-house; there was also a 'vollery' or aviary where Mrs. Walpole kept her exotic birds. The hospitality at Chelsea was as prodigious as that at Houghton but, as Walpole lived there most of the year, more constant and more expensive; the most sumptuous

---

[1] *The Norfolk Congress* (1728) is a good example of such satires.

[2] For Orford House, cf. C. G. T. Dean, *The Royal Chelsea Hospital* (1950). Vanbrugh's letter, unpublished, is in *Cholmondeley (Houghton) MSS.*, Correspondence, 1716.

banquet ever given by the Walpoles was at Chelsea in August 1729 when they entertained the Queen and the Royal children: some idea of the splendour of this entertainment can be derived from the description in the *London Journal*:

> The Dinner was in Sir Robert's Green House. A kitchen was built on purpose in the stable yards near as big as that erected for the Dinner of the Knights of the Bath, with above 20 places for Fires, etc. The fruit for the Dessert was collected a week preceding from all quarters of the Town.
>
> After Dinner Her Majesty and the Royal Family retired to the [*Octagon*] Banqueting House on the River to drink Tea; where were several Barges of fine Musick playing all the Time. After which they returned to the Green House, where the illustrious company were entertained with a ball, and afterwards supped in the same place.[1]

In 1727 the King made Walpole Ranger of Richmond Park and gave him the lease of the Old Lodge there: at once the carpenters, plasterers and upholsterers got to work and within a few months Walpole had created a charming villa for his week-end retreats.[2] There at Richmond with his hounds and his mistress, Molly Skerrett, he could find a few hours' untroubled repose. A Mrs. Burton seems to have been his housekeeper there and every few months she was paid £500 or £800, but out of this, the household expenses both of Molly and her baby daughter had to be paid. Molly, of course, had her own income derived from the considerable sums which Walpole invested for her in the annuities. One way or the other Richmond proved an expensive addition to Walpole's burdens, but it brought him more private happiness than his other homes. His delight in it may be judged from the fact that in many of his unofficial portraits, he is dressed as Ranger of Richmond Park.

Both Chelsea and Richmond were too far from St. James's for a leading minister and during the parliamentary session, or when the

[1] Quoted in Dean, *op. cit.*, p. 205.
[2] The alterations to the Old Lodge are said to have cost Walpole £14,000. E. Beresford Chancellor, *The History and Antiquities of Richmond, Kew and Ham* (Richmond, 1894), p. 218.

Court was in London, Walpole lived first at Arlington Street and then at 10 Downing Street, when the King made it over to him. Walpole refused the house in Downing Street for himself but accepted it for the First Lord of the Treasury, who has lived there by right ever since. Both the houses in Arlington Street and Downing Street were small town houses by wealthy aristocratic standards but they were an additional burden on Walpole's finances. He had to pay a high rent—£300 per annum—as well as rates and taxes on Arlington Street. He had to furnish and adorn both, for Walpole inherited nothing from his father which he felt that he could use in his homes, except a few family portraits and the splendid set of Mortlake tapestries, which still hang at Houghton, acquired no one knows when or how by his father. And finally, to complete the account of Walpole's hospitality, each year in the summer he spent a number of weeks with the Court either at Windsor Castle or Hampton Court. He took with him his cook, Solomon Sollis, and his servants and kept an open table there for all who wished to dine at his expense, and usually the four or five weeks cost him about £300.

By wealthy standards of the nineteenth century, or even the early twentieth, such a number of houses as Walpole possessed and lived in, was not exceptional. After all, the Buccleuchs rejoiced at one time in Dalkeith, Bowhill, Branxholm, Drumlanrig, Richmond, Boughton, Beaulieu and two town houses; the Devonshires in Hardwick, Chatsworth, Bolton, Lismore, Compton Place and Devonshire House. But almost all of these possessions were the accumulations of centuries, the result of judicious marriages and the happy accidents of fate by which one large estate became amalgamated with another. And behind these ducal palaces stretched the vast landed estates which alone could give them stability. Of this Walpole was well aware. The estate which his father left, worth a mere two thousand a year, would have been totally inadequate to support the new Houghton; so Walpole was faced with the necessity, not only of living and spending like a great man, but also of accumulating sufficient wealth to enable his descendants to continue to do so. To this end he bought considerable property in Norfolk even before land prices fell at the bursting of the South Sea Bubble, and he went on buying land whenever he had the chance of a bargain or the opportunity of acquiring an adjacent estate.

He more than doubled the extent and value of the Walpole property in Norfolk. In addition he married his eldest son well, if not wisely. He found for him Margaret Rolle, the heiress of considerable estates in Devonshire and Cornwall and, equally important, the owner of two parliamentary boroughs—Ashburton and Callington. The marriage proved even unhappier than his own and the couple quickly gave up all pretence of living together, but the fortune which strengthened immensely the Walpole family was secure. Certainly this marriage was a most important factor in the growth of the estate, but it should not detract from Walpole's own achievement, for the transformation which he himself brought about in the wealth and standing of his family was remarkable.

By the time Walpole had become the King's first servant Houghton ceased to be a support to his London households. Apart from a little venison, the Lynn wagons brought nothing; indeed the traffic now was the other way. When Walpole set out for his yearly visit he was preceded by his servants. Solomon Sollis took with him the luxurious foods and wines that his master was accustomed to see at his table. The simple Norfolk fare, plainly cooked, no longer sufficed. Nor was the bulk of his wine bought at Lynn as it used to be. Walpole had developed an excellent taste in claret which was, with burgundy, the really fashionable drink in spite of the high duty on French wines. He himself preferred the very best—Lafite, Latour, Margaux, Haut Brion; these great wines occur over and over again in his bills. Apart from fine claret, Walpole had a taste for hock. In 1714 he was paying high prices for the vintage of 1706 which was being imported in bottle. Old burgundy and champagne were lesser favourites but frequently drunk. His cellar always contained a large number of hogsheads of port and white Lisbon for use at his public tables or for those of his friends who preferred it. In one year he spent more on wine than the income of a prosperous country gentleman. In 1733 he bought wines worth £1,118 12s. 10d. from James Bennett, his principal, but not sole, wine merchant. Five hundred and fifty-two dozen empty bottles were returned to Bennett within the twelve-month—a consumption of over ten dozen a week. Only the French wines were bottled, the rest was drawn from the barrel as required, so to get any idea of what his household consumed this 552 dozen must be at least doubled.

As with wine, so with food. James Mill made chocolates for Walpole; in his bills each item—the chocolate, the nuts and sugar —is carefully specified and then he gives the weight of the chocolates made. The order which he received was usually for a hundred pounds (weight) at a time, which cost Walpole £17 2s. 3d., more in fact than he paid in wages to three footmen for a year. The same prodigality is to be found in all the bills and household accounts which survive—the bills for oysters in 1733 are as fabulous as those for his wine.

One cannot begin to guess at his total expenditure on food and drink but it must have run into thousands of pounds a year, and to this must be added the wages of the army of servants who helped Solomon Sollis prepare and serve it. Not that servants were expensive. Even the prudent Colonel Walpole had allowed himself and his wife a fair bevy of them, although they were an insignificant number by his son's standards, who at one point had twenty-seven men and fifty women working as weeders in his plantations. But Walpole's regiment of household servants put little strain on his resources. They were paid very little, and that not very often. Edward Jenkins, the steward, received £10 a year and by 1726 this salary was twelve years in arrears. But Jenkins did not suffer; as Walpole's steward he received a large income in tips. Walpole's porter at Arlington Street is said to have received more in gratuities than many a country gentleman derived from his estates. No wonder then that the names of the same servants appear year after year in the Walpoles's accounts!

As with wine and food, so with clothes. Old Mrs. Walpole had to be content with the clothes which either she or her friends made at home or with an occasional gown from London bought cheaply from Cousin Mann. Lady Walpole lived in different style. Mr. Joseph Windham, Linen Draper, was paid £209 11s. 0d. on September 3, 1715; Mr. Turner, Laceman, £76 10s. 0d.; Mrs. West & Co., Mercers, £26 10s. 0d. on the same day—£10 was a frequent sum paid to Mr. Downs for 'my ladys stockens', and Mrs. Foster, the Mantua Maker, is always in and out of the accounts for anything from £5 to £25. Walpole's own clothes were as expensive as his wife's. On December 4, 1716, £543 was paid for 'cloth, lineings etc.' for Walpole. Lace for a neckcloth and two pairs of ruffles cost

£17 10s. od.; but his purchases were not always so very expensive, once he bought Indian neckerchiefs at 6s. each (did he remember the ones he wore as a boy, bought by his father from the tinker woman at half-a-crown?). His father had been content to buy his wigs very cheaply (two cost him £3 14s. 6d.) and he made them last for years. Walpole's wigmaker was Monsieur de Guignicour whose charges varied from £8 to £11—and a wig lasted Walpole about twelve months. There must be added to this steady drain of guineas on clothes the jewellery—watches from the French maker, De Charmes, a diamond ring for himself, necklaces for his wife; the chairmen; the coaches; the portraits which never ceased to be painted; Mrs. Walpole's more than generous support of Heidegger and the Opera; and her children's education, no longer undertaken by a village parson or old Dr. Short. The two elder boys were at Eton under the care of Dr. Bland—furnishing their rooms cost Walpole £70; their board cost £200 a year and they expected a regular supply of the best 'Bohea' tea and Lisbon sugar. The two girls went to a fashionable school run by Madame Nezerauw, at Chelsea, fashionable but expensive at £60 a year.

Walpole was open-hearted, lavish, almost absurdly generous to his friends. Walpole's father, when his brother Horatio came of age, sent him a token worth five shillings. By contrast Sir Robert paid £68 for a gold repeating watch by Quare which he gave to his own brother Horace to celebrate their success in 1715. As soon as he was in the money his relatives knew it—parcels rattled off to Norfolk, a wig for young Mrs. Turner, a riding habit complete with hat and feather for his sister, Mrs. Hamond. His old friends often touched him for a loan: Sir Richard Steele borrowed £500 in September 1716; Charles Dartequenave, a fellow Kit-Cat, took £100 from time to time.

What did all of this amount to? We shall never know, for Walpole had several bankers and none of his accounts survive with any continuity. Between August 1714 and May 1718, £152,251 17s. 8d. passed through his account with Robert Mann; of this £61,778 14s. 9d. was spent on investments, the rest went in personal expenditure. His Norfolk expenses play no part in this. Nor does it account for all his personal expenditure. Edward Jenkins did not always draw on Mann. Walpole often paid him in cash and Walpole rarely drew money for himself from Mann; Jenkins also received money from time to time for the Houghton sheep sold at Smithfield. And it is also known that at this time Walpole had another account with the bankers Gibson and Jacomb; in August 1718, whilst at Houghton, he drew £3,400 from his account with this firm for his expenses in Norfolk. Walpole had become, and remained, colossally rich.

Much has been made of the fact that at his death he left debts approaching £40,000: and this has been used to prove that he made little out of his career and that his extravagance was far beyond his means. In fact a debt of £40,000 was of no great significance in relation to Walpole's total estate—and in any case a considerable part of that debt consisted of legacies, left by Walpole, for which ready cash had to be raised. From the evidence which remains there can be no doubt that Walpole spent and created an immense fortune. Furthermore, he was able to provide magnificently for his brothers and children. Horatio, his brother, built the fine house at Wolterton from the profits of office conferred on him by his brother. His son, Horace, thanks to the sinecures given to him as a child, was able to live a long life in luxurious and whimsical elegance. The rest of the Walpole family, in their own ways, did equally well.

Walpole created for himself and his family the splendour of aristocratic life. His houses, his furniture, his pictures, horses, hounds and coaches were equal to any in the land, and in many ways he lived more extravagantly than the richest dukes. His style of life makes a vivid contrast with his father's; it requires an effort of imagination to savour it to the full, but it is worth the effort, for this contrast provides a key to some of the bitterness of political life in Walpole's day. There was at least one common feature to their lives—both were members of parliament, both were members of the governing class. The generation which separated them did not witness any revolution in the wealth of the governing class comparable to that which took place between father and son. In 1720, in 1730, in 1740 there were country gentlemen and members of parliament, living lives of simplicity equal to Colonel Walpole's. It is true that such men were far more numerous in 1700 than 1740 but they were numerous enough even in 1740 to be an important factor in politics. Many of these independent country gentlemen were not able or successful men, and unlike Colonel Walpole they saw their slender estates contract rather than expand. It was natural enough for many of them to develop a passionate hatred of courtiers, placemen and pensioners, and an intense loathing for Sir Robert Walpole himself. This hatred, which sprang partly from envy, had made them Whiggish in Charles II's and James II's reigns and Toryish or, at least, independent after the Revolution. These squires made up the country, anti-Court, party. Their bitterness, their sense of being excluded from wealth and power, gave a keen edge to the political rancour of Walpole's time, for, like his father, Walpole was not alone. Perhaps no one made quite so much as he, but there were other ministers of the Crown who acquired a very tidy fortune—Sir Thomas Osborne, Duke of Leeds; Henry Brydges, Duke of Chandos; Sir Stephen Fox and his son, the first Lord Holland—all created great and enduring wealth from the opportunities given to them by service to the King.

In some, such careers aroused envy, in others emulation. For centuries royal service had brought affluence to many gentle families and with affluence the prospect of fine marriages. It was the way in which the aristocracy had been recruited. That political success brought enduring wealth was well known. This knowledge naturally added to the competition for office and the King's favour; it increased intrigue and the formation of rival factions; it sapped loyalty and corrupted political principle. The facts of Walpole's career, when seen in terms of his personal affluence and power, provide a key to the nature of much of English political life in the seventeenth and eighteenth centuries which was personal and factional rather than ideological.

Yet in many ways Walpole's career illustrates earlier centuries than his own. The great ministers of the Crown, after Walpole, used their power to further the interests of their families, to find safe and lucrative sinecures for their brothers and children, but they refrained from taking great wealth for themselves. The Duke of Newcastle and the Marquess of Rockingham lost wealth through their political activities; Chatham and his son, William Pitt, both died poor men. North gained little from his long period of office. The great legal officers still did very handsomely and so did many placemen below the highest level, but the contrast between the two halves of the century is very marked. There seems to be no easy answer to explain this change. Possibly it was due to the increased control of all aspects of political life by the *established* aristocracy, and the nobility's own growing consciousness of itself. It would have been far more difficult for country gentlemen such as Sir Thomas Osborne or Sir Robert Walpole, born outside the circle of any aristocratic group, to achieve supreme power in the state in the late eighteenth century. And also with each passing generation nobility became more a question of birth than of either wealth or power. It is probable that behind this change lies buried a more important social revolution of which this is but a small facet. The middle years of the eighteenth century witnessed a decay in the influence of the country gentry; for centuries they had been a factor of immense importance in politics; their aspiration for wealth and power, and their envy of those who had achieved it, had helped to create that constitutional struggle with the monarchy which stretched from the reign of Elizabeth I to that of George I. By 1760 their influence had dwindled almost to insignificance and the aristocracy was supreme, and Cecils and Walpoles were as much out of fashion as Rockefellers and Carnegies today.

The two Walpoles, father and son, illustrate some of the more interesting aspects of English social and political life from 1660–1760; the prudent, intelligent, but essentially homespun father, with his ambition adjusted to those ends that were well within his reach— an increased estate and the leadership of his county—was so typical of all that was best in the gentry of his day; whereas the brilliant son, greedy for power, greedy for riches, yet creative in all that he did, was limitless in his ambition; in the brilliance of his taste and the grandeur of his opulence, he outshone the aristocratic world in which his talents had won for him and his family a distinguished and enduring place.

1955

SIR ROBERT WALPOLE'S WINE

Twice a year Sir Robert Walpole invited his more intimate friends to his new house at Houghton, a house of which he was justly proud, for he had brought the same judgement and same capacity for detail, which were to make him the foremost of our Prime Ministers, to its building and to its unrivalled collection of pictures and furniture. The pictures are now, alas, in Russia, sold by his eccentric grandson to the Empress Catherine, but the house and the furniture remain, the finest example, perhaps, of early Georgian craftsmanship.[1] Entertainment at these house parties, or Norfolk Congresses as they were called, was both lavish and magnificent. In July 1731, Lord Hervey wrote this description to Frederick, Prince of Wales:

> Our company at Houghton swelled at last into so numerous a body that we used to sit down to dinner a little snug party of thirty odd, up to the chin in beef, venison, geese, turkeys, etc.; and generally over the chin in claret, strong beer and punch. We had Lords spiritual and temporal, besides commoners, parsons and freeholders innumerable.[2]

Elsewhere Walpole's hospitality was equally generous, whether he entertained at Chelsea, Arlington Street, Hampton Court or the Treasury; in the intimate world of eighteenth-century politics, as

---

[1] I am indebted to the Marquess and Marchioness of Cholmondeley both for their great kindness in allowing me to consult the *Cholmondeley (Houghton) MSS.*, and for their generous hospitality at Houghton.

[2] *Lord Hervey and His Friends*, ed. by the Earl of Ilchester, p. 73.

much could be done, if not more, round the dinner-table than at a formal committee. It was not an abstemious age and the wine flowed. Some of Sir Robert's wine bills survive at Houghton and we know what he drank, how much he paid for it, and roughly how much wine was being consumed at his table.

But the earliest bill for wine is not Walpole's but his father's and we have a brief glimpse of the wine which Sir Robert drank in his youth. In October 1698, Colonel Walpole, Sir Robert's father, purchased from Charles Turner, of King's Lynn, thirty-eight gallons of red port wine in cask. The next month he bought a half hogshead. The following April a further hogshead of red port and at the same time half a hogshead of white wine; later in the year he bought another sixty gallons of red port and a hogshead of white Lisbon. Just before he died, in 1700, he purchased thirteen gallons of sherry. A hogshead of port cost him £15; the white Lisbon was slightly more expensive at £16. The sherry was 6s. a gallon! Now it is possible that Colonel Walpole bought wine elsewhere than at Lynn, but he was very much a Norfolk country gentleman, and it is unlikely that he went elsewhere or bought from anyone but his relatives. These bills indicate a simple but plentiful cellar, and are interesting in showing how heavily Portuguese wines were drunk years before the Methuen Treaty of 1703. It should be remembered that at this period these wines were simple table wines and not fortified with brandy as ports now are.

For a time, Walpole continued his father's practice of buying his wines at Lynn, as we see from the following letter from his steward, John Wrott, dated February 27, 1706.

Sir,

I was yesterday at Lynn where Mr. Rudkin shewed me your letter about your wine, which Mr. Kent let us see in the Custome house vault, the chests have been all opened and riffled, and no brandy to be heard of, but Mr. Kent says he will sattisfie you about that when you come downe. I shall send for the chest of burgundy to Houghton tomorrow. I have just now bought a horse for Corn: I shall take care about the wine from Mr. Harvie.

Yr. most obedient serv[t]

Jno Wrott.

The most interesting implication of this letter for students of the early history of wine is in the use of the word 'chests', which indicates that the wine was being imported in bottles as early as this date. It is impossible to tell whether all the chests contained burgundy or not, but it is clear that some burgundy was being imported at Lynn in 1706 in bottles. We know from later wine bills that Walpole had a taste for old burgundy: it was one of the most expensive wines in his cellar. Of course, this wine may have been sent to Lynn coastwise from his merchant in London.

Naturally, Sir Robert's position as a servant of the Crown required him to maintain a far more extensive selection of wines than his father, but he seems to have acquired during his youth a lasting love for white Lisbon, which figures in all of his accounts in massive quantities. In the first six months of 1733, he bought 111½ dozen of white Lisbon, a quantity which far exceeded all other wines. And, unlike his father, he always seems to have bought his white Lisbon ready-bottled. Although, after the Bottle Act of 1734, for which after all he himself was responsible, he began to purchase by the cask. It was still a more expensive wine than port and cost Walpole 24s. a dozen; a hogshead in 1741 was £18. The only other white wines which Walpole purchased in quantity were champagne and Rhenish. Very occasionally he bought Mountain and once, possibly for an experiment, three dozen of French white wine at 30s. per dozen. Obviously, Walpole did not care for it, for never again does it figure in the numerous bills which remain. He cared more for Rhenish which he purchased from Ludovick Schaart & Co., but only one of their bills survives for the last half of 1733. Then, he bought twenty-five dozen at 36s. per dozen. This wine appears to have been ready bottled for, although bottles and hampers are charged for, there is no mention of corks, which are always charged, if the wine was drawn and bottled by the merchant. There is one very interesting mention of vintage Rhenish in a bill, for 1715, from James Haymans. This item occurs:

for 6 Doz: of Hoghmer of the Year 1706 att 36s.
   per doz.   010: 16: 0
(1706 is underlined in the bill.)

Again there is no mention of corks, nor a charge for bottles, which would seem to imply that the wine was shipped, bottled, as a vintage year. We may presume that the wine referred to is Hochheim, and so this is the earliest reference to a vintage wine of this district being sold in England. We know from the Duke of Chandos's cellar-book that connoisseurs of wine were interested in Rhenish vintages, for Chandos discussed in 1732 with the firm of Hallungius, of The Hague, the purchase of the years 1666, 1684 and 1696, but this was very probably a question of casks, whereas Walpole's bill refers to a bottled vintage year, from a specific district, and of age when the wine would have been at its best.[1]

Of other white wines champagne is the most frequently mentioned. It was bought in small amounts, usually two or three dozen at a time, but, on occasion, Walpole sent for a couple of bottles. He never seems to have bothered much with sherry and only on two occasions did he buy any sack. Three dozen pints cost him 18s. a dozen in 1733, which was an increase of 3s. on the Palm sack which he bought in 1719. Once he bought a hogshead of Canary sack and there are two or three references to Mountain but, by and large, his interest in white wines was confined to Lisbon, champagne and hock.

In red wines it is quite clear that he preferred claret to port, or his guests did, for claret dominates the years 1732 and 1733 for which complete bills exist. And it is the only wine which Walpole bought during these years by the cask. Ordinary claret was £36 per hogshead and the best £45, and Walpole preferred the very best, buying four hogsheads of Château Margaux at a time and a hogshead of Lafite regularly every three months. The clerk of his wine merchant, James Bennett, must have known Bordeaux, for he is the only early eighteenth-century clerk, whom I have yet met with, who spells both Margaux and Lafite correctly; usually Margaux appears in the most extraordinary forms—Margoose, Margos, Margon, in fact any way but the right way. The only other named claret in Walpole's bills is Pontac, a popular wine in England at that time. From the frequency of purchase it would seem that the wine was quickly drunk, whilst young, and there is no reference to any

[1] For the Duke of Chandos's wines, see: *The Life and Circumstances of James Brydges, First Duke of Chandos*, by C. H. Collins and Muriel I. Baker, pp. 188–91.

purchase of old claret. The same is not true of burgundy. On the very rare occasions when Walpole bought this wine, it is always described as 'old burgundy' and at 4s. the bottle (24s. in modern money), it was by far the most expensive wine which he possessed. Red port occurs, of course, quite frequently, but it occupied only a modest position in his cellar.

From these bills, too, we can get an idea of the very large yearly expenditure of Walpole on wine. In 1733, he spent £1,118 12s. 10d. with James Bennett, and £48 2s. 0d. with Schaart & Co. And there may have been accounts with other merchants which have not survived—certainly there were purchases of arrack at Lynn, possibly of brandy and various wines, too. But even if nothing had been bought at Lynn, the expenditure with these two merchants alone would be equivalent to about £7,700 today. From the return of empties, carefully kept and audited, we know that the consumption was prodigious. During 1733, 552 dozen empty bottles were returned to James Bennett. This represents probably only the major part of the consumption of Walpole's household.

Nor was wine Walpole's only drink. Very early in life he was famed for his hogan of which three or four casks were brewed every year at Houghton. This, and arrack punch, were always in plentiful supply at his famous Norfolk Congresses. At times, when his friends were using his house during his absence, they were so tempted by his hogan that they broached a cask and got his permission afterwards. But principally he drank wine, and wine of limited range, but certainly judged with a connoisseur's palate. Obviously he was not very interested in variety and his cellar does not compare with the Duke of Chandos's with its wines, ranging from Samos to Kill Priest. On occasion Walpole would ask a friend to send him anything of interest, discovered on a journey abroad, and, in 1716, William Willis sent him white Sieges from Barcelona, Banibofar from Majorca, and a hogshead of Hermitage from Avignon, but Walpole stuck in the main to his Lafite and Margaux with the obstinate loyalty which was so much a part of his nature.

From these bills can be gleaned a little knowledge of how the wine trade worked and of current prices. Claret was usually bottled at Walpole's cellar by his merchant, and the merchant charged 4s. for drawing a hogshead; bottles were half-a-crown a dozen, 2d. a dozen returnable on empties; long French corks, half-a-crown a gross; wine bottled at the merchants was sent out in hampers which were far from cheap—3s. for a four-dozen hamper. In fact there was nothing really cheap about wine in the early eighteenth century: even labour was expensive—fifty dozen bottles cost 6s. to be carried from London to Chelsea—no free delivery in those days. But one aspect of a wine merchant's life remains unchanged. In 1736 Walpole's merchant was still waiting patiently for settlement of his 1733 bill.

These bills are invaluable for presenting us with a picture of the drinking habits of the aristocracy in the early eighteenth century. In spite of high duties it was a very long time before claret was ousted by port, which, in the early eighteenth century, was a squire's drink.

1951

SIR ROBERT WALPOLE'S FOOD

IT is possible to discover something of Sir Robert Walpole's taste in food from a series of letters from his steward (1700–7) and from a miscellaneous collection of bills which survive for 1733.[1] Both sources also throw a great deal of light on the organization of his household. They make an excellent contrast. The letters illustrate the simple living of a young country gentleman making his way in politics; the bills show the extravagant expense to which the first servant of the King was doomed.

Between 1700–10, Walpole was a poor man—mother, brothers and sisters all had claims on his estate, so too had his uncles and aunts; frequently he did not know where to turn for five guineas, therefore any economy which helped his housekeeping was welcome. So the estate in Norfolk was expected to provide him with all his luxuries and as many of his necessities as possible. Once a week Wrott would send two or three boxes, or a couple of hampers, to Lynn where they would be put on the wagon for London, a journey which took three or four days. If bulky, the goods might be sent by sea from Lynn or Wells. For safety's sake Wrott would send Walpole a description of the contents of the boxes, and drew his attention to anything particularly choice which he felt ought to be eaten by Walpole himself.

'I drew off the wine the next day after you went from home,' wrote John Wrott on December 7, 1702. 'There was tenn doz.

[1] In this, as in the previous essay on Sir Robert Walpole's wine, I am deeply indebted to the Marquess of Cholmondeley for allowing me to quote from documents at Houghton.

of it, and my Lady had two doz. home with her. There is five doz. bottles of hogan[1] in the baskett with a hamper and box of apples directed for you, comes by a Lynn vessell, called the Catherine of Lynn, John Thompson master . . . I never heard whither the things I have sent came safe to hand by the waggon and coach. There comes up this weeke by the coach, two turkies, a brace of pheasants and two brace of partridges, and by the waggon one shott[2] and two geese. I think by the next return of the waggon, the brawne will be fitt, and the swanns, and some puddings and links, may be sent up, . . . be pleased to lett me know what collars of the brawne should be sent, and what kept at home. I think the brawne will afford four good collars and two little ones. . . .' Sometimes food was not so plentiful (January 26, 1702).

'Corn could kill but one hare with his Beagles on Satturday but being as I am informed a very well hunted one, I was desireous you should have the eating of it yourself, so it comes up by the coach this weeke and it have to accompany it I think a very good turkey. . . .'[3]

Geese and turkeys and collars of brawn made up the bulk of food moving from Houghton to Walpole in London. At times Wrott found the geese very useful in other ways.

'It will be necessary,' he writes on November 23, 1702, 'to examine the geese well before they are spitted, there being something of value in one of them.'

Walpole, however, was something of a gourmet. His servants knew it and his friends knew it and he himself was thoroughly aware of it.

Like all gourmets he loved mushrooms and his housekeeper bottled them for him and sent them up to London; but when he was a great man they adorned his table in profusion and Norfolk could no longer supply him. In September 1733, Mr. William Ward kept him regularly supplied; purchases were made every three days, sometimes as much as 15s. worth at a time. On this scale a jar was useless.

[1] Strong beer for which the Walpoles had long been famous.
[2] Young pig.
[3] It is remarkable that the hare was in a fit state to be sent to Walpole.

Throughout his life, his friends, knowing his weakness for good food, sent him presents either to keep themselves in mind or as a generous gesture for kindnesses received. Charles Turner, of Lynn —one of the patrons of Henry Bell, the great Lynn architect— regularly sent Walpole a couple of barrels of oysters. A very welcome gift, if the huge bills for oysters in 1733 are any indication of Walpole's love of them. On another occasion, when Walpole's fish ponds at Houghton had become foul and needed cleaning, Sir Henry Bedingfield offered to supply him with the best table pike. These with carp and tench were regarded as necessities of the aristocratic dinner-table. Of course, far more freshwater fish were eaten; without ice and with slow transport, only salted sea fish could travel far from the coast, whereas freshwater fish could be bred in ponds in the garden. But when he could get it, Walpole preferred sea fish. His London bills contain no carp, no pike, no tench but plenty of soles, flounders, lobsters, shrimps and, on occasions, cod. Although a Norfolk man, he seems not to have cared for herrings—a strange weakness. There were times when Walpole's kitchen must have been festooned with haunches of venison and collars of brawn for these were the two presents of food which carried considerable distinction; the haunch of venison particularly so; the best haunches were those from a buck which had been killed cool; unlike the hare, the best venison was thought to come from a stag which had been shot standing and not hunted.

But Walpole himself had his fancies and, although obviously disapproving, Wrott loyally carried out his orders and got hold of what his master wanted, difficult though it might be. In June 1706, Walpole fancied ruffs.[1] His cousin, Thomas Turner, was asked to look out for them; Turner, who lived near the fens, entered enthusiastically into the project.

'I have bespoke,' he writes, 'six dozen ruffs and ree(ve) they shall be sent to Houghton the first that are taken which will be in August.'

They arrived earlier, but less plentifully, than was forecast. About three dozen were netted and sent to Houghton on July 24. Their arrival obviously worried Wrott. He wrote to Walpole on August 7.

[1] A wader and migrant, rather like a snipe—ceased to breed plentifully in England in the nineteenth century and probably becoming rare in the early eighteenth century.

I think the ruffs and reves are now fat and I feel there will be danger of their dying if they be kept too long, therefore the sooner you have them up the better, and I know no safer way than to kill them and send them by the Lyn coach . . . be pleased to let me know when you will have them sent.

And perhaps with his tongue in his cheek, he added: 'John Cornwell brought here a couple of young shielducks which I shall send by the waggon.'

According to John C. Phillips, of Boston, Mass., quoted by André Simon in the *Dictionary of Gastronomy*:

The flesh of the shelduck is very rank and the bird unfit for the table even when skinned. I find but one writer who considers the bird edible and it is probable that his taste was not very discriminating.

There is no knowing whether Walpole ate the ducks and if he did, how they were cooked. *Lamb's Cookery*, the one cookery book in his library, is silent on shelduck.

But apart from an occasional flutter with ruffs or shelduck, Walpole's table, during his early years, consisted of plentiful but plain Norfolk fare, raised on his own estates. But, as he rose in the world, his way of life became too complex and his household too vast for Houghton to be of much assistance to him. By 1733, apart from Houghton, he had a house in Arlington Street, another in Chelsea, and a lodge in Richmond Park which he used for discreet week-ends and to enjoy a day's hunting.

To complicate matters further Walpole, as First Lord of the Treasury, entertained publicly a great deal. He had his 'days' either at St. James's Palace or at Hampton Court when the King moved there in the summer. On these public days politicians, members of the Court or aristocracy, could eat at Walpole's expense at his table. As far as I know Walpole was the last First Lord to keep open house in this way. Of course, he was not always present himself at his own public days, often he was too busy; but it was an easy way to please. Hanging about the Court in the hope of getting an audience with the great was a wearisome business for the minor politicians; and a free meal came handy. Also the right to dine openly, one might say, ostentatiously at Sir Robert's table indicated to the world that one was in favour, a man to be reckoned with. It might be thought that the royal household would provide the food and cooks for this service, even if it was charged to Walpole. Not a bit of it; Walpole had to provide the food and his own cooks. In consequence the bills are staggeringly large.

Statistics are boring; in any case the food seems to be weighed in strange and unknowable quantities—bushels, pecks, crans, barrels, lasts. Yet there is one quantity, I must say, which impressed me. Walpole's usual order for chocolates was 100 lb. (weight) at a time, at a cost of about £17—that is roughly £130 in modern money; and, as good economic historians are suspicious of monetary conversions, it was more than he paid his housekeeper or his steward for a year's wages and it would more than have paid for three footmen; it was nearly as much as a labourer got in a year, and a labourer had to support his family. His bills for oysters, fish, game and meat were all on the same scale; his total outlay on food cannot be computed, but it must have been well over £1,000 per annum—a sum considered more than adequate to maintain a country gentleman in tolerable comfort. It was a prodigious expenditure, but in keeping with Walpole's nature; he loved splendour and was not afraid of ostentation. But the contrast between his manner of life as a young Norfolk squire and the way he lived in his greatness, particularly his hospitality at his Norfolk Congresses, did not escape the keen eye of the satirist.

'There was one dish,' wrote one of these Grub Street hacks, pretending to describe a dinner at Houghton, 'that shocked many of the spectators, which was an English collar of brawn, stuck with French lilies, instead of rosemary. At this many were offended, and said the times were hugely changed with our Land-lord (i.e. Walpole) and his taste, and way of living strangely altered: For they remembered whan he had like to have overturned the whole table, upon seeing some French kickshaws upon it, which he said was poison to an English constitution. But now forsooth nothing but French sauces will go down. . . .'[1]

---

[1] *The Norfolk Congress, etc.*, p. 5. I am grateful to Lady Cholmondeley for drawing my attention to this satire of Walpole's table.

But, of course, all this magnificence was not mere display; it had a purpose. In the intimate world of eighteenth-century politics as much could be done round a dinner-table as at a formal committee. Walpole liked a dinner-party for pushing his own aims and for cajoling those reluctant to follow him. And they were valuable to the minor politician, for an invitation to Houghton or to Arlington Street was an indication of Walpole's favour, an indication which doubtless would be noted well by lesser men. And as he savoured Walpole's delicacies he could be certain that soon haunches of venison, barrels of oysters, collars of brawn and hampers of wine would be flowing into his own kitchen.

1951

THE FIRST EARL OF SHAFTESBURY

THE career of Anthony Ashley Cooper, first Earl of Shaftesbury, has a singularly serpentine quality. He joined Charles I at the raising of his standard at Nottingham, but by 1644 he had come to terms with Parliament, and proceeded to lead their forces in Dorset with success. The war over, he discreetly withdrew from public affairs, and busied himself with local government and the cultivation of his estates. Once Cromwell was securely in the saddle, he emerged again to play his part. He was promoted to the Council of State, but he soon found himself in opposition to Cromwell. In the confusion which followed Cromwell's death, his instinct led him to Monck, a wise judgement that was rewarded at the Restoration by a royal pardon for his past, a barony and a place in the Treasury.

His abilities were obvious and great. He became Chancellor of the Exchequer in 1661, an office which he retained until 1672 in spite of avowed opposition to the repressive Anglican policy of the government. Like Charles II, but for totally different reasons, he supported toleration, so that it was not this issue which finally alienated him from the King. In 1669, Shaftesbury supported the scheme to legitimize Charles's son, the Duke of Monmouth, in order to scotch the succession of James II, whose avowed Catholicism was regarded by many politicians as a national danger. Devoted as Charles was to his son, he could not bring himself to violate the principles of hereditary monarchy. Furthermore, his own inclinations and the persuasion of his mistress, the Duchess of Portsmouth, were leading him into close alliance with France. Without Shaftesbury's knowledge, the King signed the secret treaty of Dover in 1670. An attempt to buy off Shaftesbury's increasing opposition to the royal policy, by an earldom and promotion to the Lord Chancellorship, failed. The struggle at Court ended by his being dismissed from high office in 1673, and even stripped of his local honours in 1674.

Shaftesbury was not to be repressed. He fought back, agitating for the dissolution of the Parliament which had sat since 1661, attacking the King's most powerful minister, Danby, and stimulating the fears of the public of a Romanist revival, fears which finally culminated in the hysteria of the Popish Plot. Yet throughout this time, Shaftesbury was willing to negotiate, and when the crisis of the Popist Plot was at its height, he got back into office as Lord President of a large and reconstructed Privy Council, but one in which Charles put no trust. Within a few months, Shaftesbury was dismissed and back in opposition. He railed against the prorogation of Parliament, clamoured for the exclusion of James, yet at every stage was ready to enter into discussions with the leading ministers. Until he was finally outwitted at the Oxford Parliament by Charles II, who dissolved it before he could be stopped, the prospect of Shaftesbury's return to power was never remote. But the failure both to exclude James and to keep Parliament in session ruined him. Yet his popularity in London was so great that Charles was frustrated in his attempt to prosecute him for high treason; the Grand Jury of London threw out the bill. Shaftesbury, however, knew that this was the end. He fled to Holland and died there in 1683.

It was the contemplation of this career with its mixture of violence, intrigue, opportunism and principle, which led Dryden to write his famous and hackneyed lines:

> For close designs and crooked counsels fit,
> Sagacious, bold and turbulent of wit,
> Restless, unfixed in principles and place,
> In power unpleased, impatient of disgrace;
> A fiery soul which, working out its way,
> Fretted the pigmy body to decay.

And Dryden's judgement of Shaftesbury has been universally accepted by historians, Whig as well as Tory. No one had a good word to say for him. Bishop Burnet disapproved; Macaulay considered that immorality appeared in Shaftesbury 'in its most malignant type'. Others have referred to him as 'brutal', 'treacherous' and 'unscrupulous'. Most modern academic historians have found it easier to ignore him. Yet, for twenty years, Shaftesbury was the most considerable figure in politics. It is hard to believe that his success was due entirely to a Machiavellian opportunism, or that John Locke would have remained the devoted *factotum* of a cynical immoralist. Shaftesbury's bad press began with Charles II, who nicknamed him 'Little Sincerity'. It was a brilliant jibe, half true, utterly damning.

It is obvious that all contemporary accounts of Shaftesbury are distorted, all a little unfair, but behind them we recognize the man as he was—small, taut, cold-hearted, a man of nerve and wit, dexterous in business, ravenous for work, certain in decision; a man greedily ambitious, but so highly intelligent that his ambition had to be clothed in principle. His grave weakness was an unawareness of men, a failure to grasp the inadequacy of Monmouth as a solution of the country's dynastic problem. This, and this alone, brought about his final downfall.

The easy criticism of Shaftesbury's methods must be discarded if we are ever to assess his true importance. He lied; he cheated; he used monstrous imposters such as Titus Oates and Beddoes. He willingly suppressed evidence. He did not care if the innocent suffered. He was prepared to incite mobs, to exploit blind prejudice in order to further his own cause. The Popish Plot was a nightmare of cruelty and horror. Yet these were methods which Charles II did not hesitate to use when it suited his purpose. Against the death of the aged and innocent Earl of Stafford must be balanced the execution of Algernon Sidney. The stakes were high. The English throne tottered in the seventeenth century, and statesmen not infrequently went to the block. Ventures were desperate; and success achieved its own morality. It was a world alien to our own; an angry bitter age full of duplicity and lies and always close to *civil* war. It can be admitted that Shaftesbury's methods were detestable, but only so long as it is remembered that Charles II's were no better and no worse. Idolatry of the Stuarts is as stupid as the denigration of Shaftesbury.

The first and most important fact about Shaftesbury is that he was never at any moment of his career an isolated demagogue. He was intimately related to that section of the aristocracy which afterwards brought about the Revolution of 1688. Many of them gave him a cautious support; even more approved of his attitude to politics and society. He believed that political power should be firmly placed in the hands of the aristocracy rather than in the King's. The one fundamental belief of Shaftesbury's life was that political power should be enjoyed in direct proportion to the ownership of property, a view which Locke was to immortalize in his *Two Treatises on Civil Government*. A corollary of this, equally firmly held by Shaftesbury and by Locke, was that foreign policy should be subservient to the country's economic needs. Shaftesbury's hatred of France was due to the fact that Louis XIV's government was a negation of these two principles. Royal absolutism such as Louis's was inimical to the authority of property. France also was our greatest commercial rival. Shaftesbury's dislike of Roman Catholicism arose from the powerful support which it gave to royal absolutism, particularly in France. Popery, arbitrary government, France, were, he thought, synonymous. It was this attitude, consistently held and resolutely pursued, which brought Shaftesbury his wide popularity. But the great and powerful in the land trusted him because he was one of their own kind; more clever and more venturesome, but absolutely and certainly one of themselves; to them he was no mob-stirring demagogue, bent on democracy and the destruction of that patriarchal society which they cherished. He was their preserver and advocate.

The circumstances of birth had placed Shaftesbury firmly in the middle of the wealthiest and most aggressive sections of English society, a position which he deliberately consolidated by marriage. His wealth was derived from his grandparents. Sir Anthony Ashley confessed to gross peculation in the expedition against Cadiz, but he was a client of Cecil's and came to no harm. His loot was naturally invested in land and he married his only daughter to Sir John Cooper, who was as land-hungry as himself and as devoted to the increase of his wealth. When Shaftesbury came into his inheritance at the age of ten, his vast estates situated between Southampton and Tewkesbury made him one of the most considerable landowners in south-west England. Whatever his abilities, his property singled him out for political and social distinction.

Shaftesbury was quick to realize the value of alliance with families as great as his own. Buckingham, Cecil, Leicester, the great statesmen of England before the Civil War, had tended to surround themselves with lesser men, with clients in the true sense. At seventeen, Shaftesbury deliberately suppressed the longings of romantic love for the sake of the daughter of Lord Keeper Coventry, a judicious if cold-hearted action which brought him within the circle of political influence. After her death he allied himself with the Cecils and Cavendishes by marrying Lady Francis Cecil, sister of the Earl of Essex. His third marriage, to Margaret Spencer, niece and ward of the Earl of Southampton, made him a relation of the Russells and Montagues. He married his eldest son to a daughter of the Earl of Rutland. His nephew was George Saville, afterwards Marquess of Halifax. In fact, Shaftesbury was related to almost all of those aristocrats who invited William of Orange to England and by so doing—successfully—achieved their Dukedoms. All were not his ardent supporters; many preferred to play a watching game; but he had a great deal of approval from them, and without it he could never have achieved his dominant position in the House of Commons. Many a little beggarly corporation returned Shaftesbury's men because such was the wish of its patron. It was only by the conglomeration of many such interests that parties could be made in the seventeenth century.

Shaftesbury and his relatives were not merely landowners. His own estates lay in one of the great cloth-producing areas of the country, a trade whose fortunes were intimately affected by foreign affairs. The slump, caused by the Thirty Years War, had been influential in attaching many Wiltshire weavers to the Parliamentary cause. Had Shaftesbury remained a royalist in the Civil War, his influence in his own country would probably have been greatly diminished. But he was more closely connected with trade than this. Early in life, Shaftesbury had become the owner of sugar plantations in the Barbados. In 1647, he dabbled in the slave trade. In 1663, he became a proprietor of South Carolina, for which John Locke drafted a constitution. In 1671, he acquired the Bahama group; by 1672 he was the largest landowner in Bermuda. He was an original director of the Hudson Bay Company, attending its meetings assiduously. He possessed considerable African interests.

He advocated illicit trade between America and the Spanish Main, in defiance of Spanish regulations. For Shaftesbury, commerce was as vital a part of his wealth as his great estates in Wiltshire and Dorset. In this, too, Shaftesbury was exceptional only in the range and extent of his interests. Few rich noblemen kept their wealth solely in land. It was their sheet anchor; the justification of their position in society, but for many it was only the foundation of their riches. Both Southampton and Bedford possessed extensive property in London, which boomed after the Great Fire; cloth from their Devonshire estates was still sold at the Russells' back door. This rich variety of economic interest broadened the outlook of many noblemen, and made them more sympathetic to the aspirations of London and her merchants than to the Court; and lack of a coherent attitude amongst the aristocracy was the final undoing of the Stuarts.

Birth, marriage, economic interest, these were strands which tied many of Shaftesbury's followers together; but more was needed to assure the violent support which Shaftesbury's campaign for the exclusion of the Duke of York induced. There was, of course, religious prejudice. Shaftesbury played remorselessly on this theme; the fear of plots and revolutions was whipped into hysteria until men lost all sense of values. But it was, and remained, largely a method of agitation, the means by which Shaftesbury thought he could win not only political power but also those modifications of the constitution which he considered desirable. A too close concentration on anti-Popery and the problem of Exclusion has distracted attention from an important and vital part of Shaftesbury's aims, without which he could never have secured the support of men who had believed in the constitutional experiments of the Commonwealth.

Shaftesbury wanted to see political power based on Parliament, but not Parliament as it then existed; the possibilities of royal corruption were too great. He wished to reform it; he wanted a House of Commons rooted solidly on wealth. He demanded a high property-qualification for its members and for its voters. The machinery of election was to be regularized and purified, the expenses being borne not by candidates but by a county rate. The liberties of the subject were to be protected and, in this, Shaftesbury achieved a modest success in the passage of the *Habeas Corpus Act*.

Foreign policy was to be brought firmly under the control of Parliament; and so were ministers. Judges were no longer to be appointed during the King's pleasure. Religious toleration, except for Catholics, was avowed. Here was a programme, probably the work of Locke as well as Shaftesbury, which could command the respect of men of goodwill, who believed such a programme was as certain to preserve the wealth of England as the royal policy was liable to destroy it. To them Catholicism could only end in subservience to France, by which English commerce would be lost. Therefore it was imperative, before all else, to secure a Protestant succession; hence, exclusion became the focal point of battle. The weighty support given to Shaftesbury in the Commons never for one moment conceived that Exclusion was all.

And there was a third element which Shaftesbury exploited, an element which must be present in all violent political issues— envious hatred. The religious hatred has been noted time and time again. Certainly there was violent religious feeling; certainly it was important, in some ways decisive. But there were other hatreds, other envies, which went just as deep. There was the country gentry's hatred of London, of sophistication; their rancour towards those who enjoyed pension and foreign gold. Such an attitude Shaftesbury found easy to exploit. Their envy and their hate enabled him to bind the most intractable of all political classes to his cause. The support of the country gentry was as essential as was the support of London, of his noble friends and relatives, or of the old forces of discontent. His genius lay in moulding these divergent groups to a common purpose, and in making crystal-clear all that was dangerously involved in a Catholic King. It was not, as many would have us believe, a simple choice of religion. All was at stake; the wealth of the country, its liberties, the design of life which was being forged in the long struggle with the Crown.

In the end, the country came to Shaftesbury's solution, for the Revolution of 1688 justified all for which he struggled. His failure was due to his obstinate insistence on Monmouth and to impatience. He should have accepted Halifax's scheme of limitations. Doubtless, they would have been broken, but time was needed to prove the full folly of the Stuarts. In 1680, the memory of the Civil War was too near for men to wish to push the issue, if need be, to the decision of the sword. Shaftesbury himself may have been willing to secure the consent of the Crown by force, due perhaps to fear for his own safety if he lost the issue of James's succession. Certainly, he drove too recklessly, and too violently, so that, before he was out-manoeuvred by the King at Oxford, his party was disintegrating.

For all his failure, Shaftesbury is the most important statesman between the Restoration and the Revolution, the bridge by which the politics of the Civil War and the eighteenth century are linked. At no point did Shaftesbury toy with republicanism or advocate the destruction of the monarchy. He made his effort at reform through the constitutional channels available to him; he regarded Parliament as the final arbiter of all dynastic or constitutional problems. Indeed, his demonstration of the power of the Crown so unnerved Charles and James that they immediately set to work to destroy what qualities of independence it possessed, a task which led them on to attack the whole political structure of their country, and ended in their own ruin.

From the day Shaftesbury died in exile in 1683, the tide set sharply against him until he has become an object of scorn, ridicule and hatred, so that he is the least valued of all great English statesmen. Yet, in vision and in courage he was incomparable in his generation. But the country had to suffer the bitter years of James's reign before the wisdom of his violent opposition to Popery and arbitrary designs was learnt. He may have been greedy for power, and immoral in his methods, but his life was spent in preserving the growing might and prosperity of his country as well as its privileges and liberties. As such, he demands respect and honourable treat-ment.

1953

PART II
AFRICAN STUDIES

THE DISCOVERY OF
WESTERN AFRICA

In 1698 William III decided that it was time to have geography taught to William, Duke of Gloucester—the only surviving son of Princess Anne—and a series of maps of simplicity and clarity were especially drawn for the purpose. One was devoted to Africa. The Niger, rising in a great lake close to the Nile, runs in a thick bold line, straight to the Atlantic; two great inland oceans, near the Zambesi, provide the headwaters of the Nile: Congoland is there, but no Congo. The centre of Africa is empty; its emptiness disguised with three names largely and beautifully printed—Negroland, Nubia, Abisinia: the space between them is dotted with little brown, fluffy mountains. Here and there, the imaginative geographer has planted a large town. In the heart of the Ituri forest is Ambiancantiva, and Gago lurks behind the Quaqua coast. In essence, the map is the same map that Leo Africanus drew for Pope Leo X in the early sixteenth century; the coastal outline is perhaps more precise, but the ignorance of the interior is equally profound. Nothing had been learned in 200 years, and nothing much was to be learned for another century. Yet Africa was Europe's neighbour, athwart the great Mediterranean and Atlantic trading-routes. Why was this ignorance so complete and so enduring? And why was the ignorance so dramatically dispelled in a few years at the beginning of the nineteenth century?

The deliberate and conscious exploration of Africa by Europeans started in the fifteenth century; Genoese, Catalans and Portuguese were all involved, but the leadership, given by Henry the Navigator, made the Portuguese rôle the dominant one. Europe was desperately short of gold. But it was known that sources of gold existed beyond the Sahara; and enterprising men conceived of the possibility of sailing down the coast in order to get into direct contact with the mines and so cut out the Sahara and the Arab trader. Henry had other, more altruistic motives. The legend of Prestyr John, and his lost Christian kingdom, haunted him and, more than the quest for gold, inspired his passionate interest in Africa. The Portuguese navigators explored the West Coast, pushed round the Cape, sailed up the East Coast, and found in Abyssinia their Prestyr John. The gold was more elusive. They managed to collect a little on the Guinea Coast, which was renamed vain-gloriously the Gold Coast. Native rumours led to a frantic search on the Zambesi, but the effort was fruitless. The ruins of Zimbabwe were a poor consolation for men dreaming of El Dorado. As precious metals from America flooded Europe, the interest waned in African sources of gold. Nor did the interest in Christians endure much longer. The Portuguese had fought brilliantly to stop a violent Moslem attack on the Abyssinian Kingdom but the friendly feelings of the Abyssinians had been destroyed by the over-ardent, crusading, zeal of the Jesuits, and the Abyssinians, backed by the Coptic Church, closed the country to Europeans. By 1530, the first drive to the interior was over.

For the next two centuries, Europe was too occupied with its empires in America and in the Far East to bother with such an inhospitable land as Africa. The coast was jungle or desert. There seemed to be no great rivers leading to the interior. The natives were hostile and comparatively well armed. It is true that such conditions did not deter great Spanish explorations in the jungles of South America but there the appetite for gold had been whetted by the Aztec and Inca discoveries. In Africa there was not even the rumour of riches. And again, European effort, available for exploration, was small. There was a limit to men, to ships and to capital and it was natural that they should be directed where the positive gains had already been made.

But Africa was not completely deserted. In the south, about Capetown, where white settlement was possible, the Dutch estab-lished a provisioning station for their East Indiamen. On the East and West coasts, the Portuguese lingered on in mouldering and desolate settlements. But about the Guinea Coast, there was a roaring trade in slaves, the one successful commercial result of the early explorations. This trade in slaves dominated the European-West African relationship for over two centuries, and it was the slaves who brought the few scraps of knowledge about the interior which were gained during this time. They were so few because of the nature of the trade itself. The coast was desperately unhealthy. The slave caravans from the interior came down to the coast irregularly: the supply was, therefore, always speculative and uncertain. It was quickly realized that the most economic method of slaving was by single ships, sailing from slaving post to slaving post, until they had a full cargo. In consequence, there were no European settlements of importance and no European lived in West Africa long enough to collect more than scraps of information about the interior from the slave traders. Richard Jobson, an Englishman, and William Bosman, a Dutchman, were the only two navigators whose reports on the conditions on the coast are of real value for this period.

Jobson was a most attractive character, full of curiosity, and lacking all bias towards native customs, and his book is one of the masterpieces of the literature of West African discovery. He would have made a great traveller, but he was unable to venture from the coast for fear of losing his ship. The majority of journeys in the seventeenth and early eighteenth centuries were, like Jobson's, excursions rather than journeys, confined to the slaving rivers of the Senegal, Gambia and Calabar. They added little to knowledge. They touched only on one vital geographical problem. The results of their journeys seemed to indicate that Leo Africanus was wrong and that the Niger did not flow into the Atlantic. But it was an indication only; many travellers, and most armchair geographers, were confident that Leo was right and that the way to the interior lay up the great western rivers. The existence of the Niger, and the fertile land about it, had been known since ancient times, but whence it came and where it went, like the sources of the Nile, was one of the great geographical mysteries. At the end of the eighteenth century a complex variety of strategic, commercial, scientific and humanitarian factors made the solution of the problem an urgent necessity.

II

In 1788 the African Association was formed for the discovery of the interior parts of Africa. The aims of the Association were commercial as well as scientific. It was hoped to find new markets for the rising output of British goods. Wedgwood and others of the more far-seeing pioneers of the Industrial Revolution were foundation members. Humanitarian motives were not acknowledged in the Association's manifesto but the subscribers' list, with Wilberforce, Clarkson and Fox prominent, makes it quite clear that the Clapham Sect saw an opportunity in the foundation of the Association to foster its crusade for the abolition of the traffic in slaves. The government of William Pitt, eager to secure the support of the intellectual and politically active groups, gave the Society its benevolent encouragement and allowed it to use the consular service for the collection of information. The Association, therefore, focused on Africa in general, the Niger in particular, the attention of a variety of political, scientific and humanitarian groups whose interests were not necessarily compatible; but, for the time being, Africa and its interior seemed to offer an answer to their own needs and aspirations. It is necessary to look at them more closely.

The President of the Association was Sir Joseph Banks, on the threshold of being the most important political force in English scientific circles. He was a botanist by interest and as such had taken part in Cook's voyages in search of the *Terra Incognita Australis*— that mythical continent of the Eastern Pacific about which geographers both French and English wrote with such certainty, of its fertility, of its population, of its resources, and even of its civilization. Throughout the middle decades of the century the French and British governments, in anxious rivalry, sent expedition after expedition to scour the Pacific. 'Commerce was the sinews of war.' This was a self-evident truth to merchants, politicians, admirals and generals. A vast new continent, discovered and exploited by our commercial rivals, would have been a sharp blow at the strength and wealth of Britain. Hence the willingness of the government to subsidize the important scientific and geographical discoveries of Cook. But these discoveries, although strategically and economically useless, whetted the public appetite and gave a new and widespread interest in the unexplored regions of the world. Furthermore, they created a body of young men eager to pursue the scientific interests which they had developed. The foremost of these was Sir Joseph Banks who realized that the interior of Africa hid the most exciting geographical problems of his day.

The hopes of commerce switched from the Pacific to Africa with the same ease. Amongst the merchants there was a greater sense of urgency. In 1783 America had left the Empire. For some years British merchants and financiers had confidently predicted America's economic collapse, but no collapse came. And as yet no one realized that the political separation of Britain and America did not entail disastrous economic consequences, so that in mercantile circles the discovery of new markets seemed an urgent problem. For centuries rumours had filtered through to Europe of the wealthy civilized cities of the Niger. The mirage of Timbuktu, rising above the deserts of the Sahara, lured businessmen to half a century's scientific and philanthropic extravagance, alien to the nature and discipline of their world.

The loss of America had caused a profounder, more unconscious cause for the growth of interest in Africa amongst the ruling classes and in government circles. Instinctively, Britain turned to India. Long before the loss of the American colonies, British policy in India was being changed by men of forceful and desperate character who saw in the political chaos of India fabulous plunder. The plunder was obtained but only by the assumption of administrative and political responsibilities of an imperial magnitude. By 1788 the axis, Britain-India, with its extension to Australia and the Far East, was recognized as the strategic basis of the British Empire, and athwart this axis lay the vast, unexplored, unmapped bulk of Africa. Unwilling as nineteenth-century British government was to increase the strain of Imperial responsibility, the strategic importance of Africa was so obvious that any sign of interest by another European power led to instantaneous, frequently too instantaneous, action. But it also meant that all explorers from Mungo Park to Mary Kingsley could count on the benevolent and sympathetic interest of the government.

Yet the major driving force for the exploration of the interior of Africa was not to emerge from any of these factors. Science, commerce, strategy were world-wide in their implications, and it required complex and particular circumstances to focus their combined interest on Africa. But there was one other social and political force which grew steadily in strength and stature from very humble beginnings in the 1760's to become the arbiter of government policy by the 1840's whose very *raison d'être* was Africa, and more particularly West Africa, and that was the movement for the abolition of slavery. The story of the Anti-Slavery Movement has been told by one of the greatest historians of Africa[1] and there is no need to recapitulate it here. By 1788 the humanitarian movement, led by Wilberforce and Clarkson, had become a powerful force in English social and political life. Slavery had been declared illegal in Great Britain and, in 1786, a committee of abolitionists decided to make an attempt to re-establish at Freetown in Sierra Leone those Negroes to whom freedom had brought destitution; later, in 1791, the loyalist Negroes from America, whose settlement in the more inhospitable regions of Nova Scotia had proved unacceptable, were sent out after them. With a brutal and rational coarseness, typical of the eighteenth century, a covey of whores had been collected from Long Acre and packed off with the Negroes. The Negroes, largely old and mostly domestic slaves, did not take easily to a peasant's life in tropical Africa, nor did prostitutes make the best of wives. It was natural that the Committee for the Relief of Poor Blacks, which later developed into the Sierra Leone Company (1791), should view the activities of the African Association as complementary to its own purpose. The survival of Freetown, as a port and settlement, would obviously be easier if it were to become the channel of trade to a prosperous hinterland. The abolitionists were men of monumental obstinacy and Himalayan optimism and, in spite of the failure of Freetown and failure in discovery, they clung to this hope with adamantine faith. Their faith was strengthened because a prosperous hinterland and a legitimate trade, legitimate in contrast to the illegitimate traffic in human beings, was essential to their wider purpose, to their crusade against slavery and the slave-trade.

Nevertheless, the humanitarian movement was, in the beginning, only one of many factors leading to a new and more urgent interest in Africa, and certainly the African Association, which planned and

[1] Cf. Sir Reginald Coupland, *The British Anti-Slavery Movement*, Home University Library (Oxford University Press).

financed the early explorations, kept carefully away from the question of abolition. Yet there can be no doubt that the political skill of the humanitarians and their powerful organization for propaganda were more responsible than any other body of men for keeping alive an acute interest in African affairs. They certainly created the reading public which devoured edition after edition of Park and Clapperton and Lander. As the years pass, the question of abolition, absent in Park, becomes a dominant theme in the narrative of the explorers.

III

Whether in favour of abolition or not, the travellers could not ignore the slave-trade. Park was not an abolitionist, and Brian Edwardes (who wrote up Park's notes for publication) was in favour of slavery; yet one of the most harrowing accounts of the dreadful slave caravans which brought the slaves from the interior to the coast occurs in Park's pages, the more effective because so plainly, so unemotionally related. This centuries-old trade permeated all of West African society and created conditions of great difficulty for explorers, and so must be described.

The trade was in two directions—one across the Sahara to the slave markets of Cairo and Baghdad; the other to the coast for shipping to America. The former was the more terrible. The wastes of desert were scattered with bones of slaves whose stamina failed. And yet there was an even darker side to this traffic. The highest price paid in the slave markets of the Middle East was for eunuchs. This specialized trade was fantastically wasteful of human life. According to Barth, the most accurate and scientific of West African explorers, the traders considered that Allah had been kind if ten out of a hundred boys survived the operation. The traffic to the coast was less barbarous, the journey less arduous, but the volume was far greater in extent. In consequence, tribal life had been more greatly disturbed.

Slaves were obtained in a variety of ways. The children of slaves were, of course, always slaves. A man through poverty or ill fortune might have to sell his children, his wife, or even himself. Slavery, too, was a convenient punishment for malefactors breaking tribal custom. This was a profitable perquisite for the chief, hence the powers of chiefs tended to grow and they became more brutal in their use. But most of the slaves were acquired in war, by raiding the more primitive tribes who lived in wild country between the fertile Niger valley and the coast. War became very profitable and military empires were prosperous. The brutal and blood-thirsty empires of the Ashanti and the Hausa were the inevitable consequences of slaving. Once acquired, the slaves were sold to Moslem traders—usually men of mixed Arab and Negro blood—in return for guns, ammunition and finery. When one or two traders had collected sufficient slaves they would join together in a caravan, the male slaves manacled, and march to Cairo or the coast. At Cairo the slaves would be cleaned up and fattened for sale; on the coast they were herded together in pens to await the slaving ships. The longer the ship took in arriving, the greater the mortality amongst the slaves, and a more fearsome prospect of the dreaded middle passage.

On board, the slaves were fettered ankle to ankle, wrist to wrist. They were made to lie on their sides to take up less room: the space between decks was rarely more than four feet. There were no sanitary arrangements. The food was usually horse beans and water. For exercise, they were taken out to be danced in their chains at the end of a lash. In such conditions many men may want to die; almost the only way to commit suicide was to starve themselves to death. Hundreds of Negroes, of course, attempted this, but ships carried an instrument which Clarkson, the abolitionist, purchased in Liverpool. When produced as evidence of the cruelty of the trade, it chilled the Privy Council. The instrument was the mouth-opener, a type of chisel, used to break through the teeth in order to force the Negro to eat. Dysentery, inevitable in such filth, released many from the torments of the crossing. To prevent the spread of disease, the dying as well as the dead were thrown overboard to the waiting sharks whose presence distinguished the slaver's wake. Only a few men were appalled by these conditions; the majority, white and black, accepted them as a part of the vast and inevitable brutality of life. To many explorers these sufferings were no worse than they themselves accepted without complaint.

As so much and so vital a part of the slave-trade was in the hands of white men, the coastal tribes and Arab traders did not at first suspect travellers of the intention of helping to abolish their trade, but they did suspect them of planning to take away their livelihood. They could not conceive that there could be any other reason for wishing to penetrate inland, and when travellers told them that they sought knowledge not slaves, that they wished only to discover from whence and to where the great River Niger flowed, they thought it was but another example of the white man's cunning, and their hostility increased. It was this background of fear, jealousy and tribal war, created by the slave-trade, which added so immensely to the task of the first explorers in West Africa.

IV

The African Association tackled the problem of the Niger initially with great sense and judgement. Elaborate questionnaires were devised and sent out, with the help of the government, to British consuls in Africa. The replies were disappointing. The Niger flowed westward to the Atlantic; it was, in fact, the Gambia or Senegal or both. Or it flowed eastward either to join the Nile or to evaporate in a vast lake in Central Africa. The myths and rumours of centuries were uncritically repeated. It was clear to the Association that inquiry would have to give way to exploration. It was also clear to the Association that if exploration was to be undertaken, there were only two possible routes: either across the desert from Tripoli via the oasis of the Fezzan to Kano and Sokoto, towns whose names were familiar from Arab traders although no white man had seen them; or, alternatively, up the Senegal or Gambia, through the Mandingo country to the legendary Timbuktu. The third route from Morocco across the Sahara to Timbuktu, afterwards used with such brilliance by Caillié, was rejected mainly on political grounds.

The Association's first choice for an explorer was not British but American, John Ledyard. Ledyard, a friend of Thomas Jefferson, was a curious and reckless character. When little more than a child he had forced his way on to Cook's third expedition.[1] After this he decided to walk round the world. He was too impatient to wait for permission from Catherine the Great's officials before crossing Russia, and he had reached Yakutsk in Siberia before the Russians caught up with him and returned him to their border in Europe.

---

[1] It was, of course, because of this expedition that he was known to Sir Joseph Banks and, no doubt, Ledyard was Banks's own choice.

The offer from the Association arrived opportunely at this moment. He hastened to Cairo but there he was held up, caught fever, and died. The Association's next choice was Lucas, who had spent many years in North Africa, partly as a slave in Morocco, and partly as Vice-Consul in Tripoli. He knew Arabic well but perhaps he knew too much of the Arab traders for, after reaching Fezzan, he cautiously returned. He added precision to the current knowledge of the desert, but he did not extend it.

The African Association had not been content to press their attack through the desert alone: in 1790 Major Houghton had set out from the Gambia, but soon after crossing the Faleme he was attacked by natives, or slave-traders, and killed; but, before he was murdered, he had sent back sufficient information to establish almost definitely that the Niger flowed to the east and that, in this respect, Leo Africanus was wrong. After the failure of Ledyard and Lucas, and the disaster of Houghton, the Association was naturally discouraged, and it is probable that the attack on the Niger problem may have been halted had not Sir Joseph Banks come across a remarkable young Scots enthusiast for natural history, Mungo Park.

Mungo Park is one of the most outstanding figures of African exploration. He was the son of a poor Lowland farmer, but his sister married James Dickson, the gardener and botanist, who was known to Sir Joseph Banks. After qualifying in medicine at Edinburgh, Park became a ship's surgeon and whilst in Sumatra he collected eighteen different varieties of fish. Dickson put him in touch with Banks and he published with his encouragement a paper in the Transactions of the Linaean Society. Through Banks he learned that the Association were considering another expedition. He at once volunteered and he was immediately accepted: on May 22, 1795, he sailed from Portsmouth. He was just twenty-three years of age. He returned to England on Christmas Day 1797, having accomplished a most remarkable journey in which he had shown powers of endurance and fortitude rarely equalled. Park was deeply religious, a convinced Calvinist, and it was this faith—that all he suffered was predestined—which carried him through such pain and sickness. It is this that gives a saga-like quality to his plainly told tale.

He had plunged into the interior with one servant—a small negro boy called Johnson—two asses and a horse. Ill-equipped as he was, he was soon robbed of his possessions by Moslem slavers. He was kept prisoner in terrible circumstances for three months: when at last he escaped, he did not turn back to the coast but plunged further into the interior, now without guide, servant or trade goods. He reached the Niger, discovered that it flowed to the East, travelled along until his life was once more endangered and then struggled back to the coast. Only his immense stamina and iron courage enabled him to survive for he was desperately ill for over seven months and he could never have got back but for the kindness of a negro slave trader, Karfa Taura.

Park's journey caused a great stir in geographical circles and for nearly ten years widely conflicting theories were built on the data which he brought back. The leading armchair geographer was Major Rennell, a robust didactic scholar, who was quite prepared to dismiss any evidence in conflict with his ideas. Through the courtesy of Napoleon, the notes of a young German explorer, Horneman, who died after reaching the Niger, had been sent back to England. Horneman had made a strong plea for the view that the Niger was a branch of the Nile. Rennell would have none of it. He was determined to prove that the Niger flowed into what he was pleased to term 'the great sink of Africa', and there evaporated. When Reichard, a German geographer, pressed on him the true solution, Rennell maintained, firstly, that if the great delta in the Bight of Benin was the mouth of the Niger, it would be known; and, secondly, that the Kong mountains, a convenient and mythical range, ran east and west across Africa, cutting off the Niger basin from the coast. The same mountains were used as an argument to dispose of Maxwell's theory that the Niger and Congo were one, although Rennell used valid arguments as well, pointing out that for a 4,000-mile river the mouth of the Congo would have to be greater and the freshwater area vaster than it was.

Park, bored with life as a general practitioner at Peebles, was convinced that he could prove Maxwell right. He obtained the support of the Association for a novel and revolutionary type of expedition. Hitherto, exploration had been conducted by single Europeans travelling alone or in company with slave caravans. In 1805 Park assembled forty-five Europeans. This party, apart from Park, was composed of his brother-in-law, Dr. Anderson, and another Scot, called Scott; five naval artificers to build a boat on reaching the Niger; two seamen to look after the artificers. Protection was provided by thirty-five soldiers from the West Coast garrison under the command of Lieutenant Martyn. The West Coast garrison at the time of the Napoleonic War contained the very dregs of military life, and Lieutenant Martyn himself proved to be a man of cheerful, lunatic brutality whose favourite sport was shooting natives. For a guide, Park discovered Isaaco, a Mandingo, to whose exceptional intelligence, fortitude and devotion we are indebted for all the knowledge we have of this second expedition of Park's. But Isaaco was the only native to accompany the expedition. There were no native porters of any sort. This ill-assorted caravan, dressed in full military or naval uniform, set out from the coast a fortnight before the rains began. Only Isaaco survived.

The story of this journey is a saga: saga-like in its utter indifference to death. One by one they died and were buried, but on Park went, regardless of mortality, and a shadow only momentarily passed over his spirit when he buried his brother-in-law. Then he wrote: 'I shall only observe that no event took place during the journey which threw the smallest gloom over my mind, till I laid Dr. Anderson in the grave, I then felt myself, as if left a second time lonely and friendless amidst the wilds of Africa.'

But three weeks later, when he wrote his last words home to Lord Campden, the Secretary of State, his spirits had recovered:

I am sorry to say that of forty-five Europeans who left the Gambia in perfect health, five only are at present alive, viz. three soldiers (one deranged in his mind), Lieutenant Martyn and myself.

From this account I am afraid that your Lordship will be apt to consider matters as in a very hopeless state; but I assure you I am far from desponding. . . . I this day hoisted the British flag, and shall set sail to the East with the fixed resolution to discover the termination of the Niger or perish in the attempt. I have heard nothing that I can depend on respecting the remote course of this mighty stream: but I am more and more inclined to think that it can end nowhere but in the sea.

My dear friend Mr. Anderson and likewise Mr. Scott are both dead, but though all the Europeans who are with me should die, and though I were myself half dead, I would still persevere; and if I could not succeed in the object of my journey, I would at least die on the Niger.

This was written after a nightmare journey of sickness, death and near starvation, made in the worst possible season, through hostile and difficult country. Against this background, its heroism and courage stand out in bolder relief but it also underlines a quality, less admirable but equally epic, which made Park the outstanding explorer of his age—that sublime, that utter indifference to fate, to pain, and to suffering, based on an absence of imaginative comprehension of the needs of his fellow men, and also grounded on his profound conviction of the mysterious but preordained ways of God.

The achievement was great. From inquiries made by Isaaco and by later explorers we know that this same party reached the Busa rapids, 800 miles beyond Timbuktu. And a chief of that region is reported to wear Park's ring at the present day. But the geographers at home had not the slightest idea how far Busa was from Timbuktu. They judged it to be eighty miles, and, in consequence, the brilliant achievement of Park was underestimated.

The intensification of the Napoleonic wars prevented further attempts to solve the Niger problem until after the Treaty of Vienna, except for the eccentric activities of a German, Roentgen. He intended to travel as a Moslem trader. With great, perhaps excessive, thoroughness he trained on a diet of spiders, grasshoppers and roots, and before sailing, in order to leave nothing to chance, had himself circumcized. These tribulations were suffered without reward, for the moment he set foot in Africa he caught fever and died.

During the ten years in which the problem was shelved, Maxwell's theory, that the Congo and Niger were one, had gained in favour and the first attempt in the renewed outburst of Niger exploration which followed the close of the Napoleonic wars was based on this assumption. Captain Tuckey, a valiant explorer of the Arctic seas, was to sail up the Congo, whilst two army officers, Peddie and Campbell, were to follow Park's trail. It was hoped that the two expeditions would meet on the Niger. Both were utterly disastrous.

Tuckey reached the first great Congo cataract, 150 miles from the coast, a cataract which the Jesuits had discovered in the seventeenth century. He was forced back, and Tuckey and most of his crew died of fever, and the vessel only just reached Fernando Po. The army did no better. Peddie reached Faleme but the mortality was so great that he turned back to the coast; over one hundred soldiers died. These huge losses distressed the government, and the large-scale expeditions, which Park's second journey had inaugurated, were given up in favour of small parties, travelling with Arab caravans. For such parties the less hostile and difficult trans-Saharan routes were preferred.

In 1818 Ritchie and Lyon set out from Tripoli. Just beyond Murzuk Ritchie died and Lyon returned; another failure, but a productive failure, for with Lyon's narrative were published the most beautiful colour prints of North African exploration. Also, he stirred the armchair geographers to renewed controversy; the scraps of geographical knowledge, which he had picked up from the Arabs, convinced him that the Nile and the Niger were one. Maxwell stoutly maintained the Congo-Niger theories and Rennel could not be moved from his theory of evaporation. Meanwhile Park's book had reached the West Indies and stirred the lively imagination of a planter, M'Queen. Very sensibly he collected extensive information from the slaves, some of whom had heard of Park and seen him, and from this evidence it was clear that the Niger ended, as Reichard had predicted in 1803, where it does, in the great delta of the Bight of Benin. At the same time, M'Queen pleaded earnestly for the government to take over as Crown colonies the vast new territories which their explorers had discovered, for otherwise, maintained M'Queen, the French would do so and all our labour would be lost. Both the geographical and the political deductions were remarkably accurate and when, afterwards, M'Queen was proved to be right, he assumed a position of pontifical eminence in geographical circles. Unfortunately, in the controversies which raged later in the century concerning the sources of the Nile, he was obstinately and absolutely wrong and his violent championship, in the face of obvious evidence, helped to delay the problem's solution for many years.

In 1820, the year before the publication of M'Queen's book, the government, encouraged by its very friendly relations with the Bashaw of Tripoli, had sent out another expedition across the North desert under the command of Dr. Denham and subsequently Lieutenant Clapperton, R.N. This proved to be one of the most vital and important journeys of the Niger quest. Travelling by the route, Murzuk-Kawar-Kukawa, they discovered Lake Chad. This vast expanse of water appeared to justify the confident assertions of Rennell and they thought that they had discovered his 'great sink of Africa'. But their error quickly became obvious as they travelled towards Bornu and watched the river which fed Chad dwindle to a stream. At Kukawa, the capital of the Bornu, the party split, Clapperton pushed on towards the Niger; his companion, Oudney, died, and he reached Kano alone, in January 1824. 'Arrayed in naval uniform I made myself as smart as circumstances would permit. . . . I might have spared all the pains I had taken with my toilet; for not an individual turned his head round to gaze at me, but all, intent on their own business, allowed me to pass by without notice or remark.' Kano was, of course, the great trading centre of the Western Sudan and strange costumes of remote tribes were a commonplace, so that the tattered blue and gold of Clapperton's uniform would easily pass unnoticed. Once Clapperton had made his presence known to the Emir he was warmly received. Even more ardent was his reception by Sultan Bello at Sokoto who drew for him a map of the Niger and pointed out how easy it would be to reach his country from the sea. These views were embodied in a letter which Clapperton carried back to George IV and, in return for the trade we were to bring, Bello promised to stop the traffic in slaves to the coast, for Clapperton had made it crystal clear that friendship with Great Britain could only be obtained at the price of suppressing the slave trade.

At last the dreams of the abolitionist seemed to be coming true. Clapperton had discovered large, prosperous towns and friendly and intelligent native rulers who appeared to appreciate the advantages of legitimate trade to the slave trade. Clapperton was promptly dispatched in 1825 to blaze the river route to the Western Sudan, along which the trade was to flow. But when he and his party arrived off the Niger delta no one had heard of Rakah, which Sultan Bello had so confidently named as the port commanding the river's termination. So Clapperton landed at Badagry and made his way north through the Yoruba country. His companions died and he and his servant, Richard Lander, were desperately ill. Yet miserable and wretched as he was, he did not consider return. After immense privations they reached Kano; for a month Clapperton rested and then pushed on alone to Sokoto. Here he found hostility instead of friendship. The repeated statements on his previous journey that British friendship could only be secured by the abolition of the slave trade had given the Arab traders food for thought. They were also worried by the prospect of a river route from the coast to the Western Sudan which would cut out their lucrative caravans. During Clapperton's absence they had worked hard on the religious and xenophobic prejudices of the Sultan with whom, on Clapperton's return, he was no longer *persona grata*. Worn out by ill health and disappointment Clapperton died. Destitute and sick, Lander determined to make his way down the Niger alone; he reached Zaria at the confluence of the Niger and Benue but there he was captured. Escaping, he was forced to leave the Niger and make his way across country to the coast.

The results of this exploration were deeply disappointing; it was clear that friendship had given way to hostility and that the prospects of easy trade up the Niger into Western Sudan were, even if practical, very remote. But Richard Lander, like so many of the great African explorers, was a determined and obstinate man. Like Park and Clapperton before him he thirsted to get back and so he accepted with alacrity a meagre grant of the government—£100 for himself and his brother; £100 a year for his wife during his absence —and set off once more for Africa. They reached Busa in 1830, made their way easily to the confluence of the Benue. After a brief period of captivity by the Ibo, they got free and set off by boat down the river, reaching the sea in November 1830. At last, the Niger problem was finally solved; Reichard and M'Queen justified: Rennell and Maxwell reduced to obscurity. And Richard Lander, the domestic servant from Cornwall, achieved immortality as explorer and author. His books are the most interesting of all the great narratives of West African discovery; the adventure is there, the courage, the endurance, the qualities of spirit which we admire so much in Park and Clapperton, but there is also a naïve charm, an artificial elegance of style and manner, so much at variance with the

subject-matter that one's amusement is vastly increased.[1] Take, for
example, this description of a ju-ju tree:

> The huge branches of the fetish-tree, groaning beneath their
> burden of human flesh and bones, and sluggishly waving in con-
> sequence of the hasty retreat of the birds of prey; the intense and
> almost insufferable heat of a vertical sun; the intolerable odour of
> the corrupt corpses; the heaps of human heads, many of them
> apparently staring at me from hollows which had once sparkled
> with living eyes; the awful stillness and solitude of the place,
> disturbed only by the sighing of the conscious wind through the
> sombre foliage, or at intervals by the frightful screaming of
> voracious vultures, as they flapped their sable wings almost in my
> face—all tended to overpower me; my heart sickened within my
> bosom, a dimness came over my eyes, an irrepressible quivering
> agitated my whole frame, my legs refused to support me, and
> turning my head, I fell senseless into the arms of Jowdie, my
> faithful slave! Pasko assisted to bear me away from the scene of
> blood; and the two blacks emptying a calabash of water they had
> brought with them on my head, face and breast, I slowly revived,
> and after a slight refreshment, pursued my journey by another
> path.

However, the Niger quest was over; its course was known from
Sansanding to the sea. But there was much still to be learned; no
one but Park had travelled from Timbuktu to Busa; the course,
extent and importance of the Benue was unknown; the intricate
mass of the delta was unexplored. There was still great ignorance.
Nevertheless, there was the immeasurably important discovery that
the West Sudan could be reached from the sea, a fact of vital consequence for the development of West Africa.

V

The vital consequence was quickly perceived at home, and once
again events in England were curiously consonant with the rhythm

---

[1] There is no reason to believe that Lander was not the author of his own narratives.
I have a copy which he gave to Sir Richard Vyvyan, inscribed in a very fine hand
'from the author, R^d Lander'.

of West African exploration. The steam boat was growing out of infancy and the steam boat made river navigation possible, where sailing boats would have had a hopeless task against wind and current. One of the most enthusiastic supporters of the steam boat was a Liverpool merchant, Macgregor Laird. Liverpool had lost the slave trade but not its interest in West Africa. Already there was a growing trade in palm oil and the Liverpool merchants were eager to extend the area of their trade. Nor was the humanitarian movement dead. The slave trade had been abolished; the emancipation of slaves in the West Indies was about to take place. Subject to the remorseless pressure of the best organized propaganda machine in Britain, the government had forced treaties on one foreign power after another for the suppression of the trade. A squadron of the navy patrolled the West African coast in an attempt to enforce them. Once more there was the problem of the freed slaves. What was to be done with them? Where were they to go? Reluctant as the government was to embark on any colonial policy, or to attempt the responsibilities and costs of a settlement, yet the pressure of the humanitarian movement, through the great voting strength which it possessed, kept the British government actively engaged in West African exploration for the next twenty years in spite of repeated disaster and in spite of the complete failure of legitimate trade to prosper.

The first attempts at river navigation were largely exploratory, as much a test of the steamships as of the possibilities of commerce. The first two iron ships to make a sea voyage, the *Quorra* and the *Alburkah*, entered the Niger delta in 1832. Macgregor Laird was himself on board with both the Landers. A doctor, Oldfield, accompanied them, and Lieutenant Allen, sent by the government for surveying, gave the expedition an official air. The first season was neither very successful nor very disappointing. A part of the delta was explored and the vessels struggled up the main river to Lokoja at the confluence of the Benue. Laird, himself, even managed a short trip up this river. The cost in lives had been grave—eighteen men had died before they left the delta. The prospects of commerce seemed poor. Laird returned to England and left Lander in charge. The next season he and Oldfield got well beyond Lokoja, as far as Rabba, in addition to navigating a hundred miles of the Benue.

Lander was so elated with his success that he determined to make a second exploration before the water fell and made navigation impossible. The *Alburkah* was sent up river but Lander, following with supplies, was attacked by natives. He was mortally wounded and he died, on February 2, 1834, at Fernando Po. His death in some ways marked the end of the great epoch of West African discovery —the exciting period of the Niger quest which will be for ever associated with Park, Clapperton and Lander.

Yet his death did not bring an end to the exploration of the river. Each of the Macgregor Laird expeditions had set out from Fernando Po, a volcanic island in the Bight of Benin, technically belonging to Spain, but it was a base for the anti-slave squadron and a British naval settlement was maintained there until 1834. The inhabitants were primitive aborigines, freed slaves, half-castes and a curious cosmopolitan collection of Europeans. In 1834 these were governed, with their own consent, by John Beecroft. John Beecroft had begun life as an apprentice seaman. For ten years he had been a prisoner of war in France. Released in 1814, he rejoined the merchant service. He was with Parry's expedition in the Davis Straits and this presumably gave him a taste for exploration. Between 1835 and 1842 Beecroft made a number of journeys and explorations, in steam ships, of an importance which is usually overlooked. After 1842 administrative duties prevented further exploration, for in 1843 he was appointed Governor (unpaid) of Fernando Po by the Queen of Spain. In 1849 he became British Consul at Fernando Po with jurisdiction over the coasts of the Bight. In 1854 he died. The story of this remarkable man is too little known, for he was one of the great pioneers of the Nigerian trade, a magnificent forerunner of the later nineteenth-century traders. His journeys between 1835 and 1842 were not only journeys of exploration of the Niger, Benue and Old Calabar, but trading journeys as well, in which commercial relations were cautiously established with the difficult tribes of the forest and coastal belts. Behind Beecroft were the Liverpool merchants, Laird and Jamieson, who saw their faith being justified both in the river steam boat and in legitimate trade.

Unfortunately for Laird and Jamieson, Buxton and the leaders of the humanitarian movement had more grandiose views. In spite of the glaring and continued failure of Sierra Leone, they were determined on another settlement for freed black slaves on the Niger river. Their arguments were the same specious arguments which they had used so frequently. A grateful colony of freed negroes, happily engaged in the peaceful arts of agriculture, would promote commerce and extend Christianity. They shut their eyes to every fact—to the war, the rapine, the savagery; to the horrors of the climate and the ravages of disease. The government twisted and turned. It was preoccupied with French aspirations in the Indian Ocean and the Persian Gulf. It was weighed down with the burden of India. But the humanitarians dominated the imagination of the middle class, and the middle class voted. Against its judgement, and the vigorous opposition of Laird and Jamieson, the government finally gave way.

A great expedition was organized. Three ships, specially equipped with the latest ventilating devices, were placed under the command of very capable officers of the Royal Navy, and the crews consisted of selected personnel. A model farm, complete with the latest equipment, was embarked. The Rev. Samuel Crowther, afterwards the first black Bishop of the Niger, accompanied the expedition to spread the light of the Gospel. Lokoja, at the Benue, was reached with difficulty. The model farm was disembarked and established on a strip of ground, purchased from the local chiefs. Then the fever struck. Within two months forty-eight of the 145 Europeans were dead. The ships with great difficulty were worked down the river. Some of the West Indians attached to the expedition were butchered in the delta. The model farm was stranded. The government, never enthusiastic, abandoned the expedition. The *Wilberforce*, with a few officers and a black crew, got through to the model farm and evacuated it. This was the end of large-scale exploration in West Africa.

For a few more years, probably owing to the pressure of the humanitarians, whose ardour, if damped, was not extinguished, the government maintained a modified interest in West Africa and subsidized exploration. It was natural that there should be a return to the desert routes and to the small expedition. In 1850, James Richardson set out from Tripoli with two distinguished Germans— Dr. Heinrich Barth and Dr. Adolph Overweg. After the usual tribulations of robbery, blackmail and insult, the party, reaching the Western Sudan, split up to carry out independent explorations.

Richardson soon died. Overweg lasted long enough to make a survey of Lake Chad in a collapsible boat, but by August 1852 Barth was alone. For the next few years he explored with exceptional thoroughness the country between Bornu and Timbuktu, which he reached in September 1853, having covered that part of the Niger from Busa to Kabara, the port of Timbuktu, which only Park had traversed, and which had never been described.[1] The account of these journeys of Barth still remains the most important and authoritative work on these regions and it is a mine of information on tribal customs and habits.

The continued existence of Barth was known in England and several relief expeditions were planned. Towards the end of 1854 he met in the Sudan Dr. Alfred Vogel, another German who had been sent out to help him, and, more surprisingly, two sappers, Corporal Church and Private Macguire, who had accompanied Vogel. They soon afterwards parted company; Vogel and Macguire set out to explore the country towards the Nile; Barth and Church made for home. Unfortunately Vogel and Macguire were murdered and the country between Lake Chad and the Nile remained unexplored for many years.

The necessity for relieving Barth also provided the government with an opportunity to make one further river exploration, not on the disastrous lines of 1841, but organized by Laird and Jamieson and led by Beecroft. Apart from rescuing Barth, the government hoped that the expedition would help to pay for itself by trading, and detailed survey work was also to be carried out. Unfortunately Beecroft, the pioneer of this type of river exploration, died before the expedition started. His place was taken by Dr. Baikie, R.N. Although Barth and Vogel were not rescued, the voyage of the *Pleiad* was a complete success and the methods of Laird and Beecroft thoroughly justified. Quinine had been extensively used as a prophylactic and not one single member of the crew, African or European, died. This, too, was a discovery of immense importance for exploration and trade in tropical Africa.

[1] René Caillié, a Frenchman, had made the journey to Timbuktu and back in 1826— a remarkable journey related in a remarkable book. Caillié had been preceded at Timbuktu by Major Gordon Laing but he was murdered and left no account of his journey.

This journey of the *Pleiad* marks the end of the great epoch of discovery. There were vast territories, untrodden and unmapped, but the essentials of the problems were solved. The course of the Niger was known. It could be used as an easy channel of commerce with the Western Sudan. The results for Africa were profound. As the years passed, steam ships followed the *Pleiad*'s trail; hulks were moored where trade was brisk—convenient, easily movable, easily defended warehouses. Resentment of Arab tribes and of native chiefs was bred by the envy and fear of English trade; so yearly a gunboat patrolled the river to demonstrate the power of Britain. French, Spanish, Portuguese merchants followed the British; commercial relations with the natives and between the Europeans were complex and difficult. In that rough and brutal world, the knife, the fist and the gun settled arguments; lying, cheating, swindling were rife. Authority was needed: consulates were established; in 1872 their powers were extended. As year followed year, European power and influence grew, the sinews of trade bound even more firmly the Western Sudan to the Niger delta, and this, for Africa, was cataclysmic.

For centuries the Sudan, the rich, fertile Savannah lands of the Niger basin, had been separated from, but linked to, the Mediterranean by the great Saharan desert. In culture, religion and way of life it was the remote fringe of the Middle East, but essentially a part of the Old World; a Moslem from Turkey or India would not feel alien there. These bonds had been formed by trade, by the great desert caravans, which brought salt from Egypt or Morocco and returned with slaves, gold and ivory. Strung across the desert were the great oases—Taghaza, Arawan, Ghat and Agades—their fertility maintained at the cost of countless slaves. But salt, cheap and plentiful, could now reach the Sudan from the coast. As the authority of Britain grew, the supply of slaves diminished. The desert ate its way into the oases; the caravans declined and almost ceased, and a relationship of a thousand years was broken. The motley, primitive cultures of the forest and the coast and the civilized Sudanese were bound together in a common destiny by the great River Niger.

VI

Before the voyage of the *Pleiad* interest in West Africa was growing less. The development of the steamship had given a new importance to the Suez route to India, coaling stations were needed, and the unwelcome aspirations of the French to create a new empire in the Indian Ocean had to be circumvented. By 1840 we had acquired Karachi, Aden and Socotra, and Captain Owen had surveyed the eastern coast of Africa. By 1850 the French had been stalemated in Zanzibar. Indian army officers were being encouraged to explore the eastern African interior. The Niger problem solved, geographical speculation turned noisily and avidly to the sources of the Nile, stimulated by the discovery, in 1849, of snow-capped mountains near the Equator. In the 1850's, the exposure by David Livingstone of the East African slave trade sent the humanitarians in full cry on a new scent. And then the searchlight of publicity—Burton's quarrel with Speke, Speke's suicide, Livingstone lost, Stanley hewing and hacking his way through darkest Africa.[1] In consequence West Africa was left to the missionary and to the trader, until, in the 'nineties, public opinion realized with a shock that the French and the Germans were absorbing, quietly and efficiently, those vast tracts of Africa which the British had discovered.

An Indian summer of exploration set in, largely diplomatic, military and strategic in intent. In 1885 Joseph Thomson made his journeys to Sokoto and Gando and brought back his treaties. Lugard's mission to the Borgu was equally profitable in 1894. In 1889 Sir Claude Macdonald, and in 1904 Captain Claud Alexander, cleared up what remained of the mysteries beyond the Benue and Lake Chad. The difficult coastal region and the complex mass of the delta were the object of long and detailed exploration by Sir Henry Johnston and Roger Casement. The accounts of their travels are not without interest but they cannot be compared with the narratives of the heroic epoch of Niger travel nor with the one great outstanding personality of their own time—Mary Kingsley.

Tropical Africa in the nineteenth century was a challenge both to curiosity and compassion, and Mary Kingsley was more than usually endowed with both. Those frank grey eyes could observe the most bestial acts of primitive religion with that utter detachment which was so necessary for understanding. She never condemned anything but hypocrisy, pomposity and stupidity, and her honest and sane explanations of the more grotesque aspects of native life—

[1] See 'The Search of the Nile', pp. 193–202.

which Victorian England, nurtured on missionaries' tales, found so difficult to comprehend—helped to establish a sound scientific approach to primitive custom. She quickly grasped that the Englishman's conscience was too easily satisfied with contributions to missionary funds which were often wasted. She saw that many missions, through bigotry and prejudice, were doing more harm than good and that the British attitude wanted to be radically changed. Yet she was not a philanthropist. Trade, for her, was the fundamental relationship between Africa and England, but trade which was mutually advantageous and not trade which was ruthless exploitation of primitive people. She was aware that only through trade could Africa afford those necessities of civilization, health and education, which would enable the pagan tribes to grow out of primeval terrors of which their horrible and degrading religion was the expression. She was a great pioneer; along with Lugard and Johnston, she helped to create a new attitude to African problems, an attitude which was completely honourable and a violent contrast to the brutality, rapine and murder of the rubber-hunting Europeans of the Congo.

The story of African exploration closed on the same high note of courage, blended with, and humanized by, intellectual curiosity. Perhaps the most remarkable feature of these men—Park, Clapperton, Lander, Barth—was their astonishing capacity to endure. There have been explorers of far greater competence, for more often than not they took the wrong gear and started in the wrong season, but it would be difficult to find men who bore with such indifference the pain and suffering which was so frequently their lot.

All, and each of them, responded greatly to the grandeur of their quest and displayed that heroism appropriate to men who were to be the vehicle of the changing destiny of a continent and a world.

1950

THE SEARCH FOR THE NILE

FROM the days of Herodotus, the rise and fall of the Nile waters were mysteries upon which generations of men speculated—usually in vain. By the beginning of the nineteenth century, the Blue Nile, and its influence upon the flow of the Nile itself, had been discovered by Jesuit missionaries and by the great Scots traveller, James Bruce. About the origin of the White Nile there was infinite surmise. Snow-capped mountains, the mythical Mountains of the Moon, or a vast inland sea were the most favoured sources. All geographers endowed the river with enormous length, placing its source in the heart of South Africa. French interest in this problem, stimulated by Napoleon's invasion of Egypt, was at first greater than the British. After Napoleon's defeat, many French officers entered Egyptian service; others returned later to help Mohammed Ali in his exploration of the Sudan; and by 1840, the French had travelled to within four degrees of the Equator, where the Nile was still a wide, smooth-flowing stream, obviously far from its source. This fresh knowledge interested the professional geographers; but the problem of the Nile failed to capture the public imagination, which was enthralled by the quest for the Niger and preoccupied with the horrors of the West African slave trade.

French interest had not been confined to Egypt. The loss of her great Indian possessions still rankled, and Frenchmen dreamed of a new empire based on Réunion, Madagascar and Zanzibar; rich islands, conveniently and strategically placed to control the greatest of the routes to the East via Suez. Although the British government had little desire to add to its colonial burdens, it could not ignore this new threat. Uninterrupted use of the Suez route—even before the canal was cut, the most satisfactory and quickest for the new steamship service—was of vital importance to imperial interests. To protect it, both Aden and Karachi had been seized in 1839; in 1843 Palmerston forced the French to abandon a project of establishing themselves on the East African coast. The Sultan of Zanzibar, who ruled vast undefined tracts of East Africa, was given special protection; and French intrigues against our paramount influence were neatly thwarted by Sir John Kirk, the friend of Livingstone. Into this sphere of British interest swarmed Indian traders who, as British subjects, required protection. The missionaries followed the traders; anti-slavery agitation was soon in full force, raised to a fever pitch by David Livingstone's revelations of the iniquities of the Arab trade. Public interest, which had been focused for generations on West Africa, switched dramatically to the East. It was not long before the search for the Nile sources began in earnest. The solution took nearly half a century and involved some of the greatest of African explorers—Burton, Speke, Livingstone and Stanley.

In 1849, two German missionaries reported the discovery of snow-capped mountains on the Equator. For good measure, they also reported the existence of a vast inland sea from information supplied by Arab traders. The fertile imagination of the armchair geographers was soon at work on this promising material. M'Queen, whose successful prognostications about the Niger had given him an exalted idea of his own infallibility, pronounced that the Germans' mountains were the Mountains of the Moon, long known to the ancient world as the twin sources of the Nile, a view which he upheld with adamantine obstinacy until his death, no matter what fresh evidence was brought back by the explorers themselves. Others were more cautious, agreeing with Livingstone that white quartz glinting in the sun could look remarkably like snow. W. D. Cooley dismissed the mountains as irrelevant; he plumped for an inland sea, about the size of the Caspian. So that the matter might be decided by observation, the Royal Geographical Society accepted an offer from an Indian army officer, Captain Richard Burton, who expressed a desire to lead an expedition 'primarily for the purpose of ascertaining the limits of the Sea of Ujiji'. In August, 1857, the expedition left the coast opposite Zanzibar on a journey that was to lead to the century's most acrimonious and tragic controversy in geographical circles.

Burton was a wild, flamboyant character, arrogant and reckless of convention, thoroughly at home in the company of semi-civilized people; the more peculiar their private habits, the more he relished their society. His interest in sex was rabid—his consuming passion which he made a vain attempt to disguise by a pseudo-scientific, anthropological jargon. He loved to shock. Utterly self-centred, yet suspicious and acutely sensitive to criticism, he would have been a difficult companion for any man; for Speke he was intolerable. John Speke was a fresh-faced, fair-haired giant, handsome, reserved, inhibited. He came from an ancient Somerset family, and respected the principles and prejudices of his class. Yet within himself he carried about a despair which drove him to seek death in Africa. Speke's difficulties were too deeply buried for Burton to recognize that they existed; and he was aware only of the simple, conventional Speke of outward appearance. What was worse, they distrusted each other. They had been together on a previous journey when Burton had reached the forbidden city of Harar in Abyssinia. On their return, they had been attacked by Somalis. One of the party had been killed, and Speke badly and Burton lightly injured. There is a strong suspicion that Burton did not behave with that reckless bravery which he liked to assume was natural to him. Burton was certainly aware that Speke suspected his courage. He may have invited him to join him on this new expedition in order to wipe out these suspicions. Speke accepted because any danger was better than none, and he wished to crown his long leave from the Indian army with a discovery of major importance. His eagerness proved his own undoing.

The first stages of their journey were smooth enough, apart from the awkwardness caused by Burton's increasing hostility to his companion, and by the quiet, but effective, response of Speke, who made Burton feel both a coward and a cad; but once they got beyond Tabora, the centre for Arab and Zanzibar traders, their difficulties began in earnest. The tribes, tormented by the slavers, were extremely hostile. Burton was frequently delirious with fever; Speke had a bad attack of ophthalmia. In this condition, they reached Lake Tanganyika, where Burton reported that 'my purblind companion found nothing to grumble at except the "mist and glare" before his eyes'. But 'mist and glare' was all Speke could see of the lake to which he had toiled in agony. They then returned to Tabora to rest, having already made a major discovery. Burton, at least, had seen the vast inland sea of which rumour had reached London. Furthermore, they had learnt from an Arab trader that there were three vast lakes, not one. Eager to settle the Nile problem outright, Speke believed that he could do so by visiting the great lake to the north of Tanganyika. He was anxious to make an additional journey; but Burton was equally determined to stay in Tabora (Kazeh). They parted company. According to Speke, Burton was 'most unfortunately quite done up, but most graciously consented to wait with the Arabs and recruit health'. Burton's version gives a somewhat different reason:

My companion, who had recovered strength from the repose and comparative comfort of our headquarters, appeared a fit person to be detached upon this duty; moreover, his presence at Kazeh was by no means desirable. To associate at the same time with Arabs and Anglo-Indians, who are ready to take offence when it is least intended, who expect servility as their due, and whose morgue of colour induces them to treat all skins a shade darker than their own as 'niggers', is even more difficult than to avoid a rupture when placed between two friends who have quarrelled with each other. Moreover, in this case, the difficulty was exaggerated by the Anglo-Indians' complete ignorance of Eastern manners and customs, and of any Oriental language beyond, at least, a few words of the debased Anglo-Indian jargon.

Speke returned triumphant. He had discovered Lake Victoria Nyanza, which he concluded was the great reservoir of the Nile. For Speke the problem was settled; but, to his immense irritation, Burton refused to accept his discovery. He rightly pointed out that they had no positive evidence that the lake and the river were connected: for this Speke had only a native report. Burton implied that Speke's ignorance of the language made it unlikely that he would have understood any report correctly. Speke was infuriated by Burton's obstinate determination not to believe a word of his report. Violently angry, they made their separate ways to England;

but, before they parted, Burton had secured a pledge from Speke not to discuss their discoveries in public until they had both arrived. Fatally, Speke broke his pledge. He was betrayed, perhaps too easily betrayed, into indiscretion by a reporter he met on the boat home. When Burton reached England, he found Speke the idol of the hour, his discoveries everywhere accepted, apart from the obstinate M'Queen, with whom Burton went into immediate alliance. Burton stressed the weaknesses of Speke's theory; but none would listen. Burton was ignored; and the Royal Geographical Society voted large sums to Speke and sent him out at the head of a new expedition.

This expedition was grandiose and elaborate. The Sultan of Zanzibar provided an escort of Baluchi soldiers. The porters were freed slaves, who were to spread the virtues of the anti-slavery campaign among the natives. Immense quantities of merchandise were carried to interest the natives in the prospects of English trade. After Tabora, difficulties began for Speke and Grant. The Baluchi soldiers were the first to desert; the freed slaves followed them. Hostile tribes extorted from Speke most of his merchandise as the price of allowing him to pass through their territory. Fever-ridden and destitute when they sighted Lake Victoria, they were saved by the curiosity and courtesy of King Rumanika, and by the generosity of M'tesa, the Kbakka of Uganda. The rich fertile lands about Lake Victoria were heavily populated, the natives being dominated by an aristocracy of Abyssinian origin. These large well-organized countries were ruled by absolute monarchs, who lived in huge palaces, attended with elaborate ritual by a host of court officials. Both Rumanika and M'tesa were highly intelligent, filled with curiosity about the strange white men who had suddenly wandered into their midst. But Speke was shocked. Shocked when M'tesa offered him a page as a target, in order to demonstrate the power of the rifle; shocked when the Queen sent him a brace of virgins in a state of nature—they were quickly clothed and hurried off to homes and husbands in Zanzibar; shocked by the facility with which the King killed his courtiers for trivial offences; shocked even by the size of Ugandan beauty: 'She could not rise; and so large were her arms that, between the joints, the flesh hung down like large loose-stuffed puddings.' One regrets that it was not Burton, rather than

Speke, who discovered Uganda, for his curiosity would have matched M'tesa's.

Disengaging themselves with some difficulty from the attentions of the Kbakka, Speke and Grant made their way to the Ripon Falls and began to follow the northwards flowing Nile; but they failed to hold its course, being driven off by Turkish slavers from Egypt, who took a hostile view of the presence of white men. It was with great difficulty that Speke reached Gondokoro, where he met Samuel Baker, a wealthy big game hunter, travelling with his Dutch wife. Speke told him of the native report of yet another great lake; and burning with a desire to emulate Speke, Baker hurried up the Nile, undaunted by terrible privations which his wife heroically shared. Having forced his way to the lake, 'I was determined to honour it,' he wrote, 'with a great name. As an imperishable memorial of one loved and mourned by our Gracious Queen and deplored by every Englishman, I called this great lake "the Albert Nyanza". The Victoria and Albert lakes are the two sources of the Nile.' Baker's high confidence was matched by that of Speke, who wired from Alexandria: 'The Nile is settled.' In his elation, he was unmindful of Burton for whom the problem of the Nile was far from settled.

As Burton was quick to see, there was all the difference in the world between intuitive conviction and demonstrable proof. Lake Tanganyika had never been circumnavigated; it was rash of Speke to deny the possibility of its emptying into the Albert Nyanza. Furthermore, he had dismissed out of hand the persistent rumours of great mountains near Lake Albert, insisting that they referred to Kilimanjaro and Kenya, and that they were irrelevant to the Nile problem, whereas, in fact, they were vital to it. Again, the actual course of the Nile from the Ripon Falls to Gondokoro had not been traced either by Speke or Baker. Such were the obvious weaknesses of Speke's arguments upon which Burton and M'Queen seized; and controversy grew so fierce that it was decided to hold a public debate between Burton and Speke at the British Association meeting at Bath. When the day arrived, Burton paced up and down the platform, like a tiger impatient for its kill; the minutes passed but Speke did not appear. Then at last a message came through to say that he had been found dead. During the morning he had been out shooting; whether his death was an accident or deliberate no one

can say. But its effect on the Nile question was definite and disastrous. Opinion swung violently in favour of Burton and M'Queen
and no one would listen to Baker's confirmations of Speke's theory
when he returned; for a greater explorer than Baker declared himself
in favour of Burton. During his visit to London between his second
and third African journeys, Livingstone became convinced that
Speke was wrong; and his reputation was so great that geographer
after geographer tumbled over himself to tear Speke's theory to
shreds. For another twenty-three years, the Nile problem continued
to vex the geographical world and to absorb the energies of the two
greatest of African explorers, Livingstone and Stanley.

Livingstone's youth was dominated by poverty and suffering;
tragedy had dogged his early manhood. But he was one of those
rare men whose natures were deepened and rendered more com-
passionate by personal disasters. The brutalities of the African slave
trade appalled him; yet, quixotically, he seems in the end almost to
have accepted it as a part of the intolerable lot of men. Contact with
own kind and creed was difficult and unnecessary; alone, in the heart
of Africa, his life found its purpose. Remote from the world, given
to profound and concentrated thought, he was gradually consumed
and dominated by a fixed idea. It was God's purpose to reveal to
him not only the source of the Nile but also Merowe, the lost city
of Moses, which would prove to an unbelieving world the validity
of the scriptures. The search for the sources of the Nile dominated
his life and destroyed him.

Stanley was made of harder metal. Born a bastard, he had been
educated in the brutal school of orphanages and workhouses. As a
boy he had been forced to fend for himself. This struggle suited his
nature, which was violent, resourceful and decisive but cruel and
unforgiving, the whole bound together with formidable willpower
and high unthinking courage. By 1870 Livingstone had been lost
for several years in the depths of Africa; and Stanley, then working
as an American journalist, saw the tremendous publicity value of an
organized search. He persuaded the proprietor of his newspaper to
let him go, with superlative efficiency organized a model expedition
and, although he had had no previous experience of Africa, got it
in record time to Lake Tanganyika and to Livingstone. At their
dramatic meeting at Ujiji, Stanley was swept away by a hero

o

worship for Livingstone which he was destined never to lose. Together they explored Tanganyika, proving that it had no Northern exit and thus destroying for ever Burton's theory of it as a Nile source. Yet their discoveries complicated, rather than solved, the problem.

After Stanley's departure, Livingstone began his last fatal expedition—a journey of nightmare intensity that took him to the waters of the Congo, which even he, in his more lucid moments, could not believe to be the Nile. But it was the new problems his journey raised that drew Stanley back to Africa, where he was to remain the most commanding figure in the field of exploration for the next quarter of a century. His methods were novel and terrifying. Without hesitation, he left his white lieutenants to die. He described with unthinking frankness how he had lashed a native woman into silence. The maxim-gun and the dog-whip helped him to drive a red trail across the heart of Africa. But his expeditions never failed, and they revealed unbelievable riches. He discovered the vast navigable waters of the Congo, soon to be the bloodstained highway of rubber-hunting Europeans. Death and disaster for Africa followed in Stanley's wake; for he showed how ruthless violence could overcome all dangers, all difficulties, and reduce the fiercest tribes to subjection. The public, which had venerated Livingstone, was obstinately hostile to Stanley. The heroic quality of his exploits; his immense capacities as a leader and organizer; his fantastic powers of endurance; his magnificent will—these were ignored, as criticism seized on the vulgarity of his publicity and the ferocity of his actions. So spectacular were Stanley's discoveries that interest was distracted from the problem of the Nile's origin. He and Livingstone had destroyed a part of the Burton-M'Queen thesis; Baker and Speke were more or less reinstated; Lakes Victoria and Albert were regarded as the twin sources; and only M'Queen, immensely old and immensely obstinate, still clung to the theory that the Nile's ultimate source was Mount Kenya.

Finally, in 1888, apart from a few technical details, Stanley solved the whole problem. Emin Pasha, a strange, attractive German, had established himself on Lake Albert as the governor of the Egyptian province of Equatoria. Cut off by the Mahdi from Egypt, he was thought to be dead until a letter from him reached Europe. Fantastic rumours were soon abroad of the immense stocks of ivory which he had amassed; and an Emin Pasha Relief Fund was quickly over-subscribed. Stanley, who was naturally chosen to lead the relief expedition, decided to proceed via the Congo and then cut across to Lake Albert. This landed him in the heart of the Ituri forest, the most impenetrable region of Africa, which effectively destroyed his expedition. When he staggered to the shores of Lake Albert, broken in health and almost destitute, he was met by Emin Pasha, fresh and immaculate on the deck of his steam-launch, who entertained him with champagne at a delectable luncheon. For once the joke was on Stanley, but not for long. He had come to relieve Emin. It mattered nothing to him that Emin did not wish to be relieved, that all he wanted was stores, mainly ammunition, which Stanley always had in abundance. But Stanley's willpower carried the day; and Emin, Egyptian officials and servants, were packed up and sent off on the long dangerous journey to Zanzibar. A little time before they were due to leave, there was a morning of exceptional clarity; and Stanley was astonished to see a range of snow-capped mountains some seventy miles distant. Emin himself, though he had lived for years on the lake, had never before seen them. They were the legendary Mountains of the Moon, the Ruwenzori. Stanley made a rapid exploration, discovered Lake Edward, traced the river connecting it with Lake Albert and settled the Nile problem once and for all. This done, he bundled Emin and his caravanserai to the coast. The mountains were back on the map, this time in the right place. The problem of the Nile had taken forty years to settle. Its solution, like the solution of the Niger problem, created even greater difficulties.

None of the Nile explorers journeyed to Africa for the sake of exploration alone. In all their minds, there was the question of trade and of colonization. Livingstone wrote ecstatically of the Shiré highlands; and naturally Stanley's reports glowed with the economic possibilities of Uganda and the Congo. The Victorians, of course, regarded trade as the vehicle of a higher civilization, whose blessings and virtues would be readily appreciated by the African—'Philan-thropy at five per cent', as Stanley phrased it. When the traders and the missionaries followed in the wake of the explorers, both were immediately successful. The International Africa Association, whose President was the King of the Belgians, owing to the boom in rubber, caused by the invention of the bicycle, became one of the wealthiest corporations in Europe.

But its methods were so vile, and the wastage of human life so appalling, that public opinion in the end forced the Belgian government to take over the company; and so the Belgian Congo was brought into being. Explorers, traders, concession hunters and missionaries had implored the British government to take the Uganda territories under its protection. These great kingdoms had been at war with each other for centuries; and to their natural rivalry they now added the additional incitement of religious fervour, for they adopted different brands of Christianity. But the British government was reluctant to accept further colonial responsibilities; and it needed the threat of German imperialism to force it into action. German plans of aggression, however, finally determined the British government to agree to the dismemberment of the Zanzibar Sultanate. Through the usual technique of bogus treaties, the Germans had already obtained control of the vast territories of Tanganyika, a country, discovered by Englishmen, where trade was largely in the hands of British subjects. To check any further extension of German influence, in 1886, and again in 1890, England agreed to the partition of East Africa by agreements that gave rise to Kenya and Uganda. These countries bore little relation to ethnological regions; but in East Africa at least there was not the immense diversity of law, custom, religion and degree of civilization that British administrators found in Nigeria. Except for Uganda, moreover, much of the land was empty and capable of white settlement. With security and good government, the native tribes have increased with great rapidity; and today East Africa faces problems similar to and as grave as those of South Africa. Explorers are the harbingers of changing destiny; in their wake must follow all the problems inherent in the clash between sophisticated and primitive civilizations. But, for the most part, explorers are ignorant of what they forbode. They are drawn to their task not by simpler motives, but by reasons more personal and more profound. It was their own strange, desperate necessities which drew Speke, Stanley and, above all, Livingstone, to Africa. There, and there alone, they found an answer and a solace; in action, or in the acceptance of suffering, the rare nature of each was fulfilled.

1952

CECIL RHODES

BELOW the belt of African tropical forest stretched a vast savannah land, sometimes fertile, sometimes desert, but more frequently betwixt and between. From the north waves of nomadic pastoral tribes of Bantus had pushed steadily south, driving out the more primitive peoples into the inhospitable desert fringes. From the south a white nomadic race, the Boers, had pushed north. Inevitably the two migrations clashed savagely and bitterly; but the rifles of the Boers brought them victory. The defeated tribes either stayed on in subjection or quitted to find new lands free from the whites whom they learned to hate. In their conquered country the Boers set up great homesteads and lived out their simple, rough and pious lives in the wide open veldt. They were a hard race, believing that they were chosen by God to be masters, a faith which they sustained with the gun and the whip. They were not gregarious; many preferred the isolation of the great plains with the nearest neighbour miles away. A proud, bigoted, tough, primitive people yet possessing great courage and a sense of their own, if no one else's, destiny.

After the Treaty of Vienna, Cape Town had passed into British hands and the early decades of the nineteenth century witnessed a steady immigration of English-speaking people into South Africa. They were much resented by the Boers. Indeed for many Boers the situation was so intolerable that they trekked over the veldt to escape into the Transvaal where they had set up their own Free State. From the beginning the Bantus, the Boers and the British lived in a harsh disharmony. The disorders of the frontier regions constantly forced the British government to extend the area of its sovereignty: every extension increased the suspicion of the Boers that the British intended their destruction. The natives saw their land gobbled up by each new wave of white settlers, Boer or British; clashes were frequent, wars not uncommon, yet intense and continuous strife was prevented by the very vastness of the country. Black or white could move off into the great empty lands and brood revenge.

In 1867 a Boer farmer of Griqualand West noticed a bright pebble with which his child was playing. It proved to be a diamond. The next year he managed to get a larger one from a witch-doctor. It is now the Star of South Africa, ranking as one of the world's finest diamonds. News of his discovery spread; miners, speculators, the pioneers and the riff-raff drifted in; diggings were rich and began to yield diamonds. As life became more feverish and violent, the British government decided that it must take control of Griqualand West. The claims of both the Boer republics, the Orange Free State and the Transvaal, were ignored and the flag hoisted. No one knew how many diamonds lay beneath the arid veldt. The British government was moved more by the need to check the turbulence of the unruly mining town than by a desire for riches. A canvas town, called Kimberley, sprang up at the diggings which were brought under a closer control and more orderly exploitation.

In 1871 Cecil Rhodes reached Kimberley in search of a fortune. He was the sickly son of the vicar of Bishop's Stortford who had been sent to Africa for his health. He had farmed cotton and tobacco with his brother in Natal. For most of the time he had been left, young as he was, in sole charge of the farm, for his brother, Herbert, was a restless character who could not settle. News of the diamond diggings had quickly drawn Herbert to Kimberley where he had bought four holdings.

Fortunes were easy to make for the diamonds were plentiful and easy to find. But most of the diggers were feckless men, readily satisfied with what they earned, quickly tired, easily frightened by difficulties. And difficulties soon appeared. The soft sandy soil was soon exhausted, and beneath there was a shelf of hard shale (the reef) and below that blue clay which was rumoured to be lacking diamonds. The deeper the diggings, the greater the problems; roads fell in, water flooded the mines; litigation devoured earnings already much reduced by the diamond glut. It was easier to take a profit and quit.

But Rhodes had a mania for possession. He also believed, and rightly, that there would be diamonds in plenty below the reef. Furthermore he owned the one pump at Kimberley. The price which he had paid for it was wildly extravagant, and it nearly ruined him. Yet like so many of his risks, it was brilliantly judged, for his pump became a tax on other diggers. They paid his price for having their water-logged holdings emptied. Rhodes saved and bought, bought and saved. He lived frugally for he knew that his one constant necessity was ready cash in order to buy at once any holding which came on the market. The only luxury which he permitted himself was an education at Oriel College, Oxford.

It began in the nature of an insurance policy. He had failed to take certain risks, thereby losing thousands, simply because he lacked, in case of failure, the safety net of a profession. At least so he told himself but there was undoubtedly, as later appeared, a deeper yearning. No sooner was he at Oxford than his studies were broken by the threat of tuberculosis and he was forced back to Kimberley for two years to recover. He returned once more to Oxford. And when his business compelled him to interrupt his course yet again, he still persevered and finally took his pass degree. By that time his wealth was so huge that a safety net was quite unnecessary. Yet he needed a sense of purpose. Philosophy was his magic, his religion, his key to the unknown. He struggled to master Aristotle although it was quite beyond his simple, naïve, childlike mind; he felt that somewhere there was an answer which would give meaning to the violent longings of his powerful spirit. Wealth, ownership, power over fellow men, these were delectable but insufficient. His struggles with philosophy were barren but it was at Oxford that his will achieved coherence and direction and the purpose came. Strangely enough through Ruskin.

'This is what England must do, or perish,' Ruskin wrote. 'She must found colonies as fast and as far as she is able, formed of her most energetic and worthiest men; seizing every piece of fruitful waste ground she can set her foot on, and then teaching these her colonists that their chief virtue is to be fidelity to their country, and that their first aim is to be to advance the power of England by land and sea.'

It became Rhodes's profound conviction that the British were a destined people. At twenty-four he sat down and drew up his first will; he dedicated his not inconsiderable fortune to a secret society which was to bring the whole civilized world under British rule, and, incidentally, recover the United States for the Crown. By a mysterious process Oxford had crystallized the limitless, megalomaniac phantasies of a child. His own mania for possession had become the driving force of a conscious political ambition. Men of great wealth have often dreamt childlike dreams, fancied themselves like Rhodes as cast in the mould of a Roman Emperor. Politicians have at times lifted their eyes from the immediate and seen the vision of a world created to their desire. Mostly such dreams are harmless. They become a known folly or remain a secret, cherished only by the holder. Usually they belong to men who lack the ruthless will and obstinacy of heart essential for builders of empire. And the times are rarely propitious, though more frequently so than is desirable for the safety of mankind. With Rhodes the time and the place were peculiarly propitious. Africa offered the chance of colossal wealth. Its vast empty lands were peopled by primitive black tribes or scattered Boer farmers, slender obstacles to a man who lacked all sense of public morality.

Throughout Rhodes's Oxford career his fortune had continued to grow, partly through the care of his partner Rudd, but also due to his own unceasing vigilance. But he was not the only man to have grasped the desirability of acquiring a monopoly of diamond production. A young East End Jew, Barney Barnato, starting with a few boxes of cigars, had built a fortune commensurate with Rhodes's. They fought a bitter ruthless war, driving up the price of shares and driving down the price of diamonds in an attempt to ruin each other. But Rhodes's ideas were brighter and quicker. He regimented native miners, insisting that they should live in strictly controlled compounds. It half ruined the tradesmen of Kimberley but saved Rhodes the loss of three-quarters of a million a year in diamond thefts, a handy sum in his fight with Barnato. Rhodes, too, compelled loyalty; Barnato did not. Rhodes's friends kept their shares, Barnato's secretly traded with Rhodes. In the end Barnato was cornered and he was forced to amalgamate, but Rhodes insisted on his own conditions; the most remarkable was that the profits of the amalgamated company could be used for political purposes. Barnato hedged, and remained resistant to Rhodes's cajolery. Rhodes blandly offered to make Barnato a gentleman by securing his entrance to the Kimberley club which had, hitherto, refused him membership. To this exquisite privilege was added a seat in the Cape parliament. Barnato succumbed. The diamond mines became a vast monopoly whose profits were controlled by Rhodes to direct more or less as he wished.

And there was gold in Africa as well as diamonds. Rhodes had been an early speculator in the newly discovered goldfields which lay in the Rand of the Transvaal. The same mixture of boldness and shrewd calculation led him from success to success until he became one of the greatest magnates in gold. For years in the 'nineties he was drawing between £300,000 to £400,000 a year from these interests. As with the profits from diamonds, so with the profits from gold; Rhodes insisted that they could be used for political purpose.

Rhodes's achievement was a rare one. His fortune was of the same order as that of the great multi-millionaires of nineteenth-century America: it may even have exceeded their's. But Rhodes's was made much more quickly than Rockefeller's or Carnegie's and his monopoly was more absolute than their's. It is doubtful whether any other man in the history of the world has made so much money before his fortieth birthday. Such success fortified his megalomaniac tendencies which were further strengthened by the adulation of his intimates. He lived like an Emperor. He bought a mountain for his garden. Interested in Gibbon's footnotes, he started to have his authorities translated, printed and illustrated for his own sole use. Whatever he commanded was done. Yet he was a lonely and un-happy man. His brooding face with its strange heavy lidded eyes bespeaks an unquiet heart. The pleasures of great wealth were care-lessly and casually indulged but they never absorbed him. They brought him no ease and they failed singularly to dull his aching ambition. He wanted to mould the destiny of South Africa in such a way that Englishmen would become aware of their dedicated future which was to own the world.[1]

The discovery of diamonds and gold created difficult social and economic problems for South Africa. The unskilled labour was black. Mining communities led to the disintegration of tribal life and to the growth of an ever-increasing black proletariat. And these workers lived either in terrible squalor or in the closely-guarded compounds with their severe regimentation. It was not long before they acquired leaders and sympathizers who gave a political twist to their sense of injustice. Furthermore the prosperity of the gold and diamond fields depended on transport, but an efficient system was difficult to achieve without the close co-operation of the independent Boer republics who distrusted and feared the industrial developments within their own territories. Gold and diamonds were a magnet to aliens whose attitude to life was in violent contrast to the simple pastoral ideals of the Boers. Again, such riches could not fail to raise the cupidity of other nations. There were still great empty regions of South Africa free from the control of any European power. England's enemies found in the anxieties and jealousies of the Boer republics a rich field for diplomatic intrigue; so that the destiny of South Africa became linked with Europe's. Each of these problems deeply concerned Rhodes for they were interwoven with the sources of his wealth. He or his associates would have been driven into politics no matter how alien they might have found them. But, of course, Rhodes had every intention of being a statesman. Indeed the making of his wealth had gone hand in hand with his career in politics.

Rhodes, aged twenty-seven, entered the Cape parliament in April 1881, representing Berkley West, the constituency of the diamond fields. At the same time he bought a share in the *Cape Argus* to make certain that his speeches were fully reported. His power was soon felt. He organized the representatives of the diamond fields to oppose the government because of its failure to build the railway to Kimberley; an attack which helped to bring about the fall of the ministry. He was appointed to a commission to investigate

---

[1] 'As I walked, I looked up at the sky and down at the earth and I said to myself this should be British. And it came to me in that fine exhilarating air that the British were the best race to rule the world.' Quoted Basil Williams, *Rhodes*, p. 55.

the conditions of Basutoland; he disagreed with his colleagues and presented a minority report. His verdict was accepted by the Assembly. His mark was quickly made. He sought out influential men and tirelessly put forward his doctrine of expansion to the North. But he adjusted it to reality. He would have nothing to do with schemes for independence. South Africa was too poor, too weak to stand alone; expansion could only be achieved with the co-operation of the home government. And too, Rhodes thought, with the co-operation of the Dutch at the Cape. There were too few white men in the colony and far too many black to permit a fratricidal strife to divide them. But he was a realist enough to know that little help and much hindrance could be expected from the Boer republics. Also his idea of the rôle of the home government was at this time not much to the liking of the Colonial Office. South Africa was to absorb and rule the new territories; the home government was there to provide defence, or as Rhodes phrased it, 'the government of South Africa by the people of South Africa with the Imperial flag for defence'.

His main concern was with the narrow strip of fertile territory which ran between the Kalahari Desert and the Transvaal. This territory was the best land of the Bechuana tribes, a restless people made more restless by the steady increase of white settlers in their country. Already two semi-independent Boer republics had been established. Furthermore the Germans had taken over the great territories of South West Africa (Damaraland and Namaqualand), thereby creating the grave danger of a common frontier with the Transvaal.

Rhodes considered this situation imperilled the great route to the interior which ran through Bechuanaland. If blocked by the Germans or by Boer republics, all hope of expansion to the North would have to be abandoned. In the end the door to the interior was kept open; southern Bechuanaland was declared a Crown colony, the rest a protectorate; but the solution had been a bitter lesson for Rhodes. The Imperial government had handled the situation ineptly. The Boers had been insulted which affected the Cape Dutch whose goodwill Rhodes knew to be essential for South Africa's success. Rhodes himself had been accused as a warmonger and more or less driven from Bechuanaland. Yet the decision not to put this territory

under South African rule, whatever the motives, has proved a
blessing to these tribes which still enjoy their vast homelands free
from the fear of the worst types of racial discrimination.

Rhodes felt the Bechuanaland decision as a personal humiliation,
but his interest in the North was not diminished. He resolved to
take matters more firmly into his own hands; to lead and let governments follow. Beyond Bechuanaland lay the rich fertile lands of the
Matabele and Mashona, stretching to the Zambesi, territory which
Rhodes longed to possess not only for its reputed wealth in minerals
but also needed to fulfil his dream of a British Africa. But the Boers
of the Transvaal were already negotiating with Lo Bengula, the
Matabele warrior king, a treaty of friendship which included mining
rights. Rhodes breaking in on the High Commissioner's Xmas party
in 1887 persuaded him to send a mission to Lo Bengula. The Boers'
diplomacy was scotched, Lo Bengula went over to Great Britain.
A more prolonged effort was required to extort the concession of
full mining rights from the reluctant chief whose warriors were
highly suspicious of the swarm of white adventurers that circled
about his kraal at Bulawayo. More spectacular was Rhodes's triumph
in obtaining from the British government, in spite of much opposition, and great misgivings in Whitehall, a royal charter for a company which was to

1. To extend the railway and telegraph northwards towards the
   Zambesi.
2. To encourage emigration and colonization.
3. To promote trade and commerce.
4. To develop minerals and other concessions under one powerful
   organization so as to avoid conflicts between competing
   interests.[1]

This was tantamount to delegating to Rhodes and his partners the
right to create and govern a new colony. At least this was Rhodes's
interpretation and his intention. He assembled a tough band of
pioneers, organized on military lines, and waited for the inevitable
clash with Lo Bengula, and waited with a certain impatience, for as
he said 'so long as the Matabele do not molest my people, I cannot
declare war against them and deprive them of their country, but as

[1] B. W. Williams, *Rhodes*, p. 135.

soon as they interfere with our rights I shall end their game'. Lo Bengula was a shrewd man with an all too limited idea of the vast issues involved in the little pieces of paper which he solemnly sealed with his great elephant seal. He sensed the power of the white invaders of his country and dreaded a clash with them. But his tribes were organized for war; they lived for little else—and could not be restrained. The clash came; Rhodes won and Rhodesia was born.

It had been handled in Rhodes's own way and it was so much easier for him to do it, for he had become Prime Minister of the Cape as the pioneers set out for Rhodesia. Every doubt and hesitation felt by the High Commissioner for the brutal and savage acts in the North were roughly brushed aside by Rhodes. Success achieves its own morality and by 1895 Rhodes had added a country nearly half the size of Western Europe to the Empire. Both in London and the Cape there were few who could view him without idolatry.

As Prime Minister of South Africa Rhodes displayed great shrewdness in winning and keeping the support of the Dutch party. This was partly due to the care with which he attended to their special interests and partly to his attitude to the native problem which was close to theirs. He believed in firm paternalism. The natives were to work so that through work they might attain civilization. It would be time enough to talk of their enfranchisement when they achieved civilized status. Segregation was regarded as desirable for them and a benefit to their masters. These principles were unexceptionable to Hofmeyer and his Boer colleagues. Their natural suspicion of Rhodes was allayed.

With Rhodes himself the insidious corruptions of power were at work. The rape of the Matabele lands had been carried through with a rough disregard of human life. And it had been carried through impatiently, for Rhodes was finding any check to his will provocative and irksome. Wealth and power were breaking down the restraints of his temperament. His impatience may also have been strengthened by his growing knowledge of the weakness of his own body. Always sickly, the immense strain of his career was telling on his heart. But these two factors—the stimulus of his overwhelming success and the consciousness that his time might be short —go towards explaining the tragedy of his closing years.

The trouble was the Transvaal. The inrush of settlers once gold had been discovered had disturbed the Boers, but the wealth which they brought was not easily rejected by a poor nation. Fearing that their power and their traditional attitude to life might be swamped, the Boers had steadily refused to enfranchise these *Uitlanders* as they called the foreign settlers. To Rhodes, who was one of the largest gold proprietors on the Rand, it was an intolerable situation. But it was made worse by Kruger's casual method of giving monopolies in coal and dynamite which forced up the price and acted as a further tax on the goldfields. Furthermore his tariff policy and his obstinacy about railways added yet more grievances. And Kruger was a man of monolithic obstinacy—with a closed mind. He and his people would rule and rule in their own way. The *Uitlanders* must rest content with the wealth which they had won. He was the greatest obstacle to Rhodes's dream of a united South Africa stretching from the Cape to the Great Lakes. But Rhodes could brook obstacles no longer; he had never been patient of them. Early in 1895 he took a grave decision. The grievances of the *Uitlanders* were to be used as an excuse for a revolution in the Transvaal which would be supported by the 'police' of Rhodes's Chartered Company massed on the border. The intolerable wrongs of their fellow countrymen were to be set right by violence. The technique employed was the technique with which we are so sickeningly familiar. The difficulties of an alien minority were to be used to destroy the independence of a nation. The methods of Rhodes and Hitler will bear comparison as will their attitude to race. The guilt does not belong to Rhodes alone, for the evidence that the Colonial Secretary, Joseph Chamberlain, also knew of the conspiracy is very strong.[1] Such a plot was utter folly. Its ramifications were so extensive that the Boers were quickly aware of their danger. The Germans who were rapidly building up an empire in East Africa allowed their sympathy to be known to Kruger. As it turned out the revolution and the raid were complete fiascos, but fiascos of sinister portent.

The guilt was never placed squarely on Rhodes even though he had to resign the Premiership and quit the Board of his Chartered Company. Everything possible was done to obscure the evidence

---

[1] See *The Jameson Raid*, J. van de Poel; for the most favourable view of Chamberlain's rôle, see J. L. Garvin, *Joseph Chamberlain*.

and in this the Colonial Office was not slow to help. Kruger, thoroughly alarmed, read too much into the sympathy of Germany, and prepared for the war which he knew to be inevitable. Chamberlain realized that a war with the Boers would justify the past. Yet wars are never made by individuals; neither Rhodes nor Kruger nor Chamberlain was ultimately responsible for the Boer War when it came. Like the Bantus before them, the Boers were being crushed by an unmanageable historical process. In the Rand there was wealth and power, linked with the fortunes of the great industrial nations of the Atlantic Ocean. This was alien to the simple agrarian society which governed the country in its own interests. But the ruthless disregard of the law of nations, the brutal use of force, these cannot be ignored, nor can Rhodes escape responsibility. And worse, the whole concept of empire was degraded by this war so that progressive and liberal opinion became anti-imperialist with fatal consequences, for only the early application of a liberal and progressive policy could have stayed the empire's decline. Indeed all the repercussions of this war were disastrous. The Kaiser interpreted the frequent defeats of the British army to an inherent incapacity to fight and our ultimate success to supremacy at sea which allowed reinforcements to be landed by the navy; an interpretation which led him to regard the British army as irrelevant and to concentrate on immediate increase in his fleet, both factors of ill-omen.

Before the war was over, Rhodes was dead. He was taken and buried in his granite grave, high on the Matoppo Hills in the country which bears his name; the same hills which witnessed his slaughter of the Matabele warriors.

In his short life Rhodes had done more than any single man to mould the immediate future of South Africa. His methods were rarely honourable; his ends questionable. They have made the agony of Africa more bitter. The tragedy of Rhodes lay within his own nature. His wealth and power gave him an incomparable opportunity, but his vision was too limited, too naïve, too crude; responsibility rotted in his hands.

1953

PART III

MEN AND BOOKS

HISTORY AND BIOGRAPHY

ACADEMIC historians have always been aware of the dangers inherent in biography, particularly of the full-scale political biography which tends to distort the general history of a period to fit the needs of a character study. Nevertheless, this last fifty years, which has seen such a rich development in psychology, has witnessed a further decline of interest in biography among professional historians in this country, if not in America. During the same period, however, a biographical technique has been developed for exploring difficult problems of political and social history.

The decline of academic historians' interest in biography is very marked. The generation of Holland Rose and Basil Williams were prepared to devote years of research to biographical studies and to attempt to produce authoritative lives in two, or even three, volumes. The present generation of professional historians occasionally venture into the field of biography—but more often than not in the form of a large-scale essay, and mark the fact that it is something of a *jeu d'esprit* by leaving out all references. Although in some cases the result has been brilliant—Sir John Neale's *Elizabeth I* and Mr. A. J. P. Taylor's *Bismarck* are two outstanding examples—the best biographies have been written in recent times by non-academic historians. Mrs. Cecil Woodham Smith, Mr. R. W. Ketton-Cremer, Sir Philip Magnus, Iris Origo and Miss C. V. Wedgwood, among others, have produced biographies of outstanding quality. In each a natural insight into human character, enriched by the deeper knowledge of the present time, has been applied to biographical facts to re-create men and women with a reality which carries the conviction of great art.

The timidity of academic historians can be appreciated, for in each of these biographies the authors have had to take risks which professionals are taught to avoid. They were forced to decide, in the light of their own understanding, on facets of the psychology of their subjects where the evidence was but flimsy or tentative. It is, however, curious that an academic is often prepared to make decisions on slight evidence so long as it relates to questions of constitutional, economic or legal history, but once a human being enters his field of vision, he slips away in fright.

Nor can it be argued that large-scale political biographies are a matter for literary and not academic history, or that they can offer little insight into the general historical process. The nature and exercise of political power is a vital subject for the understanding of almost any period of human history, and more particularly of eighteenth-century English history when politics were of such a personal nature. Furthermore, few periods of our history have been subjected to such close research in the last fifty years, research which has revolutionized not only ideas about politics but also ideas about personalities. The characters of George III, Charles James Fox and Edmund Burke, among others, have been revealed, albeit incidentally, as not at all what previous generations of historians have assumed them to be, yet there has been a biographical study of only one of them—Burke—and that by a gifted amateur, Sir Philip Magnus. From 1760 to 1790, George III was mainspring of political activity; his temperament and actions influenced profoundly not only questions of detail but also the broader issues of policy. He was a loquacious man (a fault of his mental instability) and so left an immensely valuable record of his hopes, intentions, attitudes. His contemporaries enriched this source by keeping records of equal volume. In consequence the material for George III's life exists in super-abundance. No adequate life has been written.

Yet professional historians complain that the old picture of George III, as a tyrannical king deliberately exploiting his prerogative powers to impose his will on an unhappy kingdom and empire, continues to exist in textbooks. It is likely so to continue as long as the truth about George III has to be quarried from technical monographs or from his own correspondence. A full life of George III of the quality and scholarship of Sir John Neale's *Elizabeth I* would dispel legends far more quickly than professional lamentations, endlessly reiterated. And what is true of George III is true of a score of figures, medieval and modern, whose reassessment is long overdue—here are a few of the first rank only: Henry II; Edward III; Henry V; Somerset; Oliver Cromwell; William III; William Pitt; Disraeli. And all of these historically important characters are more comprehensible to us than to our ancestors, not merely because our sources of historical evidence are richer but also because we know more of the vagaries of human behaviour. Modern psychology has presented the historian with new techniques of interpretation; unfortunately the majority of academic historians show no signs of applying them. There are a few honourable exceptions, notably in contemporary historical studies, but this generation of professional historians as a whole have avoided the difficult problems posed by human character, in marked contrast with scholars in other fields of study. Literary criticism has gained immeasurably from developments in modern psychology and the biographical study of great writers is in quite a different category from historical biography.

★　★　★

Although professional historians have eschewed biographical studies, they have developed a biographical method, using it as a technique to study a particular field of political or social history. The method employed is to study not one but hundreds of lives—to create a biographical dictionary directed towards a definite historical question. Perhaps the most formidable exponent of this technique was Sir Lewis Namier, who used it to find out just who were the Whigs and Tories and Independents of the early years of George III's reign. Under his microscopic analysis, the two-party system, so beloved of the Whig historians, vanished, leaving a wealth of factions and interests behind. He has shown how impossible it is to talk of a Whig party in the 1760's. Important decisions on policy were frequently decided haphazardly, according to the dictates of personal ambition or factional loyalties. The study of individual men reveals the complexity of motive in political behaviour which the broad study of political history tends to obliterate. The confusions of reality are historically reconstructed and no one can doubt that this use of a biographical technique has been brilliantly justified.

Yet the method has its dangers. Although immediate reality may be a confusion of events, decisions themselves create a coherent dichotomy of politics. The welter of personal motives may obscure political actions which men are forced to take, nevertheless they take them, and political doctrines acquire a validity irrespective of the motives of those that adopt them. Also, in the context of eighteenth-century society, demands for favours and influence are likely to be more vocal and therefore more evident in historical records than the impalpable influences of public opinion, and it is interesting to note that in recent discussions of eighteenth-century politics, Junius and Wilkes get short shrift. There is also this further danger. The most vociferous and clamorous politicians were those either in office or on the verge of obtaining it, or full of hope that a successful opposition might bring them to it. These men were obviously deeply concerned about the personal factors in political life, but all parliaments contain scores of silent voters—men with little prospect of any advancement beyond their status as M.P.s.

These members had little need to compromise their principles; there was little to stop them from acting according to their conscience. This, too, could be moulded by changing circumstances. The influence of these independent men is to be found in the course of events and in the growth of political attitudes. The biographical method does throw some light on their characters and actions, but it is likely to belittle their effectiveness. Furthermore, even active politicians at the centre realized that such men needed to be influenced by ideas and by political programmes and so they were forced to clothe their greed for power in the respectable guise of a political doctrine. Fox's attitude to monarchy may have been the result both of pique and of the desire to protect power gained. It was, however, an attitude which could be intellectually justified and one which could, and did, attract men by its obvious political advantages. The revelation of human motive which is the inevitable result of close biographical study can over-simplify the complexity of political action. Yet as a technique it has fully justified itself—giving, as it were, extra dimensions to the study of political and constitutional history.

★　　★　　★

The grave misfortune is that this technique has been almost confined to political history where it has obvious disadvantages. There are problems of social and economic history which cry aloud for its use. The great debate on the gentry has been vitiated by a lack of the knowledge which the biographical method would give. Neither the late Professor Tawney nor Professor H. R. Trevor-Roper has the depth of material available to make a really safe generalization as to whether the gentry were rising or falling. Until the gentry has been acceptably defined as a class and until individual members of it have been studied in detail in a selection of regions—Home Counties, Midlands, West Country, etc.—no answer is possible. And this is a perfectly feasible task. The patient research of many generations of antiquarians and local historians has provided scholars with an unresolved mass of biographical material which demands to be used for the investigation of the problems of social history. The great volumes of the new edition of G.E.C.'s *Peerage* contain the answers to a host of problems related to the English aristocracy—its social mobility; its relations with trade; the effects of intermarriage—important questions which could easily be answered from the material available. Only work needs to be done. Discussion about the nature of the Civil War will proceed in the same prejudice and obscurity that has marked it for generations until a scholar settles down and finds out just who composed the Eastern Association—where these men came from—their professions, their education, their families and the extent of their property—a laborious task, perhaps, but quite practicable. Indeed the biographical technique has hardly been applied at all to the problems of social history which still, unfortunately, remains largely evocative and sentimental rather than scientific and historical. And to the academic historians' ignorance of modern psychology, one might add also sociology, which, although a young and as yet tentative discipline, is profoundly important to any investigation of history.

The vast accumulation of biographical data by local historians has not, however, gone entirely unused. Several academic historians have realized its value to give immediacy and validity to the general descriptions of their periods of investigation. Perhaps the most obvious exponent of this method is Dr. A. L. Rowse, and the sparkling vigour and sharp impact of his writing results from his use of

the short biographies of almost forgotten men. His descriptions of
the Borderlands in Elizabethan times are full of brief lives, or of
moments of lives, and a picture of society as a whole is created from
the study of individual men and women. This again has its dangers,
as with political history; the complexity of human existence, once
re-created, carries conviction, but, although we realize more directly
what life was like, the result is less easy to understand. The vivid,
confused, truthful picture of the past is also more obscure. Unless
severely disciplined to precise historical questions, there is always
the danger that this technique will decay into a mere literary device.

★   ★   ★

America has not witnessed similar developments, and there the
political biography still holds a proud position. Lives of Abraham
Lincoln in four, of George Washington in seven volumes are not
exceptional achievements. Most major figures of American history
have been encased in vast new literary mausoleums. Unfortunately
piety in nine cases out of ten guides the pen. Often these biographies
are the work of research teams and the judgements are often those
of its least perceptive member. Most English historians eschew
psychology like the plague, but their American counterparts seem
unaware of its existence and their discussion of motive is, in consequence, exceedingly naïve. These massive studies are valuable as
factual compilations; the majority are useless from the point of
view of analysis. Perhaps an awareness of the shortcomings of these
team biographies, with their platitudinous judgements, has led to
the development in America of a different kind of biographical
approach—the mass publication of the entire literary remains of
great men or of influential historical figures. The great editions of
Horace Walpole's letters, of Boswell and Jefferson papers, and now
of Burke's, Franklin's, Adams's, Roosevelt's, etc., are, in a sense,
biographical studies. By skilful editing and scholarly presentation
the life of the man is re-created in his own words. In some ways this
is much the most satisfactory of all biographical techniques—at least
for those who are addicted to the vagaries of human existence. It
needs, however, not only stamina, but also an insatiable interest in
humanity, to get through the millions of words that Walpole and
Boswell bequeathed to posterity. Certainly the lives of these two

men will be known at a greater level of detail than any two previous men in history—and that in itself is a biographical achievement of no small magnitude. The cost of such an enterprise must, however, render it rare; only America in a period of great prosperity could afford such studies as these. And it may be the singular fate of Horace Walpole and James Boswell that their lives will be recorded in greater detail than any other two lives in the history of mankind.

The last fifty years, therefore, have witnessed remarkable changes in the relations of history and biography in England. Academic historians have, for the most part, ignored, either intentionally or unintentionally, developments in modern psychology which have so enriched the study of literature. They have, in general, preferred to explore other fields of history. Yet this flight from large-scale biography has been countered by a development of a biographical technique by which means hundreds of brief lives are used to investigate problems of political and social history. This technique, in spite of its obvious pitfalls, has a great future for by its use new light can be thrown on problems which have baffled generations of economic and social historians. Indeed by its use social history may cease to be evocative and sentimental, and take its place amongst the more exact fields of historical scholarship.

1956

G. M. TREVELYAN

GEORGE MACAULAY TREVELYAN is the heir of a great tradition. His great-uncle was Lord Macaulay who, with Gibbon, is the chief glory of English historical writing; his father, Sir George Otto Trevelyan, was also a historian of great distinction, a most important figure in the development of Anglo-American understanding; for his great work on the American Revolution did much to dispel ancient prejudice. With this inheritance it is not surprising that G. M. Trevelyan has a high sense of the duty of a historian. For him the writing of history, like the writing of poetry, is a part of English culture, a culture not limited to the few but available to all men so that it might deepen their understanding. History, then, for him, has a literary and moral purpose. His inheritance made this attitude clear enough to himself but it required an obstinate courage to maintain it, for the view was no longer fashionable amongst academic historians. They preferred to treat history as a science; to concentrate on evidence, techniques, statistics, and if the public found the results unreadable that did not matter, for history was a specialized study by professionals for professionals. In the face of such opposition Trevelyan had to define, and defend, his attitude, and this he did in his volumes of essays, *Clio: a Muse* (1913), and *An Autobiography and other Essays* (1949). For anyone wishing to study the whole of Trevelyan's works, these books should come first and be followed by the *Memoir* of his father (1932), the book on Meredith (1912), the *Life of Grey of Fallodon* (1937) and the delightful little history of Trinity College (1943), for these make clear his personal inheritance, the background of tradition which fed that rare poetic imagination, perhaps his greatest gift.

I

In his *Autobiography*, written in the evening of his life, he writes:

> More generally, I take delight in history, even its most prosaic
> details, because they become poetical as they recede into the past.
> The poetry of history lies in the quasi-miraculous fact that once,
> on this earth, once, on this familiar spot of ground, walked other
> men and women, as actual as we are today, thinking their own
> thoughts, swayed by their own passions, but now all gone, one
> generation vanishing after another, gone as utterly as we ourselves
> shall shortly be gone like ghosts at cock-crow.

He made the same moving affirmation when he became Regius
Professor of Modern History at Cambridge in 1926:

> The appeal of history to us all is in the last analysis poetic. But
> the poetry of history does not consist of imagination roaming at
> large, but of imagination pursuing the fact and fastening upon it.
> That which compels the historian to 'scorn delights and live
> laborious days' is the ardour of his own curiosity to know what
> really happened long ago in that land of mystery which we call
> the past. To peer into that magic mirror and see fresh figures there
> every day is a burning desire that consumes and satisfies him all
> his life, that carries him each morning, eager as a lover, to the
> library and the muniment room. It haunts him like a passion of
> almost terrible potency, because it is poetic. The dead were and
> are not. Their place knows them no more and is ours today. Yet
> they were once as real as we, and we shall tomorrow be shadows
> like them.

There is one beautiful example of 'imagination pursuing the fact
and fastening upon it' in his own early work, *Clio: a Muse*, which
illustrates how much his poetic imagination, blended with such
wide ranging human sympathy, is stirred by the visible memorials
of a past time.

The garden front of St. John's, Oxford, is beautiful to everyone;
but for the lover of history its outward charm is blent with the

intimate feelings of his own mind, with images of the same
College as it was during the great Civil War. Given over to the
use of a Court where days of royalty were numbered, its walks
and quadrangles were filled, as the end came near, with men and
women learning to accept sorrow as their lot through life, the
ambitious abandoning hope of power, the wealthy hardening
themselves to embrace poverty, those who loved England prepared to sail for foreign shores, and lovers to be parted for ever.
There they strolled through the garden, as the hopeless evenings
fell, listening, at the end of all, while the siege guns broke the
silence with ominous iteration. Behind the cannon on those low
hills to northward were ranked the inexorable men who came to
lay their hands on all this beauty, hoping to change it to strength
and sterner virtue. . . . The sound of the Roundhead cannon has
long ago died away, but still the silence of the garden is heavy
with unalterable fate, brooding over besiegers and besieged. . . .

This has an incomparable beauty of tone: having read such words
as these, who could doubt that here was a great artist at work; at
work in a medium, the writing of history, in which scholars have
been plentiful and artists rare. But why did Trevelyan choose to use
his gifts of imagination in history rather than in poetry? The answer
to this question is manifold, but one overwhelming reason cries
aloud in the three quotations given above, this is his preoccupation
with Time. Many artists—Wordsworth and Proust immediately
spring to mind—have been deeply moved, one might almost say
that their art has been controlled, by the sense of the loss involved
in the nature of Time. But nowhere more than in the study of
history is the artist so acutely aware of the tragedy of man caught
inexorably in the temporal world of flesh. Each historical fact is
implicit with our doom: as the long story of man's achievement is
our one straw of hope. And this is made keener for a historian unable
to accept the fact of personal immortality, as he looks back over the
countless lives, as numberless as the sands of the sea, that go to make
our history. Those wide Border lands in which Trevelyan grew to
manhood—there were the lasting physical memorials of unknown
men which haunted him with their sense of destiny—the walls and
forts of the Romans, the villages of Saxon and of Dane, the ruined

abbeys and peel-towers, the battlefields with their forgotten dead; those to Trevelyan are what the lakes and the woods and the trees were to Wordsworth, the symbols of man's tragedy and hope.[1]

The circumstances of Trevelyan's life have done much to strengthen this feeling for the passing of time, just as the social and cultural interests of his family have had their say in directing his historical interests. Trevelyan was born in 1876; his family background was both aristocratic and upper middle class. His father's family could trace their ancestry back through the centuries, from Northumberland to Somerset, from Somerset to Cornwall, a long line of typical English gentry, never of national distinction but playing their part in the local affairs of their day. His grandfather, a successful Indian civil servant, married Macaulay's sister who introduced the atmosphere of middle class culture with its piety and its liberal views on politics and society. Trevelyan's father knew intimately the great figures of Victorian civilization, at the same time he was accepted as a member of aristocratic society.[2] His marriage with Caroline Philips, the daughter of a Manchester merchant, free-trader, Unitarian, friend of Cobden and of Gladstone, strengthened the family ties both with liberalism and the middle class. And so Trevelyan grew up amidst all that was best in the late Victorian world of art and politics, imbibing its liberalism, its free-thinking, and its culture to which his own nature was so responsive. The background to his life was the country houses of an earlier age, particularly Wallington, the great house in Northumberland, which his father inherited in 1886. Here, he was able to savour that stable, English country-life which had endured for centuries.

Time has not been kind to this early world of Trevelyan's. Of the great houses in which he lived as a boy, Welcombe, his mother's house near Stratford-on-Avon, is a British Railways hotel, and Wallington in Northumberland has been given to the National Trust, of which he himself has been an ardent supporter and a munificent benefactor. For the Trust has helped to preserve many of the great houses of England and much of the loveliness of the wilder countryside of cliff and fell which have meant so much to

---

[1] Cf. Trevelyan's essay 'The Middle Marches' in *Clio: a Muse* (1913).

[2] Not the same, as Trevelyan is careful to stress in his admirable memoir of his father, *Sir George Otto Trevelyan: A Memoir* (1932).

him. But far more has been lost, and now the pace has accelerated; in another generation the civilization which Trevelyan knew as a young man will have passed and then his occasional works, his essays, memoirs and the biographies of his friends will not only help readers to understand his own works but also have great value as historical documents in their own right. Yet one cannot doubt that the passing of this world, of which he is intensely aware, has given a keener edge to his preoccupations with history, particularly with those aspects of nineteenth century English history which are linked with his own and his parents' past.

Trevelyan's education was the same as any rich young man of his day; preparatory school in Berkshire, Harrow, and then Trinity College, Cambridge, but of course with him it was more formative. His interest in history had developed very early, particularly in military history. At Harrow he was exceptionally fortunate in his history masters, Robert Somervell and George Townsend Warner. Somervell had a rare gift of teaching boys to write well and Townsend Warner was a scholar of distinction.[1] As a freshman at Cambridge he fell under the spell of Maitland, the great English medieval and legal historian, of Cunningham who was founding the study of economic history, and of Lord Acton, the greatest Catholic historian of modern times, whose learning and wisdom were unrivalled. But he fell foul of Seeley, Acton's predecessor in the Regius Chair of History; Seeley was an ardent champion of scientific history and loved to denounce Macaulay and Carlyle; to one Trevelyan had his family loyalty and the other had illuminated his first year's work at Cambridge. Ever since he has been a devoted admirer of the superb imaginative quality of Carlyle's work, especially the *Cromwell* and the *French Revolution*.

Naturally, with his background, Trevelyan was drawn to the liberal intelligentsia and he became a friend of Bertrand Russell, Desmond MacCarthy and G. E. Moore. Many young men at the University reject the beliefs in which they were nurtured, but the circles in which Trevelyan mixed at Trinity helped to strengthen the liberal attitude to life which he had derived from his family. This

---

[1] Winston Churchill has said that Somervell taught him his mastery of English. To have helped produce two such masters of our language as Churchill and Trevelyan is indeed a claim to fame.

attitude was essentially protestant, infused as it was with a strong scepticism of all doctrinaire beliefs either in religion or politics. When Trevelyan came to start historical research it was natural that his interest should be aroused in a historical movement deeply concerned with the belief in individual freedom. His imagination was caught by the Lollards, by the Peasants' Revolt, by the first stirrings of national consciousness in England. It was this work which won for him the Fellowship at Trinity: it was published in 1899 with the title *England in the Age of Wycliffe*, and in the same year he issued with Powell a collection of documents which he had used as evidence, and which he thought deserved a wider currency.

England in the Age of Wycliffe achieved immediate success, and it has enjoyed a continuing popularity, having been reprinted fourteen times. It was an astonishing achievement for so young a man. Many of the views, especially on economic and legal matters, would now require modification; about the whole work there is a slight but definitely archaic air, derived very probably from its militant anti-Romanism. It is well written—even as early as this Trevelyan's style was completely under his control, and what a marvellously flexible instrument it is! The narrative moves with exceptional speed; his descriptive passages evoke the dark and the light of Chaucer's England; the analysis of social causes and human motives is crisp and clear. The book has a pace and *élan* which will carry it on through many editions yet to come. Although there is a marked bias towards Lollardy, Trevelyan's historical judgement is never darkened by prejudice, and the facts, truly ascertained, are made to give their own evidence. Even more remarkable is the skill with which Trevelyan uses narrative and descriptive writing; so, too, is his capacity to reveal motive by description of events. In this way the reader is made aware of why these conflicts and battles took place without the tedium of detailed analysis. Remarkable, too, the certainty both of the writing and the convictions of the author. In his work there is the steady affirmation of a faith that would last a lifetime, whatever Time brought forth, for it was a faith begot by inheritance and by tradition, and it is made explicit in the closing words of the book.

In England we have slowly but surely won the right of the

individual to form and express a private judgement on speculative questions. During the last three centuries the battle of liberty has been fought against the State or against public opinion. But before the changes effected by Henry the Eighth, the struggle was against a power more impervious to reason and less subject to change—the power of the Medieval Church in all the prestige of a thousand years' prescriptive right over man's mind. The martyrs who bore the first brunt of that terrific combat may be lightly esteemed today by priestly censure. But those who still believe that liberty of thought has proved not a curse but a blessing to England and to the peoples that have sprung from her, will regard with thankfulness and pride the work which the speculations of Wycliffe set on foot and the valour of his devoted successors accomplished.

II

For his work on the age of Wycliffe, Trevelyan had been awarded a Fellowship at Trinity in 1898, and a straightforward career as a professional academic historian was open to him. He began to teach for his college; he started to lecture. He had accepted the offer of Methuen to write a textbook on Stuart history, as one of their series on the *History of England*. These were all easily recognized stages in the making of a don. Then suddenly he left Cambridge. The reason he gives in his *Autobiography* is that he knew that he wanted to write literary history and that 'I should do so in more spiritual freedom away from the critical atmosphere of Cambridge scholarship'. The artist in him had dominated, and instinctively bolted from an uncongenial world, although to the outsider it must have seemed a curiously wilful gesture for a young professional historian to desert the citadel of his profession. Of course, Trevelyan has been fully justified. His output has been far greater than the majority of his generation because he was able to avoid the time-consuming hack work of academic life—the endless supervisions and lectures and examinations. But more importantly he escaped from the withering atmosphere of hyper-critical scholasticism which has grown stronger and more powerful in Cambridge during the twentieth century. The fine points of argumentative scholarship exercised with equal zest on the important and the trivial have had no fascination for Trevelyan, and he has an even stronger distaste for the shifting quicksand of historical abstraction. Again the fields of history upon which Cambridge historians were concentrating—economic, diplomatic, constitutional—were fields which offered little attraction to Trevelyan. They lacked story; they lacked drama; they lacked the warmth of human life. Because of these things, the artist insisted on escape.[1]

Away from the inhibiting influence of Cambridge, Trevelyan produced a book of outstanding quality. His *England under the Stuarts* (1904) was far and away the most impressive volume in this series published by Methuen. When the others have been forgotten, it will still be read, for it may be generations before the most dramatic century in English history is so finely portrayed between the covers of a single book. The advance on his first book is obvious but remarkable. The nineteenth century had been profoundly interested in the struggle between Crown and Parliament, for they felt that the triumph of Parliament had made their own democratic world possible. Nor were the Victorians dismayed by the intensely biblical language of Puritan thought and action, for the middle classes of the nineteenth century were equally capable of testing political issues by religious principles and expressing themselves with equal force in Old Testament terms. Nevertheless, the old Whig attitude of seeing Charles and his cavaliers as dissolute despots and Cromwell and the Roundheads as apostles of liberty had mellowed by Trevelyan's day. It was fashionable to be more than scrupulously fair to opponents in debate and, in consequence, although Trevelyan is, in his final reckoning, on the side of the Roundheads, his sympathies do not at any point in his book inhibit his imaginative insight. In many ways it has remained the least biased summary of the seventeenth century, for the last twenty years has witnessed the development of a concealed *apologia* for the Stuarts under the cloak of a more exact scholarship. The same movement has sought to denigrate Cromwell as the prototype of a fascist-dictator because of his grave failure to secure constitutional government and his resort to force—for neither

---

[1] Of course, Trevelyan was a young man of means, and could afford to quit an assured position. In any case he could easily have maintained himself by his writing, but whether the choice would have been so easy had he been without private means is an interesting speculation.

of which is he spared by Trevelyan. These Tory historians—as dangerous as their Whig counterparts—should read and re-read Trevelyan's magnificent paragraphs on the execution of Charles I, which must be quoted in full, for they demonstrate one of his greatest virtues as a historian.

> If there was any chance that the establishment of a more democratic form of government could gradually win the support of the people at large, that chance was thrown away by the execution of the King. The deed was done against the wish of many even of the Independents and Republicans; it outraged beyond hope of reconciliation the two parties in the State who were strong in numbers and in conservative tradition, the Presbyterians and the Cavaliers; and it alienated the great mass of men who had no party at all. Thus the Republicans, at the outset of their career, made it impossible for themselves ever to appeal in free election to the people whom they had called to sovereignty. Their own fall, involving the fall of democracy and of religious toleration, became therefore necessary to the re-establishment of Parliamentary rule. The worship of birth, of pageantry, of title; the aristocratic claim to administrative power; the excessive influence of the large land-owner and of inherited wealth; the mean admiration of mean things, which became so powerful in English society after the Restoration—all these gained a fresh life and popularity by the deed that was meant to strike them dead for ever.
>
> It is much easier to show that the execution was a mistake than to show what else should have been done. Any other course, if considered in the light of the actual circumstances, seems open to the gravest objection. It is not possible to say with certainty that if Charles's life had been spared Cromwell could have succeeded in averting anarchy and the disruption of the empire until opinion was again ripe for government by consent.
>
>   'This was that memorable hour
>   Which first assured the forcèd power'
>
> —that was the verdict on the King's execution privately passed by Cromwell's secretary, Andrew Marvell, a man of the world if a poet ever was such, who in the same poem wrote the lines

we all still quote in praise of Charles's conduct on the scaffold. The situation at the end of 1648 was this—that any sort of government by consent had been rendered impossible for years to come, mainly by the untrustworthy character of the King, and by the intolerant action of Parliament after the victory won for it by the Army. Cromwell, in the Heads of the Proposals, had advocated a real settlement by consent, only to have it rejected by King, Parliament and Army alike. The situation had thereby been rendered impossible, through no fault of his. But he was not the man therefore to return to his private gardens and let the world go to ruin. He took upon his massive shoulders the load of obloquy inherent in a situation created chiefly by the faults of others. Those Herculean shoulders are broad enough to bear also the blame for a deed pre-eminently his own, inscribed like a gigantic note of interrogation across the page of English history.

This is a complete realization of all that is important in a historical incident of profound significance, beautifully and confidently expressed. And the book abounds in similar passages.

Along with a deepening historical judgement, there was a growth in craftsmanship. In his earlier book, Trevelyan had been most humanly tempted to spend many pages on those aspects of his subject which contained a deeply personal interest, but *England under the Stuarts* witnesses a more rigorous personal discipline. Military and social history are kept firmly, at times almost too firmly,[1] in their place and never allowed to clog the narrative, which moves at a furious pace—surely no textbook has ever before or since been written with such a gusto. Although the general reading public gave the book an ardent reception, the professional historians received it rather coldly. It was considered only worthy of a short notice in the *English Historical Review* and the space was largely devoted to a consideration of Sir Charles Oman's preface—only ten lines being given to the book itself. The reviewer, Professor C. Sandford Terry—whoever he may have been—thought the chapter mottoes platitudinous and the success of the book questionable.[2] So great had become the gulf between professional and literary history!

[1] The battle of Dunbar is dealt with in five lines.
[2] *English Historical Review*, vol. 20, pp. 403–4.

But Trevelyan had no cause to complain, for this book fully justified his decision to break with academic life.

In the same year as the publication of *England under the Stuarts* there took place what he has described as 'the most important and fortunate event of my life'—his marriage to Janet Penrose, a daughter of Mrs. Humphry Ward, the novelist and social worker. Amongst the wedding presents was a collection of books on Italian history, including Garibaldi's *Memoirs* and *Belluzzi's Ritirata di Garibaldi nel 1849*.

Immediately the creative artist in Trevelyan saw that in the story of Garibaldi was a subject which exactly fitted his genius. It touched some of the deepest springs of his nature, and the work and study necessary for the undertaking could be woven into the fabric of his personal life, for his wife had a passion for things Italian perhaps even keener than her husband's. From a public point of view the choice could not have been more judicious, had it been made by a sophisticated journalist in search of a best-seller. The year in which Trevelyan wrote *Garibaldi's Defence of the Roman Republic* was 1906, and it was published in 1907. These were the years of the greatest liberal victory in English politics for a generation. The intellectual world responded to the optimism of the politicians. Here was the manifest triumph of that long nineteenth century tradition of liberal humanism; the final defeat of obscurantism was at hand. It was one of those rare moments in history in which the atmosphere of life is lyrical and charged with hope, when man seems his own master, and his destiny secure. Trevelyan's personal life was completely in tune with the world at large. Newly married, the father of a son and heir,[1] an established success in his chosen career in which risks had been taken and justified, this for him, too, was a time of hope.

The Garibaldi story fitted these moods. The struggles, defeats and ultimate success of Italian liberalism in the nineteenth century had seemed to many Victorians a demonstration by Providence of the justice of their attitude to life, and of its capacity to save other nations from spiritual and political obscurantism. Again, it was heroic, and personally heroic. It did not seem to be the long culmination of an anonymous historical process but the dramatic act of individual men, and of those Garibaldi was the greatest. Hence a

[1] Theodore Macaulay Trevelyan, who tragically died in 1911, aged five.

consideration of the story of his achievement did not appear to disturb historical truth. For Trevelyan personally it touched perhaps deeper springs—not only of his mind but of his heart, for within the Garibaldi story there was one of the world's greatest love stories—the passionate and tragic love of Anita.

As with many great historians, Trevelyan has a very strongly developed topographical sense. The very act of standing on the battlefield of Blenheim or on the heights of the Janiculum, where Garibaldi conducted his defence, released the springs of his historical imagination. It would be impossible for him to write well about any historical events of whose setting he was ignorant. It is necessary for him to walk over and to see, to experience with all of his senses, the locality of history. And this he had already done for Italy as he tells us in his *Autobiography*:

> But eight years went by before I ever thought of writing on any Italian theme, although during those years my chief walking-grounds were the Tuscan and Umbrian hills, and the Alban and Sabine heights that look down on the Campagna of Rome. I kept the high ground as much as I could, with the help of ordnance maps and compass. I used to prolong my walks till late into the charmed Italian night, under those brilliant stars, known and named so long ago; at the right time of year I could walk after dark, mile after mile, to the continuous song of innumerable nightingales.

So that the topographical setting for his Garibaldi was, when he came to write it, as well known to him as the wide border lands of Northumberland. All was prepared—his love of nature, his personal romance, his beliefs and attitude to life, all were pointing to Italy and to Garibaldi, but it needed that chance wedding-present to release the springs of imagination.

'I began one day to turn over their pages,' he writes, 'and was suddenly enthralled by the story of the retreat from Rome to the Adriatic, over mountains which I had traversed in my solitary walks: the scene and spirit of that desperate venture, led by that unique man, flashed upon my mind's eye. Here was a subject made to my hand, if ever I could write "literary history", this was the golden chance.'

Just as he had been unconsciously prepared to write it, so the public had been unconsciously prepared to receive it.[1] It established Trevelyan, and rightly so, as the foremost historian of his generation. It is a wonderful book, and it is a miracle that all the detailed work and the writing could have been accomplished in twelve months, yet the pace with which it was done adds undoubtedly to its quality. Had the writing been prolonged it is unlikely that the note of intense lyricism could have been sustained, for in many ways it is the most poetic of Trevelyan's longer works, certainly the most completely so. Apart from the beauty of the writing, its greatest strength lies in the handling of the narrative. This dramatic and exciting story has enthralled, and will continue to enthral, generations of readers, yet never once is historical accuracy sacrificed for the sake of literary effect. In his characters, too, Trevelyan was fortunate; both Garibaldi and Anita were simple, direct, lacking in psychological subtlety and complication; a man and a woman of epic quality. Their thought was action and their action thought. Their words expressed, and never attempted to conceal, their response to life. With them Trevelyan seems to have felt a kinship of spirit, and he was able to re-create not only the history of their deeds but also the warm human reality of their lives.

The reception of *Garibaldi's Defence of the Roman Republic* was so enthusiastic that it was impossible for Trevelyan to leave the rest of the story of the *Risorgimento* untold even if he ever wished to do so. *Garibaldi and the Thousand* was published in 1909 and, two years later, he completed the trilogy with *Garibaldi and the Making of Italy*. He had not, however, finished with Italy, for he spent the years of the 1914–18 war as the Commandant of the British Red Cross Ambulance Unit and worked with the Italian army in the Isonzo and Piave fronts from 1915 to the end of the war. He summarized his experiences of these years in *Scenes from Italy's War*, published in 1919, which proves one thing—if nothing else—that

[1] What Italy meant to men of culture in the nineteenth century is described by Trevelyan himself in his essay: 'Englishmen and Italians', published in *Clio: a Muse*.

great as Trevelyan is as a historian he would have found it difficult
to earn a living as a journalist. The book is fascinating to read
because of its singular lack of merit: history-in-the-making failed to
quicken his imagination. Finally, he wrote his last book on Italian
history in 1922, *Manin and the Venetian Revolution of 1848* (published
1923); the result of many visits to Venice and of contacts with
Venetian intellectuals during his war service. It gave him great
pleasure to write but the public received it with less enthusiasm,
and, I think, rightly so, for the intricacy of Venetian politics and
society, twisted and encrusted with traditional and personal attitudes,
and, moreover, a society as far gone in decay as it was developed
in sophistication, was not a world for the great simplicities of
Trevelyan's heart and mind.

But to return to the Garibaldi books, a theme which was peculiarly
suited to his genius. They have weathered the years remarkably
well, and they have achieved a permanent position in historical
literature. In my estimation, they rank with the works of Prescott
or Parkman, in fact with the world's best narrative histories. They
have, of course, their weaknesses; the motivation of nationalism is
largely unexplored, especially the economic and social causes; the
Papacy and papal policy, the motives of Louis Napoleon and the
French, are judged too harshly; the self-interest of British policy too
consistently ignored. Yet it remains the best, and the least biased,
account of the *Risorgimento* in any language, and acclaimed so by a
generation of Italian scholars for whom the movement for Italian
liberation was too recent and too *political* to allow such an objective
attitude as Trevelyan maintained. In many ways, these three books
are the highest achievement of Trevelyan: never again was his
theme and his imagination so completely fused. But these works
will remain as long as English literature is read, a contribution of
outstanding worth to historical scholarship.

III

Trevelyan was now established as the foremost literary historian of
his time, and naturally as soon as the war was over he was eager to
return to his study; but it was less easy to find a theme which
matched his gifts so absolutely as the Italian books. Like many
writers of great natural creative power he was always very wary of

themes which failed to touch the deepest springs of his own experience. Through his mother's family he was connected with the great movement for free trade, associated with Manchester, of the mid-nineteenth century, and before the 1914–18 war he had written a *Life of John Bright* (1913). It was not favourably received, and nowadays it comes in for little notice and less reading. The weaknesses are obvious and Trevelyan himself is very conscious of them; he did less than justice to the opponents of Bright, and the complexity of the political difficulties which faced Peel are simplified to his disadvantage. Yet the book has a very real and positive value which far outweighs these shortcomings. His grandfather had been a friend of Cobden and Bright, and he had acquired from him and his mother an understanding of the rugged moral power of the great nineteenth century liberals. In the re-creation of the past it is essential for the historian to recapture the conscious aspirations of men, and to do full justice to their ideals as well as lay bare whatever unconscious grasp they may have had of the purpose and destiny of the social class to which they happened to belong. And this Trevelyan achieves. It should never be ignored by anyone wishing to understand the power and force of the Manchester School.

His next choice was less happy: *Lord Grey of the Reform Bill* (1920). 'The theme of glorious summer (in this case the summer of Reform) coming after a long winter of discontent and repression, is, as I have said, congenial to my artistic sense. And then the background of Grey's life was my own—Northumberland.' But here his local, political and personal loyalties, his instinctively Whig attitude to life and history, got in his way; made him visualize too clearly and too simply issues which were dark and involved. The intricate interplay of social dynamics and political activity of which, at times, politicians are the ignorant marionettes is not a field for the exercise of his talents. He was too consciously aware of the final achievement of Victorian constitutional development to appreciate fully the desperate insecurity and the sharp revolutionary edge of these years; and it prevented him from seeing the Reform Bill for what it was, a rapid and instinctively cunning readjustment to new conditions by those self-same social classes which had dominated eighteenth century politics, and were to dominate English political life until the introduction of the ballot box. The real difficulty lay in this—that neither personalities nor the detailed narrative story were the crux of the historical situation—its reality lay outside formal politics and within the strained structure of society. Because of this *Lord Grey of the Reform Bill* has become outmoded: a fate which has not overtaken many other of Trevelyan's books.

The early 'twenties must have been a difficult period for Trevelyan. His last three books, judged by the high standard of success of his Garibaldi trilogy, or even of *England under the Stuarts*, had been failures. No theme had captured his imagination in the same way. Much of his creative energy was being absorbed in public work— he was a member of the Royal Commission on Oxford and Cambridge, and a strenuously active supporter of the National Trust. The writing of the *Bright* before the Great War and the *Grey* after it had entailed a great deal of work and thought on the whole range of nineteenth century history which, no doubt, like all good artists, Trevelyan thought that it was a pity to waste. Whatever the reason may have been, *British History in the Nineteenth Century* appeared in 1922. It was avowedly a textbook—in many ways far more of a textbook than *England under the Stuarts*—but its success was great. A well balanced, well constructed, comprehensive book, even in texture, beautifully written, it became the staff of life for generations of adolescent historians, bent on examination success. For the general reader as well as for the student it remains the best introduction to nineteenth century British history, weak though it certainly is on the economic side, to which very little space is devoted. Yet the importance of the book lay not entirely in itself but rather for the idea it gave to both Trevelyan and his publishers. Its success showed that it filled a real need; there was a greater: no comprehensive, single volume *History of England* of any merit had been published for over fifty years, since J. R. Green had written his *History of the English People* (1874).

This venture entailed an immense amount of work, intensive reading in fields with which he had little acquaintance and the book took three years to write. Trevelyan's own comment in his *Autobiography* on this really great achievement is almost absurdly modest.

In April 1926 my *History of England* came out. It has been, as regards sales, the most successful of my books, except the *Social*

History, because it treated so necessary a subject as the history of England at the length, and to some extent in the manner, which suited a large public, including schools and Universities. Some day, very soon perhaps, it will be replaced, but it will have served its generation.

Not only has it served its generation, there is no doubt that it will outlast it, and many more, taking its place by the side of J. R. Green's masterpiece. Let us admit its faults at once. Too little space was devoted to the development of industry, trade and finance; it has—although one might almost say 'Thank God!'—a bias, it is frankly liberal and protestant; the archaeologists might grumble a little at the brevity of its pre-history; specialists can no doubt attack it on points of detail. Yet what a massive achievement remains! Within seven hundred pages the story of the English people is told with an unmatched verve; rarely has narrative been so brilliantly sustained. Its judgements on men and affairs glitter with wisdom. Once more the deepest springs of his creative imagination had been released by the story of the race to which he belonged and of the countryside which he has so deeply loved, and in which, and this is important, he had faith. For this book could only have been written by a liberal and a humanist. Conscious though he is of the disastrous weakness of men confronted by the problem of their own destiny yet he has never been without hope.[1] This enabled him to give full and true value to the positive contributions of Englishmen to civilization and to do full justice to the aspirational side of their endeavours. His book glows with human warmth, and some of the best chapters are those in which he re-creates the world of ordinary men and women, the medieval peasants, the Tudor yeomen, the Hanoverian squires, the working men of Victorian England, all nameless now and forgotten.

[1] Cf. *Autobiography*, p. 34: 'I used to look askance at Gibbon's dreadful saying that history is "little more than the register of the crimes, follies and misfortunes of mankind". Nor do I even now wholly subscribe to it. But the war of 1914–1918 enlarged and saddened my mind, and prepared me to write English history with a more realistic and less partisan outlook. Yet, even after that war, the Reign of Queen Anne and the History of England up to the end of Victoria's reign, still seemed to me, when I came to write them, to be stories of happy endings.' This, too, was written in 1949!

But the *History of England* had a social as well as an intrinsic worth. Millions of Englishmen have derived from his book the little history that they will ever know.[1] Hence the importance of Trevelyan's attitude and beliefs.

'In answer to the instincts and temperament of her people,' he writes in his Introduction to the book, 'she evolved in the course of centuries a system which reconciled three things that other nations have often found incompatible—executive efficiency, popular control and personal freedom.'

It is his stress on these qualities, as well as on the material and spiritual contribution of Englishmen, that has given the book such enduring worth. He has laid bare the common grounds of tradition, possessed by rich and poor alike, and fortified their belief in their way of life, now so desperately challenged. And it is well that this should be liberal and humanist, stressing the genius of our race for compromise, for tolerance, for social justice, and freedom of the spirit. Yet he does not gloss the lapses; the brutality of our Irish policy is not ignored, nor the human suffering entailed in the Industrial Revolution left undescribed. This wise, just book would by itself have secured Trevelyan's place in the great tradition of English historical writing.

IV

After the publication of the *History of England*, the circumstances of Trevelyan's life once more changed course. In 1928, his parents died; he inherited Hallington Hall in Northumberland from a distant relative; and Stanley Baldwin offered him the Regius Professorship of Modern History at Cambridge, which he accepted. Many honours quickly followed, but none gave him greater pleasure than the conferment of the Order of Merit in 1930, a distinction which his father had held before him. The return of Trevelyan to academic life did not mean, however, a return to the academic chores from which he had escaped a quarter of a century before, for the duties of administration and lecturing of a Professor are not

[1] Over 200,000 copies have been sold, but in schools copies are used time and time again, and, of course, many schoolmasters base their lessons on it.

onerous and rightly allow plenty of time for creative work, and, although there was still a powerful atmosphere of destructive criticism abroad in Cambridge, his confidence in his own abilities was now unassailable.[1] And the third phase of Trevelyan's historical writing begins—his great three-volume book on *The Reign of Queen Anne*. But before dealing with this major contribution to English historical studies, there are three other books of this period which are too frequently neglected. He published a charming *Memoir* of his father, Sir George Otto Trevelyan, in 1930, which in many ways is a document of great worth for the social and cultural history of late nineteenth century England, and invaluable for understanding the compulsions in Trevelyan's own nature which made him a historian. In the same *genre* was his *Life of Lord Grey of Fallodon* (1937), a labour of love for his distinguished Northumbrian neighbour, and this book is pervaded with nostalgia for the way of life which Grey represented and which Trevelyan knew to be passing. In both of these works one is made keenly aware of Trevelyan's preoccupation with the poetry of Time and of Nature. Then, in 1934, there was a masterpiece in miniature, *The English Revolution, 1688–89*, published in the Home University Library. The social analysis of politics has never been Trevelyan's *forte* but in this book his descriptions of the social forces which brought about the Revolution are profoundly stimulating, and his realistic intuitions have been fully justified by subsequent research.

The motivation for writing the chief historical work of his life, *England under Queen Anne*, is best described in his own words:

The idea of taking up the tale where my great-uncle's history [i.e., Lord Macaulay's *History of England*] had broken off, was perhaps a fancy at the back of my consciousness. But I was more

---

[1] One of the duties of a Professor was the supervision of the research of post-graduate students and because I had the honour of being one of Trevelyan's perhaps I may be allowed one personal reminiscence. I would take my written work round to his study at Garden Corner in West Road. He would peer at it through his steel rimmed spectacles; his long legs would twine and untwine impatiently; he would growl a little to himself and then I would find myself by his side at an enormous desk while he attacked my prose with his pencil. Unnecessary adjectives would fly out, commas would be removed and then appropriately replaced, phrases would be inserted, so apt that I knew at last what I meant, and I would come away happy and inspired by sentences which were of course his, but I liked to think mine.

seriously attracted by the dramatic unity and separateness of the period from 1702–14, lying between the Stuart and Hanoverian eras with a special ethos of its own; the interplay and mutual dependence of foreign and domestic, religious and political, English and Scottish, civil and military affairs; the economic background and the social scene and their political outcome; the series of dramatic changes of issue, like a five-act drama, leading up to a climax of trumpets proclaiming King George. . . . In Anne's reign, it seemed to me, Britain attained by sea and land to her modern place in the world, having settled her free constitution and composed by compromise and toleration the feuds that had torn her in Stuart times.

It was planned, therefore, on the most considerable scale and intended to be his greatest contribution to the study of English history. But what of the achievement? Personally, I feel that in the choice of subject Trevelyan's intuition for once failed him. The Reign of Anne, unlike the Italy of Garibaldi or England of the Stuarts, was not an heroic age, and even Marlborough, who most nearly approximates to the hero, has none of the hero's simplicity and emotional force, that direct response in action to emotional need, which marks a Garibaldi or a Cromwell. The other chief characters in this part of our history—Harley, Bolingbroke, Godolphin—were men of exceptional psychological complexity, tortuous in thought, feeling and deed, whose words often bore little relation to intention, and intention none to avowed aspiration. Backstairs politics, the worldliness and cynicism of men seeking power at all costs, twisting and debauching institutions to get it, is not a world in which Trevelyan moves with instinctive ease. Furthermore, his traditional outlook on English politics distorted his vision of the Augustan age. He is a firm believer in the historical continuity of the two-party English political system.[1] In the reign of Anne, party-politicians, it is true, used party-clichés, exploited for their own purposes social animosities which lie concealed under party names, and they were prepared to enforce legislation of a party nature; but

[1] Cf. his Romanes Lecture, *The Two Party System in English Political History*, delivered at Oxford in 1926 and reprinted in the *Autobiography and Other Essays* (1949) pp. 183–99.

this is only the surface story, concealing the real drive for power and for the fruits of office. In this struggle, family and territorial connections were always, in the last resort, as strong as party. The failure of the Whigs to obtain any clear-cut and detailed definition of the constitution in 1689 led to the disintegration of politics, making the growth of oligarchy easy, desirable and certain. The system of Walpole was based on the system of Harley, sometimes using the same men and their connections, which had been fostered by the 'Tories', but which were easily adaptable to 'Whig' purposes. The straightforward conception of a two-party system does not forward the analysis of this intricate and involved period of our political history; such analysis must come from the detailed study of factions and connections, as yet largely undescribed. Nor was the unity of the period so actual as Trevelyan would have us believe; in all aspects of English history—social, economic, political, religious, constitutional and diplomatic—the play had got well and truly into its second act by 1702. In consequence, the structure of these books is to some extent artificial, and the construction does not arise so naturally from the historical situation, as it does in the Garibaldi trilogy.

But it is, of course, a work of tremendous quality; the opening chapters which draw a picture of England at the opening of the eighteenth century are outstanding for their imaginative insight, and for the warm spirit that breathes through them. Actual and vivid, they compel belief even though he lays major stress on the ease, virtue and sweetness of life of the possessing classes and glosses somewhat the brutality and suffering which were the lot of the common man. Apart from the social background the best part of the work is that which deals with the naval and military history; certainly, too, by far the best character study is of Marlborough whom Macaulay had detested and to whom Trevelyan, conscious of a major family blunder, was determined to do full justice. Full justice is, indeed, done both to his capacity as a general and to the persistence of his will in diplomacy. As in all of Trevelyan's work the narrative is treated very cunningly; the pace of the book is intense, especially in *Blenheim* (1931), the first of the three, for the battle gives a natural and dramatic climax to the book. In his second two parts, *Ramillies and the Union with Scotland* (1932) and *Peace and the Protestant Succession* (1934), there is no such natural climax, and inevitably the story is more broken up, with a consequent loss of intensity. Stylistically, these are the most beautiful of Trevelyan's books. In his earlier works there are strong traces, especially in the descriptive passages, of Ruskin and Carlyle, which to our modern taste impart a sense of straining after effect. It is possible that the writing of the *History of England*, in which every word had to count, helped to simplify his style without weakening his gift for a memorable phrase. Whatever may have been the cause, words in these books are used with absolute mastery; passage after passage stir the heart and mind with their elegant clarity and evocative beauty. *England under Queen Anne* is a great work and a great achievement, but one cannot help regretting that, in the fullness of his powers, he had not been drawn to a subject more apt to his genius.

The Mastership of Trinity College, Cambridge, is a Crown appointment, and it must have given Winston Churchill great pleasure to confer it on Trevelyan, when the vacancy was created by the death of J. J. Thomson in 1940, for they were contemporaries at school and, in a sense, rival historians, for Churchill's *Life of Marlborough* had been published about the same time as *England under Queen Anne*. This last and greatest distinction of his academic life has, as he has written, 'made my life as happy as anyone's can be during the fall of European civilization'. The depth of his feeling for his College, great in men and history, and for the beauty of the stone and buildings in which it lives its corporate life, may be seen in the pages of the little book, *Trinity College*, which he published in 1943. It will continue to give pleasure to generations, not only of Trinity men, but to all whom Cambridge has enriched.

But the most outstanding success was yet to come. Before the war Trevelyan had been working on a social history of England, as a companion volume to his *History of England* which had been mainly concerned with politics and war. In 1940, he decided to drop the early part of the work and begin with Chaucer.[1] From that point onwards the book was already written, but owing to war shortages it was not published until 1944 in this country, when it

[1] Unused fragments of the projected earlier part may probably be detected in two essays in the *Autobiography and Other Essays*. They are: 'Social Life in Roman Britain' and 'The Coming of the Anglo-Saxons'.

appeared under the title of *English Social History: a Survey of Six Centuries*. By 1949, it had sold 392,000 copies and has by now far exceeded this large total. This book must have reached thousands who do not normally read history. I was told by a friend who did his military service in the Suez Canal Zone that he saw it being read by soldiers who had left school at fourteen and who had probably never held a stiff covered book in their hands since the day they had left. And my friend tells me that they lay in their bunks for hours, reading with all the keen and eager enjoyment which they might have derived from an adventure story. In many homes it must be the one and only history book. This work is not only a social history but a social phenomenon.

Once more, as with the Garibaldi books, Trevelyan was exceptionally fortunate in the moment of his publication—1944. The war, which we were bringing to a successful end, had jeopardized the traditional pattern of English life, and in some ways destroyed it for ever. This created amongst all classes a deep nostalgia for the way of life which we were losing. Then, again, the war had made conscious to millions that our national attitude to life was historically based, the result of centuries of slow growth, and that it was for the old, tried ways of life for which we were fighting. Winston Churchill in his great war speeches made us all conscious of our past, as never before. And in this war, too, there were far more highly educated men and women in all ranks of all of the services. The 'twenties and 'thirties of this century had witnessed a great extension of secondary school education, producing a vast public capable of reading and enjoying a book of profound historical imagination, once the dilemma of their time stirred them to do so. Trevelyan's book was a beautifully timed response to the need which so many were unconsciously feeling and its nature widened its appeal, for it was the story of how the ordinary men and women of England had lived out their lives, enduring their times as best they might, and it was read by just such ordinary men and women who were enduring times as hard as the English people had ever faced, and perhaps with far less hope for their future; in such tribulation it was natural to read with avid longing of ages more gracious and more secure, and to draw strength from our chequered past.

Intrinsically the book deserved its fame, its glory, its continued and continuing success. Throughout his life the poet in Trevelyan had been drawn to a contemplation of the ordinary nameless man, caught up inexorably in Time. In volume after volume which he published on English history there were chapters which evoke the past life and lost countryside of our island. It is usually in these chapters that his writing acquires its most lyrical note. The subject, therefore, of the *Social History* touched the deepest springs of his temperament and was one which he had long contemplated. By and large, during the centuries about which Trevelyan wrote, the great contributions to our civilization were made by the aristocrats and squires and yeomen, by merchants and craftsmen, by owners of wealth, great or small; in fact by those classes with which he was instinctively familiar, and from which he derived his own ancestry. Their world is dead, their opportunity past, and it is as well that their elegy should be pronounced by one who loved their ways of life so well, and by one who could respond to their aspirations and to the beauty of the material civilization which they created, and who could accept, if uneasily, the poverty and suffering upon which it was, of necessity, based. This attitude gives a sunset glow to the whole work, softening the edges, obscuring some of the harshness, bitterness and conflict which have, at times, distracted our country, but in the main fulfilling the great purpose which he set himself.

Each one, gentle and simple, in his commonest goings and comings, was ruled by a complicated and ever-shifting fabric of custom and law, society and politics, events at home and abroad, some of them little known by him and less understood. Our effort is not only to get what glimpses we can of his intimate personality, but to reconstruct the whole fabric of each passing age, and see how it affected him; to get to know more in some respects than the dweller in the past himself knew about the conditions that enveloped and controlled his life.

There is nothing that more divides civilized from semi-savage man than to be conscious of our forefathers as they really were, and bit by bit to reconstruct the mosaic of the long-forgotten past. To weigh the stars, or to make ships sail in the air or below the sea, is not a more astonishing and ennobling performance on the part of the human race in these latter days, than to know the

R

course of events that had been long forgotten, and the true nature of men and women who were here before us.

Few books have responded so nobly to the demands of their age.

V

Such are the many triumphs and the few failures of Trevelyan's contribution to English historical literature, and it remains to assess his achievement. What perhaps is most frequently forgotten, or ignored, is the skill of his literary craftsmanship. Trevelyan is a born writer, and a natural story-teller; and this, amongst historians, is a rare gift; only Prescott, amongst the great historians, has this facility in equal or greater measure. In consequence, those episodes of history which were full of dramatic action, with a firm beginning and obvious end, have brought forth some of his best writing—the *Garibaldi* books, *England under the Stuarts*, much of the *History of England*, and perhaps *Blenheim*. As a stylist he cannot be compared with Gibbon, Macaulay, or even Clarendon, and amongst his own generation he would have to concede the first place to R. H. Tawney, but he has written passages of greater lyrical beauty than any of them, when the heart of the poet has been stirred. A poet at large in history is a unique phenomenon of our literature and will create for Trevelyan a special place in the history of English letters. Certainly, I think, it will secure a permanent niche for *Garibaldi's Defence of the Roman Republic*, which, were it fiction, would live as one of the greatest love-stories, told with exquisite feeling and poetic power. The same poetic temperament has been responsible for some of the best evocations of times past that have been written in our language. They are scattered throughout his works but brought together and continuously sustained in the pages of the *Social History*. If one quality is to be singled out, it should be this, for, of all historians, he is the poet of English history.

His work has one other great and enduring merit, the tradition within which it was written. The Victorian liberals and their Edwardian successors have made one of the greatest contributions to science and to culture ever made by a ruling class. To these by birth and by instinct Trevelyan belonged. Therefore, as time passes, his work will acquire fresh significance and become the material of history itself, for these books of his will show how these liberal humanists considered their past, from whence they derived their tradition, by what they would like themselves judged. And because he has written from such a standpoint, he has helped to inculcate into the hearts of men and women, born in more desperate times, a regard for human justice and personal freedom.

1951

THOMAS BABINGTON MACAULAY

ON the day in November 1848 when the first volume of Macaulay's *History of England* appeared, Ludgate Hill was jammed with carriages struggling to get to Messrs. Longman in Paternoster Row. Three thousand copies were sold in ten days and the pace began to increase rather than slacken. The time came when Robert Longman pressed a cheque for £20,000 on Macaulay on the grounds that he had too much money in his own account. At a guinea a volume this was a prodigious achievement for Victorian times. Although Macaulay naturally thought well of his work, its public reception astonished even him. The reviews were almost uniformly as eulogistic as they were lengthy, but the book was far more than a success of metropolitan literary society. 'At Duckinfield, near Manchester, a gentleman who thought that there would be a certain selfishness in keeping so great a pleasure to himself, invited his poorer neighbours to attend every evening after their work was finished, and read the History aloud to them from beginning to end. At the close of the last meeting, one of the audience rose, and moved, in north country fashion, a vote of thanks to Mr. Macaulay "for having written a history which working men can understand".'[1] His success at Windsor was as great as at Manchester. The Prince Consort was so deeply impressed by his book that he immediately offered Macaulay the vacant chair of Modern History at Cambridge, which Macaulay immediately declined on the grounds that if he were to lecture well he would be forced to give up his *History*. And if he were to write the *History*, his lectures would be bad. Some years later, Queen

[1] Sir George Otto Trevelyan, *Life and Letters of Lord Macaulay* (World's Classics ed.), II, p. 173.

Victoria recognized Macaulay's unique position in English life and letters by making him a peer—the first writer to achieve such a distinction.

It is obvious from the great financial rewards and public honours which Macaulay's literary works brought him that he wrote very much what his time and generation wished to read. Certainly his own sympathy with his age was greater than that commonly found amongst the great historians. Gibbon who, alone of English historians, can be compared with Macaulay to the latter's disadvantage, offended a considerable section of his reading public by his ironic treatment of the mysteries of the Christian religion. Although perfectly in harmony with the philosophic attitude of the Enlightenment, Gibbon displayed a complete detachment from the aspirations and ideals of the active part of the nation to which he belonged. Macaulay, however, was totally involved in his age—in it he found an echoing response to his own boundless energy and eupeptic confidence. Indeed, it is remarkable how closely Macaulay's character mirrors the strength and weakness of the early Victorian period. And his success must partly lie in the fact that the men and women who read him so eagerly, felt as he felt and believed as he believed: his truth was their truth. That this was so is also borne out by the fact that Macaulay now seems not only far below Gibbon in quality and achievement, but also below Michelet, below Burkhardt, and well below Ranke. He lacked the range of Gibbon, the imagination of Michelet, the penetration of Burkhardt and the wisdom of Ranke. Nor has his scholarship worn so well as theirs.[1] Even so, his qualities still claim for him a place amongst the great historians of the nineteenth century. It is likely that he will always maintain that place, and always be quite widely read. For this reason: in temperament he was very close to a fairly common variety of human personality. To make this clear, Macaulay and his time need to be described in a little more detail.

II

He was born October 25, 1800, the son of Zachary Macaulay who had recently returned from West Africa where he had been in

---

[1] In this context it is worth noting Acton's dictum, 'Resist your time—take a foothold outside it.' G. L. Kochan, *Acton on History*, p. 36.

charge of the settlement of freed slaves at Freetown.

Zachary was an evangelical, a member of the Clapham Sect, one of the Saints, a man of formidable and relentless piety. Equally formidable and equally relentless was his industry. The only holiday which he ever took was at Rothley in Leicestershire at the time of his son's birth. Not that this holiday was due to his pleasure in acquiring an heir; it was due entirely to ineluctable circumstance. Zachary had fallen from his horse and broken both arms. Naturally such a father was not slow to inculcate those virtues which he believed to be the only sure guides in a world full of sin. Like Wesley, he believed that industry was the best antidote to temptation. He insisted, of course, on absolute honesty and upon a deep respect for those institutions by which society was governed—the King, the Church, Parliament and the family. Although Zachary Macaulay was an ardent supporter of the abolition of slavery, he was no reformer. He accepted government as God-given and his desire for reform was limited to the individual conscience. Macaulay's father was, therefore, a man of certainties, one who never hesitated to judge men or events by his own rigid standards. Macaulay's mother held very much the same views as her husband but they were tempered with more obvious affection and, not surprisingly, more obvious ambition for her child. But both parents believed ardently in willpower and in the effectiveness of ratiocination—and from his earliest years Macaulay was encouraged to act like an adult. Childish behaviour or wilful attitudes were thoroughly deplored. He was expected to devote himself actively to a boy's principal task —learning.

Few parents have had a child so apt to their purpose, so willing or so eager to tread in the paths marked for him.

Macaulay possessed a formidable mental equipment in which the most outstanding and remarkable gift was his photographic memory. After having read *Paradise Lost* twice, he could recite without fault the bulk of the poem. He himself said that if Shakespeare's works were to have been destroyed, he could have reproduced them entirely from memory. A memory of such proportions naturally strengthened Macaulay's self-confidence: on questions of fact he was always right; time and time again he triumphed over less exact men. Such a faculty fed his self-assertiveness, and, as he believed that his judgement was based on knowledge, he had few doubts about the validity of his attitudes. A powerful sense of certainty pervades all that Macaulay wrote and there can be little doubt that this was strengthened by the absolute accuracy of the facts which he could recollect.

Yet essentially Macaulay's was a selective memory controlled and exercised by those preconceptions which were the very fibres of his personality. The facts were fitted into his pattern of judgement. They demonstrated the virtues of liberty and progress or they could be used to show the iniquity of those men who tried to oppose their development. Facts never became the object of imaginative exercise. Macaulay never tried to feel through them, irrespective of judgement, to the reality of times alien to his own world. He remembered what was useful to his own sharp, confident vision. The irrelevant was, however, meaningless to him. His memory was neither the stimulator of curiosity nor its servant; it was a weapon of didacticism.

A fabulous memory was not the only outstanding quality of Macaulay's intellectual make-up. He possessed an immense appetite for learning. As soon as he could read, he was wolfing down universal histories, plays, sermons, poems, classics. He mastered languages with ease and delighted in mathematical exercises—throughout his life he had a passion for doing long arithmetical calculations in his head. To memory and appetite was added order. There was nothing ragged or diffuse about Macaulay's interests. He quickly reduced his knowledge to a system. His earliest essays, even his earliest letters, are remarkable for the lucidity of their arrangement and the aptness of the facts and quotations used to illustrate his arguments. And finally to this impressive list of intellectual qualities must be added a sense of style as personal as it was powerful. At the age of five, a servant of Lady Waldegrave's scalded his legs with hot coffee, and when asked some minutes later how he did, he replied, 'Thank you, Madame, the agony has somewhat abated.' And for the rest of his life his style remained formal, balanced and frequently pompous. His public performances, either in essays or in speeches, were also loaded with erudition, yet he was never dull. All that he had to say was too pungent, too vigorous and too decided to allow a reader's interest to decay.

Macaulay was, therefore, extravagantly well endowed. He possessed a mind of exceptional range and almost incredible accuracy.

His intellectual energy displayed volcanic force, but the rapid, almost torrential, flow of his thought was confined by a strict sense of form and order. Few men have been equipped with Macaulay's ability to reduce a complex mass of fact and argument to a clear and lucid exposition. And yet these qualities were matched by weaknesses which have grown more apparent with time.

III

Macaulay's emotional make-up was exceedingly simple; as simple as his mind was complex. Although in his journal he left a detailed record of his daily feelings, it is almost devoid of those emotional experiences which provide the structure of most men's lives. Macaulay was never in love. His strongest attachment was to his family. When his sister, Hannah, decided to marry, he was surprised, pained, and then resigned to the separation realizing his own obtuse folly in never having considered such a possibility. That blow was the most grievous personal loss that he ever experienced and he buried the pain it caused him very quickly. Time and time again in his diary he refers with pleasure to the sustained happiness of his life. On his fiftieth birthday he wrote: 'Well, I have had a happy life. I do not know that anybody whom I have seen close, has had a happier. Some things I regret; but, on the whole, who is better off? I have no children of my own, it is true; but I have children whom I love as if they were my own, and who, I believe, love me. I wish that the next ten years may be as happy as the last ten. But I rather wish it than hope it.' His last sentence refers to his fear of death, one of his only terrors throughout his early life. He could, however, have 'hoped it', for this fear weakened as death itself approached and he met it with the same serenity with which he lived so much of his life.

Yet, although there was an inner core of tranquillity, based on successful repression, Macaulay was not devoid of strong feeling. He was insatiably ambitious and when writing his *History* he was constantly preoccupied with speculations as to how it would be regarded in the year 2000 or 3000. He thoroughly savoured and enjoyed the great fame which came to him, and felt that it was a proper reward for his unflagging industry and his concentration of purpose. Furthermore his feelings about public affairs or individuals could be intense: the reform of Parliament, the abolition of slavery

the duties of Englishmen in India, or Byron, Boswell, or Horace
Walpole—all aroused in him strong feelings. Heredity, education
and temperament gave him a bias towards decided moral attitudes
in which powerful feeling was blended with absolute certainty of
right or wrong. This moral passion in Macaulay, so much in tune
with the atmosphere of his age, sprang to some extent from the
directness of his own feelings. The lack of any real sympathy with
the strong, surging animal passions which could destroy and ruin
men, was a serious defect in a man who aspired to be a historian of
genius. Yet the fault lay deeper than this. It was not the moral weaknesses of men such as Boswell or Shaftesbury that disturbed Macaulay
so profoundly. There was a deeper jealousy at work.

Both in character and in intellect Macaulay was in the last analysis
a simple man—simple and lucid—no matter how intricate the
surface machinery might appear to be. On occasion he could be hot
and choleric yet always about surface matters. He lacked the roots
of life, sexual passion, and the sense of tragedy that it arouses—the
biting, painful sense of the transience of living and loving men.
Oddly enough the cool-tempered Gibbon, so much more detached
from life than Macaulay, felt these things much more strongly. At
the heart of Macaulay's being there was immaturity, an inhibition
of passion, or an inability to face where it might lead him, which
made him distrust it in other men. But unfortunately for Macaulay
creative energy is usually fertilized by the chaos of passionate life—
not always, but frequently. Consequently, Macaulay never pene-
trates to the heart of human existence. His attempts at poetry are
dreadfully banal—the metrical exercises of a clever boy in which
the emotional situations have been taken from literature and not
from life.[1] The same sterility, the same artificiality of feeling, is

---

[1] Macaulay did write one poem which displays a certain tender, heartfelt sensibility
of both thought and language—a poem about a Jacobite, whose theme, appropriately enough, is the poignancy of exile from home.

> To my true King I offered free from stain
> Courage and faith; vain faith and courage vain,
> For him, I threw lands, honours, wealth away,
> And one dear hope, that was more prized than they.
> For him I languished in a foreign clime,
> Grey-haired with sorrow in my manhood's prime;
> Heard on Lavernia Scargill's whispering trees
> And pined by Arno for my lovelier Tees.

present in most of the great descriptive passages of his *History*. Although his account of the siege of Londonderry is a *tour de force* of narrative skill, the human figures are two-dimensional, conventional characters, lacking the convincing reality which a more imaginative and creative writer would have given them.

The limitation of Macaulay's emotional range was one of the grave faults of character which weakened his powers as a writer, but it was not the only one. Creative thinking often works very mysteriously, one might almost say in darkness. Suddenly there is a moment of illumination; inconsistencies are resolved, interrelations discovered, and a new vision of reality perceived. In Macaulay's mind, however, there was no darkness, no obscurity, no inconsistency, nothing unrelated. Everything was lucid and certain. Macaulay lacked doubt; lacked the confused, groping, searching mind which is often so much more creative, except perhaps in mathematics, than a mind of absolute clarity. And paradoxically enough, though Macaulay loved facts, he did not possess a really enquiring mind. At first sight that may seem a fantastic statement, yet it is true. Macaulay took pleasure in being accurate, yet he did not love facts for their own sake, but merely to arrange them in patterns to his own satisfaction. The patterns were those of a conventional and accepting mind. He viewed the Revolution of 1688 as did the average Whig reader of his day. His vast learning became merely a brilliant illustration of commonplace ideas, for his ideas were rarely formed by his knowledge. His knowledge decorated his convictions. He saw the seventeenth century in terms of his own political beliefs, and in terms of his own morality; and he was quite content to do so. This, of course, was a crippling handicap to an historian for it produced satisfaction and decision too quickly. Lacking curiosity and suspicion, Macaulay had little or no interest in ferreting out facts for their own sake. The hope of a new or startling revelation never sent him searching in strange places for new sources. Compared with other great nineteenth-century historians he added remarkably little that was new to our knowledge of the past. Accepting too easily facts which suited his didactic argument, Macaulay committed grave errors of scholarship. Forster, Paget and Spedding had little difficulty in marshalling convincing evidence against judgements that Macaulay had made with too great confidence on too little evidence.

This severe limitation of curiosity to the accumulation of the knowledge which Macaulay wanted, was responsible for his weakness as an historian: his lack of grasp of the intricacy of human character and his over-confident judgement of it. True, his own emotional deficiencies had severely restricted his experience of the dark, passionate, tumultuous side of life, yet often creative men have lived lives as quiet as Macaulay's. They, however, have been haunted by imagination, or known the jungles buried in their own hearts, so that they were able to appreciate the difficulties and confusions of more active men. But for Macaulay the precepts of morality were as clear as those of politics and as simple. The complexity of character was lost on him and he depicted the men and women of his *History* and *Essays* in simple terms of good and bad. He never sought beyond the obvious. In consequence, Macaulay was far more successful in describing action or political debate than he was in portraying human beings.

Macaulay was, therefore, a man of formidable learning, fluent, confident, decisive in his judgements. But beneath a powerful intellect there lay a simple, rather childlike, heart. Although he was a thrusting, ambitious man, with a muscular, forceful mind, yet in certain fields of human experience he was curiously opaque. His lack of subtlety or of real creative depth proved to be no obstacle to his success. The men and women of his time loved to hear certainties; confidence was a part of the air they breathed.

IV

Although as a child Macaulay had spent hours writing vast verse dramas and world histories, it proved quite impossible for him as a young man to follow a literary career. Indeed, though he wrote a good deal, he probably did not in his early youth desire such a career. Precise scholarship did not appeal to him; and he was drawn irresistibly to politics where his intellectual capacities and immoderate fluency were bound to make him famous as well as redoubtable. His success was immediate, and within a short time he could fill the House of Commons as no other speaker could. He was no debater, no orator in the usual sense. He spoke in a loud, clear, unmodulated voice without a gesture. One of the parliamentary reporters of the time described his manner in these terms.

> Vehemence of thought, vehemence of language, vehemence of manner were his chief characteristics. The listener might almost fancy he heard ideas and words gurgling in the speaker's throat for priority of utterance. There was nothing graduated, or undulating, about him. He plunged at once into the heart of the matter, and continued his loud resounding pace from beginning to end, without halt or pause. This vehemence and volume made Macaulay the terror of the reporters; and, when he engaged in a subject outside their ordinary experience, they were fairly nonplussed by the display of names and dates, and titles. He was not a long-winded speaker. In fact, his earnestness was so great that it would have failed under a very long effort.[1]

Although he became one of the great speakers of the Commons, he was not, considering his abilities, a successful politician. He quickly lost his Tory principles, much to his father's regret, and became an ardent disciple of moderate Whig reform. He had no use for Brougham whom he considered to be an immoral, as well as a dangerous, radical. He strongly disapproved of Socialist or Jacobin sentiments—indeed he detested Wordsworth's *Prelude* because he thought its political implications too revolutionary. He believed passionately in orderly progress, gradual reform and in the ultimate triumph of technology through liberal education. He was convinced that it was England's singular destiny to disseminate these virtues through the world. For Macaulay the 1851 exhibition was the crowning glory of human achievement. He wrote in his diary of his visit to the Crystal Palace, 'I made my way into the building; a most gorgeous sight; vast; graceful; beyond the dream of the Arabian romances. I cannot think that the Caesars ever exhibited a more splendid spectacle. I was quite dazzled, and I felt as I did on entering St. Peter's.' This was the demonstration of England's industrial majesty, the final justification of the long struggle for civil and religious liberty. 'The history of England,' declared Macaulay, 'is emphatically the history of progress' and by progress

[1] Trevelyan, *Life*, II, p. 87.

he meant what he saw about him in the Great Exhibition—material progress—for he believed that the amelioration of the conditions in which man lived made him more virtuous. Macaulay saw in Francis Bacon the first great exponent of this empirical philosophy and he realized that many would mock him for his materialist outlook. 'Some people,' he wrote, 'may take the object of the Baconian philosophy a low object but they cannot deny that, high or low, it has been attained.' And after dismissing ancient philosophy as sterile and useless, he hammers home in a passionate, breathless passage the victories of empirical philosophy.

It has lengthened life; it has mitigated pain; it has extinguished diseases; it has increased the fertility of the soil; it has given new securities to the mariner; it has furnished new arms to the warrior; it has spanned great rivers and estuaries with bridges of form unknown to our fathers; it has guided the thunderbolt innocuously from heaven to earth; it has lighted up the night with the splendour of the day; it has extended the range of the human vision; it has multiplied the power of the human muscles; it has accelerated motion; it has annihilated distance; it has facilitated intercourse, correspondence, all friendly offices, all despatch of business; it has enabled man to descend to the depths of the sea, to soar into the air, to penetrate securely into the noxious recesses of the earth, to traverse the land in cars which whirl along without horses, and the ocean in ships which run ten knots an hour against the wind. These are but a part of its fruits, and of its first fruits. For it is a philosophy which never rests, which has never attained, which is never perfect. Its law is progress. A point which yesterday was invisible is its goal today, and will be its starting-post tomorrow.[1]

This outlook has been criticized as philistine, blinkered, nerveless, unimaginative. At the time that Macaulay was trumpeting his praise, Carlyle, Disraeli and others were brooding over the suffering and poverty which the Industrial Revolution had brought into being —a fact which many observers were quick to seize on. Aesthetes and philosophers deplored the frank materialism of Macaulay's outlook and modern commentators have not been much more

[1] T. B. Macaulay, *Critical and Historical Essays* (Everyman ed.), II, pp. 375–6.

sympathetic. Professor Geyl, Macaulay's most perceptive critic, maintains that this 'religion of progress' prevented Macaulay from being a really great historian. 'That feeling,' he writes, 'of absolute certainty about the superiority of the present and about the unqualified beneficence of the gradual increase of the technical and scientific knowledge at the disposal of mankind . . . must lead the historian to view the past in terms which may be entirely irrelevant and result in a picture lacking in the truth of intimacy . . . to my way of thinking, however stimulating and instructive and powerfully intelligent I may find Macaulay's work, this mental attitude toward the past is in the deepest sense unhistoric.'[1] Since Macaulay wrote the prevalent mood of European society has been one of doubt if not of despair—at least in literary and philosophic circles— and it is a mood that naturally enough is deeply antipathetic to Macaulay's own.

And yet in that way was Macaulay wrong? The material progress of mankind is the one certain, glorious triumph which no one can deny. Treating history polemically, and it can be treated polemically, Macaulay was quite right, incontrovertibly right, and in no way unhistorical except in so far as he attributed a conscious and deliberate purpose to man's evolution. But history can be more than polemics: it is also a quest for reality in which suffering, ignorance, folly, decay and failure are as valid as happiness, knowledge, wisdom, growth and success. These are the realms which more imaginative and sensitive historians, such as Ranke or Burkhardt, have made their own, and because their works have re-created a more complex and accurate reality, their scholarship is both more profound and more durable. Yet unsubtle, dogmatic and philistine as Macaulay was, he still has the best of the argument. Man's prime reason for self-congratulation is his triumph over the material universe.

For Macaulay life and history were all of a piece, the unfolding pattern of virtue, justice, progress. A gigantic, if naïve, faith infused his attitude to present politics as well as to the historic past. The same direct, materialistic commonsense made him very effective on specific political issues, but it rendered him too unyielding, too unsupple for the shifty world of high politics, where more imagina-

[1] P. Geyl, *Debates with Historians* (The Hague, 1955), p. 27.

tion and more sense of reality would have served him better. Although he reached cabinet rank before he was forty (as Secretary at War), his greatest achievement in public life was not in politics but in administration during his residence in India as a member of the Supreme Council, particularly the time that he spent as President of the Commission of Public Instruction and afterwards as President of the Law Commission.

The tasks which Macaulay tackled while he held these posts in India were completely commensurate with his abilities. His minute on Indian Education is a masterly summary of the complexity of native languages, customs and educational methods, and the difficulties which would face India unless a common language were found to meet the needs of a more uniform and complex administration and of the growth of technology. He then planned a scheme of education, primary, secondary and technical, including the production of qualified teachers; as might be expected his attention to detail was absolute and reached down to textbooks and grammars. As President of the Law Commission he set about reducing the wild chaos of Indian customary law and argued strongly for the introduction of the principles of British justice, with the consequence that one of the greatest benefits conferred by the British on India has been a reasonably unified, coherent and wise system of law. The brilliance of Macaulay's administrative ability is thus partly responsible for the excellence of Indian education and justice. On these questions the strength of his mind and character had full play; his weaknesses were of no importance. A comprehensive factual knowledge and a sense of relevance were more apt than creative imagination or a knowledge of fellow men and women. And his empirical philosophy was fully justified.

V

Politics and administration provided large opportunities for the exercise of Macaulay's singular talents; the majority of men might have been content with his achievements and the rewards which they brought. Undeniably they gave Macaulay deep satisfaction, but curiously enough they proved in the end inadequate. He had never ceased to be drawn to literature; he had started to scribble as a child and he could not stop. From the age of twenty-four he wrote regularly for the *Edinburgh Review*, and what he contributed was so novel, so exciting, that his reputation was quickly made. Macaulay in his very first essay used the pretext of a review to write a short biography of the subject of the book under discussion—in this case, Milton.

Biography had not, in Macaulay's day, become an important, regular part of the yearly output of books. Apart from Boswell's *Johnson* it was still largely a matter of short memorial sermons or pamphlets or huge and tedious compilations of ill-edited letters and memoirs.[1] In his essays Macaulay provided something fresh and exciting. Usually after a few paragraphs displaying the profound ignorance of the author's knowledge of his subject, and of course the superiority of Macaulay's, he settled down to give a short biographical sketch in which his judgements were as rapid, authoritative and final as the style was flamboyant and pungent. As Macaulay could compress a massive quantity of material into a short space and without the least confusion or congestion, he was able to give a remarkably comprehensive account not only of a man, but of the time in which he lived. Macaulay in these essays set out deliberately to startle the mind and he sought paradox rather than avoided it. He wrote them too with magnificent journalistic verve—once read, never forgotten. To give some idea of their flavour here is a passage on Horace Walpole:

> The conformation of his mind was such that whatever was little seemed to him great, and whatever was great seemed to him little. To chat with blue-stockings, to write little copies of complimentary verses on little occasions, to superintend a private press, to preserve from natural decay the perishable topics of Ranelagh and White's, to record divorces and bets, Miss Chudleigh's absurdities and George Selwyn's good sayings, to decorate a grotesque house with pie-crust battlements, to procure rare engravings and antique chimney-boards, to match odd gauntlets, to lay out a maze of walks within five acres of ground, these were

[1] There were exceptions. The works of Archdeacon Coxe, a far too neglected historian, were quite scholarly biographies, and these works mark the beginning of the modern historical biography as Macaulay's essays mark the beginning of popular biography. And, of course, Johnson's *Lives of the Poets* are in a sense precursors of Macaulay's biographical essays.

the grave employments of his long life. From these he turned to politics as to an amusement. After the labours of the print-shop and the auction-room, he unbent his mind in the House of Commons. And, having indulged in the recreation of making laws and voting millions, he returned to more important pursuits, to researches after Queen Mary's comb, Wolsey's red hat, the pipe which Van Tromp smoked during his last sea-fight, and the spur which King William struck into the flank of Sorrel.

In everything in which Walpole busied himself, in the fine arts, in literature, in public affairs, he was drawn by some strange attraction from the great to the little, and from the useful to the odd. The politics in which he took the keenest interest were politics scarcely deserving of the name. The growlings of George the Second, the flirtations of Princess Emily with the Duke of Grafton, the amours of Prince Frederic and Lady Middlesex, the squabbles between Gold Stick in waiting and the Master of the Buckhounds, the disagreements between the tutors of Prince George, these matters engaged almost all the attention which Walpole could spare from matters more important still, from bidding for Zinckes and Petitots, from cheapening fragments of tapestry and handles of old lances, from joining bits of painted glass, and from setting up memorials of departed cats and dogs. While he was fetching and carrying the gossip of Kensington Palace and Carlton House, he fancied that he was engaged in politics, and when he recorded that gossip, he fancied that he was writing history.[1]

Rarely before had the public been regaled with such language or treated to the opinions of a scholar so absolutely confident of the morality and wisdom of his judgements. Naturally his essays brought him great popularity and his literary fame grew as he made his way in the world of politics. Macaulay himself, however, did not set great store by these essays: he did not realize that he was helping to create a new taste for short, vivid biographical studies and he himself thought of his work as being merely ephemeral. Yet he drew a deeper satisfaction from these brief excursions into literature than he did from most of his public activities and the fortunate combination

[1] T. B. Macaulay, *Essays*, I, pp. 332–3.

S

of a valuable legacy with his defeat at the General Election of 1847 brought about his decision to retire from politics and devote himself entirely to history. The last twelve years of his life were spent in writing a *History of England* from 1688 to the nineteenth century. It was planned on a monumental scale to challenge comparison with the world's greatest historians—Thucydides, Herodotus and the rest —for Macaulay's ambition was as grandiose as his conception.

He failed even to complete the reign of William III and he was honest enough to admit that his work fell short of the highest achievements in the writing of history. Nevertheless, it remains one of the great historical works in the English language, second only to Gibbon's. And probably at no time in his life could Macaulay have written a better one, for by the time he settled down to write his history his mind was formed, his style perfected and his experience completed. His beliefs were straightforward yet unshakeable. He put his trust in those same virtues which his evangelical father and mother had bred in him: honesty, loyalty, charity, industry and absolute respect for the Christian ideals of marriage and family life. If a man lied, took bribes, dabbled in treason, or fornicated, he was a bad man, so Shaftesbury and Marlborough were bad men; an occasional peccadillo, especially if discreet, could be forgiven, as William III was forgiven for having a mistress, but the combination of immorality and chicanery to be found in Shaftesbury was too much for Macaulay. These simple black and white judgements are couched in absolute terms: the *need* in a Shaftesbury or a James II for the life that they led is never explored.

Macaulay's characters, however, had to pass more than moral tests. They were required to have discovered the right side in politics. Macaulay believed that the prosperity, liberty and political freedom of his own time were the result of those seventeenth-century struggles between King and Parliament, between Church and Puritan, and between Tory and Whig. Prosperity and imperial greatness marched with liberty, toleration and Whig doctrine. William, Prince of Orange, became the embodiment of the good— the hero of the Victorian world and a maker of the nation. Although this estimate contains more truth, perhaps, than many modern critics of Macaulay would allow, it is altogether too simple, too *determined* to carry conviction. It leaves out the muddled, chaotic, stumbling nature of human activity, and in doing so distracts rather than clarifies the reality which Macaulay hoped to depict. And of course he is baffled, totally baffled, by a character as complex as the 2nd Earl of Sunderland who, after acting as James II's confidant almost to the Revolution, reappears shortly after it as the trusted adviser of William III himself.

To some extent historical events, too, had to be forced into the same mechanical pattern and they are judged by Macaulay as men are judged, according to whether they aided or thwarted the Whig cause. It was quite impossible for him to see that the Tories were largely responsible for the Revolution of 1688 although the facts stared him in the face. Indeed for a modern scholar his history of political management is naïve and jejune, weak in analysis, and unscholarly in detail. He attempted the impossible task of forcing the politics of William's reign into a rigid dichotomy of Whig versus Tory. Once more his love of clarity bedevilled the truth. He would have men and events clear cut and therefore got them wrong. The rigidity of his intellect and the simplicity of his heart are implicit in almost every page that he wrote.

Glaring as these faults are, the *History* remains a great book. By the time Macaulay was forty-seven he was naturally fully aware of his literary abilities. He knew that he possessed admirable skill in narrative, for his fabulous and accurate memory and his disciplined schematic mind could hold the complete, detailed story that he wished to tell, ready for his pen. His great set pieces, like the Siege of Londonderry or the Massacre of Glencoe, were written straight out of his head, once he had digested and memorized his materials. This, of course, gave them a wonderful fluency and unity. And although he frequently altered his words and rewrote considerably, he never had to verify the detail which he knew with such absolute certainty.

Furthermore, he had developed his style to the point where it was a complete reflection of his thought and feeling so that the full flavour of his truculent, virile personality could be savoured in every paragraph. Few historians have been so easy to read or so easy to remember once read. The authority with which he wrote induced a ready acceptance of his vision of history in the mind of his reader. Also his great intellectual powers and his personal experience of politics enabled him to re-create the political debates of William's reign in a way which can, perhaps, never be bettered. He gives the excitement of a battle to the struggles in the Commons. In some aspects of his history, too, Macaulay showed great originality. He realized from his knowledge of his own times that the political structure of a country is deeply influenced by its economic interests and by the pattern of its society, so he devoted considerable space to depicting the social habits of the late Stuart times and gave many pages, and very admirable ones, to the foundation of the Bank of England and the Recoinage.

In spite of all the criticism which can be levelled against it, the *History* remains a great work of literature and scholarship. And so do Macaulay's essays. In a hundred years England has not produced an historian of his stature. He was an intellectual giant and although he lacked the imagination, the poetry, the sense of tragedy which is present in the very greatest writers, these were almost all that he lacked. Every other quality that a great writer needs he possessed in abundance: he was able to project his mind and personality into words so forcibly that his history has become a part of our common heritage. And what some choose to regard as his prejudices command both admiration and respect. He believed in liberal virtues and faith in man's capacity to control and order not only history but the world about him. Although this led him to many false and intolerant judgements, they should not blind critics to the basic truth of Macaulay's conviction. In the material world in which he took such optimistic delight, man has made undeniable progress by the use of those qualities that Macaulay possessed in such abundance —memory, order, intelligence.

1956

JOHN EVELYN

THE timing of these two books,[1] doubtless accidental, is excellent
—one displays Evelyn as he wished to be known to his descendants,
the other reveals Evelyn when he was less conscious of the effect
which he wished to produce. The bulk of the diary has been known
for a century and a half but only in a careless transcript from which
a great deal was omitted. The letters which form the basis of Mr.
Hiscock's brilliant book have never been used before. They were
not available to scholars until Mr. John Evelyn generously deposited
them at Christ Church. The full diary and the letters permit a fresh
assessment of Evelyn's character and worth.

Mr. de Beer has been working on this edition of Evelyn's diary
for nearly thirty years—a task which could only have been completed by one who was not so much devoted to Evelyn as obsessed
by him. And not only by Evelyn, but also by the fascinating and
compulsive joys of exact scholarship. The result is monumental and
final. No other scholar need devote a fraction of his life to the
editorial problems raised by Evelyn's diary—as far as they can ever
be answered, they have been by Mr. de Beer. The annotations are
excellent and the index beyond praise. The introduction gives a
fascinating account of the methods used by the editor and an
astonishingly evasive discussion of Evelyn's character, for Mr. de
Beer ignores Evelyn's correspondence and the recent, and most
revealing, researches of Mr. Hiscock.

Although it may seem ungracious to carp at so devoted and so
valuable a labour, yet it does seem to me that Mr. de Beer, along

[1] *The Diary of John Evelyn*, edited by E. S. de Beer (O.U.P., 6 vols., £15 15s.); *John
Evelyn and His Family Circle*, by W. G. Hiscock (Routledge and Kegan Paul, 25s.).

with so many other recent editors, has carried some of his annotations to a point of pedantry that is almost ludicrous. Does any reader need to know that a bracket has been inserted to close a parenthesis, that Evelyn put a bracket the wrong way round, or even that 'secretary' may read 'scecretary'? In spite of the excellence of the Oxford University Press's typography, the weight of annotation grows as tedious to the eye as Evelyn's endless abstracts of sermons to the mind.

And what of Evelyn himself and his diary? The latter possesses little value for the historian—most facts are better known from other sources: even the vast abstracts of sermons, which constitute the bulk of the new material, add little or nothing to church history. Although Evelyn moved on the fringe of great events his discretion was absolute. He dined frequently with Pepys, but he recounts next to nothing of his conversation or his views. The same is true of his statesmen friends. Godolphin was a lifelong friend and for most of the time at the heart of politics. Evelyn relates the banalities of his association with him—their dinners, their casual meetings and interests; for the rest there is silence. The same is true of his other highly placed friends—Clarendon, Sunderland and the others. Doubtless reasons of prudence restrained Evelyn. His nature tended to secrecy and discretion, and, to put it mildly, he lacked courage. During the Civil War, although young, vigorous, rich and a royalist, he slipped abroad to safety. Curiously enough, however, during the plague he behaved with exemplary fortitude—a Commissioner for the Sick and Wounded, he resolutely refused to leave London and his duty. Once caught up in danger Evelyn could live through it, even though he was unable deliberately to choose a violent hazard. Certainly in a politically tempestuous and treacherous world in which some of his friends had finished on Tower Hill, he could not bring himself to commit his opinions to paper. In consequence much of the diary is disappointing and its value is less than it might have been. Nevertheless, it has two virtues. One is that Evelyn was a cool, observant man and his descriptions of other men's characters are often excellent—indeed, better than Pepys's, who, unlike Evelyn, could not meet men like Sandwich on equal social terms and so became too involved in his own feelings to observe them dispassionately. The other is that Evelyn was very typical in his interests—his curiosity, his book collections, his passion for new architecture, his dabbling in horticulture and science, his thirst for religion, are all very much of his time and class—and his diary is an excellent illustration of the intellectual attitudes of a cultivated gentleman of the seventeenth century.

Yet the diary's reputation has been inflated. Historically of small importance, it also lacks human interest. Evelyn's cool nature was given to concealment—not an attribute which makes for a good diarist. He lacked the outward-going, experience-loving temperament of a Pepys, nor did he possess the capacity for self-examination of a Rousseau or a St. Augustine. He was too intent on appearing to be a good man to reveal himself as a human being.

His diary, it is true, deceived the Victorians. They loved it, displaying as it did, they thought, the life of a good and pious example, an impression which Evelyn himself was keen to make. He wished to patch over the frailties of his own nature and present himself to his posterity as a gentleman of upright conduct and religious inclination. Mr. Hiscock shows in this brilliant book of his the far less respectable but far more human truth. Unfortunately for Evelyn, his correspondence as well as his diary has survived. And now against his lifelong addiction to sermons may be placed his facility at light erotic verse (is it not odd that the four smutty lines, inadvertently written into his diary and erased by Evelyn, should have been left out of this meticulous edition in which every misplaced comma is noted?). Evelyn posed as the apostle of seraphic love and in his *Life of Mrs. Godolphin* edified the world with his account of the spiritual ecstasies which he enjoyed with Margaret Blagge. Mr. Hiscock demonstrates, however, that his ecstasies were not so purely spiritual as he would have us believe. His love was possessive and selfish. He did his utmost to prevent Margaret from marrying Sidney Godolphin, and even tried to bring her to his home at Sayes Court to live. His confession of sins indicates that his thoughts about her may have been as human as they were intense.

Throughout these spiritual infidelities he neglected his wife and family, and from his casual references to his wife in his diary no one would suspect that she was highly intelligent, lively and well balanced. Her amused and cynical attitude to her husband's foibles was too dangerously near to exposure for him to enjoy her company for long. Her letters to her brother-in-law, William Glanville, with whom Evelyn quarrelled not about a point of theology as the diary would have us believe, but for the much more mundane reasons arising from the settlement of the Wotton estate, shows her nature to have been frank, open and direct. How the serpentine Evelyn must have disliked her, and he took his revenge by scarcely mentioning his wife in his diary. And who, from this diary, would guess that his son was an oaf for whom his father whined and wheedled until he obtained a minor place for him from the long-suffering Godolphin? But the diary is all equivocation as far as Evelyn and his family are concerned, for this self-righteous example of piety was alive with spiritual pride, a sin far, far more grievous than the fleshy peccadilloes of his friend, Samuel Pepys. And yet that is not the full story. Men loved his company. Pepys himself, who was a shrewd judge of characters whom he could meet on equal terms, reckoned him one of the most ingenious and agreeable of men. Evelyn possessed, as one may see from his portraits, great charm, a quality whose power, so effective in life, vanishes at death. Most of the curious convolutions of Evelyn's character lead ultimately to that vain self-regard which was the core of his temperament. He had at last achieved an odd, singular, but perhaps well-deserved, fate. At a time when Mr. Hiscock's revelation of his hypocrisies has made him a much more interesting human being, his diary has been rendered almost unreadable by the herculean scholarship of Mr. de Beer.

1957

POPE: THE DWARF OF GENIUS

FIRSTLY, a salute to the Oxford University Press! For many years now they have been producing superlative editions of the letters of the great masters of English literature—Jane Austen, Thackeray, George Eliot, Dr. Johnson and the rest—and there are many more yet to come. They are the product of the best traditions of English and American scholarship—nothing is missed, not a scrap; every allusion is remorselessly hunted down; and an index, of exemplary complexity, usually takes up the final volume. To some these seried volumes, bristling with scholarship, seem too lavish, a waste of time, energy and money, but not to me. Scholarship which will last for centuries is always worthwhile, a task worthy of a University Press. Far better that scholars of English literature should be thus employed than in wasting their talents on the fatuities of literary criticism, or, worse, the criticism of criticism.

Professor Sherburn has been assiduously collecting Pope's letters[1] for more than twenty years, and although his haul of new material is considerable in bulk, it is, on the whole, trivial in quality, but there are a few letters which help to elucidate a little further the strange ravelled character of Pope, that dwarf of singular genius.

*   *   *

All understanding of Pope must begin with his deformity, an ugly, terrible sight which he, as much as his friends, wished to ignore but could not. Like an ineradicable dye it stained all thought, all feeling. Deformity is commonly hideous in its effects. It corrodes character,

---

[1] *The Correspondence of Alexander Pope* (5 vols.), edited by George Sherburn (O.U.P., £10 10s.).

leading to deceit, treachery, malignity and false living; and as often as not vitiates those entangled in the sufferer's life as much as the sufferer himself. So it was with Pope. Yet cruel as was his fate, he also had his luck; luck to be born with a poetic gift as certain, as infallible as mathematical genius, a perfect instrument for the expression of his vast abilities; and luck, too, to be an Augustan, to belong to a world which looked to poetry for that social criticism in which it revelled. But, of course, Pope was far more than a satirist. He used the modes of his time to express his strong emotional nature. His poetry eased his own heart as much as Keats's did in his Odes. But Pope's heart needed to be eased of hate not suffering, detestation not pity, emotions which are as much a part of human experience as compassion. This savage, brutal attack on Sporus:

> Sporus, that mere white curd of Ass's milk?
> Satire or sense, alas! can Sporus feel
> Who breaks a butterfly upon a wheel?
> Yet let me flap this bug with gilded wings,
> This painted child of dirt, that stinks and stings;

which mounts in twenty magnificent lines to a crescendo of vituperation, is more, far more, than a brilliant satire of Lord Hervey. It expresses hatred, that intense loathing which can develop between one human male and another, an experience as common and as deep as romantic love between the sexes, but far less readily admitted. In discharging his venom so brilliantly Pope was rising above mere satire, giving a universality to hate.

★   ★   ★

There was a sweeter side to Pope's nature and some moments of forgetfulness, times when the frustration and the pain and the ape-like world were forgotten; times when the gay intelligence sparkled to its own delight. To these we owe the felicity of the *Rape of the Lock* and many of the minor poems. If he could, Pope would always have had it so, for he longed for respect, friendship, love. An adored and deceiving image of himself lurks mockingly in his poetry and his letters; it is that of a good, noble, incorruptible man, free from sycophancy, just in his dealings, loyal to his friends, direct in his purpose. Nor do the lines that express these high sentiments ring entirely hollow. They are a part of Pope's dream world, a part of that loving consolation by which he contrived to ease his pain. And, of course, such admirable virtues provided a self-deceiving excuse for his vast and rancorous hate; for the good surely have a right, a duty, to hate the bad. He could not, would not, recognize that his loathing sprang from his desolate, fatal isolation, from his little, twisted body. Only rarely were his defences broken; once they were pierced by his love for Martha Blount, and in *Eloisa and Abelard* he acknowledged his own tragic circumstance:

> Hearts so touch'd, so pierced, so lost as mine
> Ere such a soul regains its peaceful state,
> How often must it love, how often hate!
> How often hope, despair, resent, regret,
> Conceal, disdain—do all things but forget.

These moments of poignant insight were, alas, rare. Could Pope have lived with himself, face to face, he might have been one of the greatest poets of all time. The sight was too grievous, the knowledge too intolerable, and both his nature and the age in which he lived turned him away from a direct expression to a social criticism in which the ferocity of personal feeling could be transmuted into moral condemnation.

★　★　★

Although the basic structure of Pope's character was always clear enough from his poetry, his letters alone present the full picture of his strangely involuted temperament. They do not, of course, reveal Pope in direct terms any more than his poetry does. They are guarded letters, and, alas, very dull ones. They convey little. Pope's mother lived to an immense age. He was devoted to her. He mentions her time and time again (usually her illnesses which prevented him so frequently from gratifying his friends). And she remains a word, 'mother'. No picture of her is ever drawn; she might have been any old woman. Quite fruitless, too, for anyone to go to these letters in the hope of gaining fresh insight into Pope's fascinating friends—Swift, Gay, Arbuthnot, Bolingbroke and the rest. Neither character nor anecdote interested him at all. There is no sparkle in his prose, and in the dull and wearisome journey through this Sahara of correspondence it is a relief to reach a letter from Swift, from Gay, from Lady Mary Wortley Montagu or even from Bolingbroke.

No, these letters are not for the general reader unless he happens to be a connoisseur of human temperament. For him the sandy journey offers a rich reward, for the Pope of the letters makes the Pope of the poetry seem as simple as a child. Obviously he was addicted to double-dealing as compulsively as a kleptomaniac to stealing, and like other practitioners of vice, his taste grew more complicated with age. No sooner had he, as a favour, deposited manuscripts in Lord Oxford's famous library, than his lordship found that the fact was being used to justify Pope's veracity in public combat with a publisher, a fact Pope forgot to mention to Oxford. He asked, or rather begged, his noble friends to treat him like a domestic servant, but it was they who fetched and carried for him, parcelling up his Homer and protecting him from libel. He servilely ate Walpole's dinners, whilst consorting with his enemies. Having contrived presentation at Court, he immediately parodied the Royal Family. He wrote anonymous letters to secure the publication of his own correspondence; brought out two editions, one official and one pirated, both by himself. He cheated his life-long friend Swift and in the end very nearly double-crossed himself. There are other odd and very unpleasing characteristics. His delight in prevarication, his relish of the half-given lie, and his gloating in obscenity. Add to this his intelligence, discernible even in these letters, and remember his exceptional charm—the fine features, the brilliant eyes. He knew that he possessed the power to exploit it. He could, and did, entrance as well as disturb. And further, he was sensitive to the pain of others, quick to help, generous, attentive, and so, perhaps, lulled into security those he had not intended to betray. From these letters emerges a creature stranger far than his poetry reveals—a tortured, tortuous being who carried the force of genius in the tiny body of a dwarf—a fate which neither fame nor achievement, love nor friendship, but only deceit and chicanery, betrayal and revenge, could sweeten or alleviate.

1956

DANIEL DEFOE AND *THE JOURNAL*
OF THE PLAGUE YEAR

I

In 1721 the plague swept across Europe from the Levant and reached Marseilles. Men, women and children began to die like flies in Provence and it seemed as if another great epidemic was going to decimate Europe. The Dutch imposed a strict quarantine on all shipping from the East—even burning cargoes and making sailors swim ashore naked. The English government, equally perturbed, placed an embargo upon shipping from the Mediterranean. This irritated the merchant classes for memories of the Great Plague of London in 1665 had grown dim; the restrictions threatened serious loss of trade and the ministers of George I were accused of behaving hysterically. So sharp was public criticism that the government requested the help of the ablest bishop in the Church—Thomas Gibson, afterwards Bishop of London—who wrote two trenchant pamphlets on the gravity of the danger. Whether or not they also asked Daniel Defoe, the ablest of English journalists, to help them is not known. It is, however, possible, for at that time he was secretly working for the government and being paid by them. His *Journal of the Plague Year* may have been his response to the ministry's needs but he was so shrewd a journalist that he may have realized his opportunity without any prompting, for the Great Plague of 1665 had been one of the most vivid experiences of Defoe's childhood. Whatever the cause the result was a masterpiece.

Defoe had been born about 1660 in Cripplegate, London, the son of James Foe, a butcher. The circumstances of Defoe's birth and early education were humble rather than poor. He changed his name to the aristocratic De Foe later in his life for he was an ambitious man, not only hungry for fame but also for social acceptance; the former he acquired, the latter eluded him. His father was a dissenter and he intended Daniel for the ministry, sending him to be educated at the academy of Charles Martin who afterwards became the first Vice-President of Harvard. But Defoe felt no vocation. He took to trade. At first he was successful, probably he ventured abroad to Spain and Portugal. His business prospered enough for merchants to trust him to the tune of £1,700 for which amount he went bankrupt in 1692. By that time he had lived a roving, dangerous life. He took part in the abortive rebellion of the Duke of Monmouth against James II and Defoe was lucky to escape with his life. This was in 1685, the year after he had married—which unlike his business enterprises did not end in disaster, although his wife had plenty of tribulations to bear. Prudently Defoe had chosen a rich merchant's daughter, Mary Tuffley, who had a dowry of £3,700—not that it lasted long in Defoe's slippery hands.

The flight of James II in 1688 made Defoe hasten once more to arms. He joined a volunteer regiment that acted as William III's escort. Indeed riding his horse to the Guildhall of London with the great merchant princes of the City about him made success seem near. Disaster proved closer. By 1692 Defoe's creditors would stand no more. Suit after suit was filed against him. Defoe's pitfall lay in his imagination. It was too wild for a merchant. And his character was far too unstable. He loved a gamble whether on a horse-race or the speculative purchase of a parcel of civet cats.[1] Before him sparkled the mirage of great riches and of the honours that came to a great London merchant—Alderman, Sheriff, Lord Mayor, Knighthood. He knew well enough what was needed for success—in all his works he sang the praises of those nonconformist virtues—thrift, industry, caution, modesty—that his father and schoolmaster had dinned into him. In vain. Defoe was born a Projector. He borrowed recklessly and any shift would do to keep himself afloat. And the law helped him for in his day it thought the dupe as much to blame as the duper.

---

[1] These were as valuable in the seventeenth century as mink in the twentieth. They secreted a substance—musk—that was used in the manufacture of perfume. Not only did Defoe default on the purchase of the cats but also he involved his mother-in-law for £400.

Yet shipwreck was inevitable. He talked his creditors round with promises and avoided a debtor's prison. Having failed as a merchant, he took to manufacture. He went off to the marshes of Tilbury and made bricks and tiles. He prospered enough to pay some of the debts and flourished like a gentleman.

In the 1690's the air was full of projects and inventions. It was an atmosphere that suited Defoe like a glove. His schemes, put forward with all the skill of his superbly realistic imagination, attracted the attention of the government. He became a known man, friendly with the great. He revelled in a new world. He started to write pamphlets, some for government pay, some to release the teeming ideas that his excited imagination threw off like fireworks. He was a natural writer, fluent, direct, trenchant. He discovered too that he had a happy turn for doggerel. Sneers from the Tories about William III's Dutch birth led him to write *The True-Born Englishman*, whose vigour may be judged by this description of England:

> We have been Europe's sink, the jakes where she
> Voids all her offal outcast progeny.

His poem achieved fabulous success, quickly running through twelve authorized and nine pirated editions. Defoe wallowed in the notoriety. With his brick works thriving and his sales soaring, he lived high. His ebullience proved his undoing. William III died; Queen Anne succeeded, and with her the High-Church Tories came to power. Defoe pulled their leg. He wrote a masterpiece of irony—*The Shortest Way with Dissenters*. Written as if by a Tory, it solemnly recommended that nonconformists be exterminated. At first people were taken in; then a gale of laughter swept the country. The infuriated government ordered Defoe's arrest. They caught him and put him in the pillory where the public treated him like the hero he was. But jail followed. He hated it. He sold himself to the government and became a sort of spy. He travelled up and down England, reporting all that his sharp, observant eye and quick intelligence seized upon. Later he used these experiences to create one of the greatest travel books written about England—*A Tour Through the Whole Island of Great Britain*. Spying was not Defoe's sole task for the ministry; it had also bought his pen. As well as pamphlets, he wrote a newspaper, *The Review*. This he wrote almost entirely single-handed, often in impossible conditions, three times a week for seven years—a truly astounding achievement. This alone would have given Defoe an immortal place in English letters, even had he never written a novel, for *The Review* can be compared without disadvantage to Addison's *Spectator*.

Governments fell, the dynasty changed, the years passed and Defoe lived a hand to mouth existence. He dodged creditors for a time, deceived both his government and the opposition, and received pay from both. But he was nearing sixty, an ageing man of brilliance, marred by his own unstable temperament. And then suddenly his genius flowered. Between 1718–23 he wrote *Robinson Crusoe*, *Moll Flanders* and *The Journal of the Plague Year*, all works of great and enduring quality, as well as several others that were about as fine. And the flame died as quickly as it had flared. He lived for a time rather grandly in Stoke Newington but soon the creditors crept back, old quarrels restarted, new ones flourished. He had to go into hiding, a pathetic old man dodging from cellar to garret. And he died on April 24, 1731, in lodgings; alone, without friends or relatives. He had lived a strange life at variance with the principles in which he believed, overwhelmed by instincts he could not resist, but endowed with such talent that his name will live as long as the English language lasts.

II

Defoe did not achieve acceptance among the writers of his day. Addison called him 'a false, shuffling, prevaricating rascal'; Swift sneered at him; Pope scorned him; the majority ignored him. His work was alien to the polished elegance that they admired. His literary gifts were as great as theirs, if not greater, certainly they were more original, but he wrote for a different public. He did not write for a *côterie*, for the fashionable, polished upper middle-class or for the aristocracy. He wrote, like Bunyan before him, for shop-keepers, artisans, clerks, yeomen, for ordinary men and women, and he wrote as one of them. Moll Flanders, Colonel Jack, Robinson Crusoe, the saddler in the *Journal of the Plague Year* are all drawn from this class. Defoe is sensitive to their experience; he knew the horrors of poverty, the terrors of sickness, the joy of a windfall, the wonder of luck. He had known the frightening insecurity of those who had to work to live. There is little romance in Defoe's world, little affection and less love; pity there is and charity, but the excitement, the tension in his writing, springs from his concern with success. Will Robinson Crusoe survive? Will Moll Flanders achieve respectability? How will the saddler live through the plague? Cheating fate, getting the better of circumstances, surviving, these are the major preoccupations of Defoe's characters. And it is these natural concerns of ordinary men and women that give such exceptional verisimilitude to his characters whether they are pitched on a desert island, shipped to Virginia or caught in a plague. Defoe's eye was quick and observant; the human scene entranced him and he could report it in direct, vivid prose. Such a natural realist often used real events and historical material so that it is at times difficult to distinguish fact from fiction in Defoe's work.

This is particularly true of his *Journal of the Plague Year*. Some of his sources have been traced with certainty—*The Weekly Bills of Mortality*; *A Collection of Very Valuable and Scarce Pieces Relating to the late Plague in the Year 1665*; Dr. Nathaniel Hodges's *Loimologia, a Historical Account of the Plague*. These were all republished in 1720 or 1721 and must have been on Defoe's desk as he wrote. And it is almost equally certain that he made considerable use of an old pamphlet, *God's Terrible Voice in the City* by Thomas Vincent, printed in 1666.[1] From these Defoe built up the main structure of his narrative and the general outline of the plague—the way it swept from West to East; how many people took to living in ships, moored downstream in the Thames, to avoid contact with the City; the desertion of their town houses by the rich, and the flight of the poor to the woods and forests about London; the alarm of the country folk; the emptiness of the City's streets; the shut houses marked with a great red cross; the terrible carts of the dead; the yawning grave-pits; the bells that never ceased to toll. These things he learned, but on them his imagination worked, stimulating, perhaps, recollections of his remote childhood or recalling tales told him by his elders long ago. On this material, whether true or invented, his creative genius got to work and peopled plague-stricken London

[1] See Watson Nicholson, *The Historical Sources of Defoe's Journal of the Plague Year*, Boston, 1919.

T

with intensely human characters, but ordinary men and women caught in a tragedy they could scarcely comprehend. We hear again the shrieks of the dying and the lamentations of the living, witness the chicanery, the twists and cheats of men desperate for life and the heroism, the calm acceptance of fate, of the few ennobled by suffering. For the Londoners of Georgian England, waiting for the plague, Defoe's book must have been terrifying reading. But the plague never came and instead of a caution for the present, Defoe's *Journal* became a memorial to the past.[1]

No one knows why London was not attacked by bubonic plague after 1665. This scourge had swept England repeatedly since the Black Death; after the Great Plague of London only small and isolated outbreaks occurred. The disease can be transmitted by the flea of the black rat which was gradually driven out of London by the brown or Hanoverian rat. Some scientists believe this to be the reason for the plague's disappearance; others will not accept it for it took generations for the brown rat to become dominant. A few historians believe that the Great Fire of 1666 cleansed London, but this did not touch the worst plague-spots—St. Giles or Whitechapel. Modern parasitologists incline to the view that, after three centuries, human beings acquired some immunity and the bacillus itself become less virulent. Certainly the plague of 1665 was both less violent and less widespread than many other visitations. Whatever the reason, it never returned.

From the hygienic comfort of the twentieth century, the terrible calamity which Defoe described with such accurate, vivid realism seems remote, an experience that never can be repeated. But such suffering can still visit mankind—the great influenza epidemic of 1919 killed far more people. The terror for Defoe's London lay in the awful concentration of the disease. In his pages a metropolis dies before our eyes; the streets empty, grass grows where life reigned. *The Journal of the Plague Year* is a tale of horror, told, however, by one of the great masters of realism.

1960

---

[1] Some scholars hold that the 1721 disease was a virulent form of smallpox and not bubonic plague.

HENRY FIELDING
AND *JONATHAN WILD*

HENRY FIELDING's great-grandfather was an earl, one grandfather an archdeacon, the other a judge, his father a soldier who, in the fullness of time, became a general. By ancestry, therefore, Fielding would seem to belong to the highest circles of eighteenth-century English society. In fact, he lived a hand to mouth existence, often debt-ridden, friendly with few of the great, but drawn to men like William Hogarth, the painter, whose savage satires on tawdriness, cruelty and poverty portrayed a world which Fielding knew at first hand. Success played hide and seek with Fielding and affluence came but slowly, so slowly that Death was already lurking in the wings by the time Fielding had really prospered. His was a tough life, and more often than not a sad one, yet made endurable and significant by the huge appetite, the wonderful gusto, the irrepressible humanity which Fielding brought to living. He loved human beings, particularly the odd, the gullible, the transparent man of good intentions. He knew enough of the baseness of men to guard his spirit with an ironic shield but his irony never crushed his instinctive wonder or turned his hope to despair.

He was born on April 22, 1707, the eldest son of Edmund Fielding, a soldier of fortune, active in Marlborough's wars, by Sarah, the daughter of Sir Henry Gould, the judge. Something of an heiress, his mother inherited a small estate which her father carefully entailed on his grandchildren to the exclusion of their feckless father. By the time Henry was eleven, his mother was dead and his father, who had already dissipated what money he had by gambling, soon married again, this time an Italian and a Roman Catholic. He quarrelled violently with Lady Gould who started proceedings against him partly to get the little estate out of his clutches and partly to shield the children from the Roman Catholicism of their step-mother. The father lost, and Henry, who had been packed off to Eton, was brought up with his sisters by his grandmother, partly in Salisbury and partly in London. His father went on living his rackety life, running through two more wives but climbing slowly up the military ladder, and always spending any money that he could lay his hands on. Nevertheless Fielding remained attached to his father, thoughtless, unreliable, probably an inveterate gambler though he was. Such a father may have strengthened Fielding's craving for the simple, good life, lived in a tranquil countryside, but at the same time he introduced him to the wild, dissolute, intensely provocative life of London that always held Fielding in its grip: thereby creating that dichotomy of illusion and reality that is one of the most attractive features of Fielding's novels.

He left Eton at eighteen, proceeding neither to the University nor the Grand Tour. Aristocratic origins he might have, but near poverty was his lot. He tried to alleviate it by carrying off a young fifteen-year-old heiress, Sarah Andrew, but her trustee preferred his own kith and kin and Fielding only succeeded in making a nuisance of himself. But London was his destiny: neither his nature nor his abilities would permit him to settle down as a country gentleman of small estate, even had he had the means to buy one.

London in the 1720's was a rip-roaring place; a vivid contrast between extravagant luxury and grinding poverty, the London of Hogarth's *Rake's Progress*, *Marriage à la Mode*, *Beer Street* and *Gin Alley*, tough, brutal, savage yet full of colour and life: luxurious and magnificent for the rich, harsh and disease ridden for the poor. It was a world in which the crafty, the sly and the hypocritical could get away with deceit and double-dealing, where the good-natured, honest man could easily be overborne, where morality was at a discount. The law was slow, expensive and witnesses not difficult to suborn. The vices and follies of mankind were written large across the metropolis. The great and powerful could exercise, usually un-rebuked, petty tyranny and the good man had to find satisfaction not in public acclaim but in private knowledge of his right behaviour. Towering over this riotous, rich, rough, ruthless society was 'The

Great Man' as Sir Robert Walpole, the King's minister, was known.
He ran politics, the Court and Parliament. Few men had ever
engrossed so much power as he or roused up such a vigorous or so
gifted a literary opposition. Swift, Pope, Gay had all tried to get
favours from Sir Robert, all had failed. So they poured out their
hate in some of the most brilliant satire England has known—
Gulliver's Travels, The Dunciad, The Beggar's Opera were all aimed
at the Great Man. In ballads, pamphlets, burlesques and plays
Walpole was mercilessly lampooned to the delight of Londoners
who enjoyed this novel literary war with the gusto it deserved.

This was an exciting literary world that young Fielding entered
in 1729. He had spent eighteen months at Leyden University study-
ing literature and he felt fully equipped to take London by storm.
This he failed to do, but for the next eight years he wrote play after
play (twenty-six in nine years), many successful, a few original, but
all of them relying for their popularity on an ever-increasing boldness in their attacks on Walpole. Not only did Fielding lampoon
'The Great Man' and his political methods but he attacked the Court
as well; and so long as these plays were scandalous, they attracted an
audience, and made Fielding prosperous. So he lived high with open-
handed generosity, every bit as reckless a spendthrift or as gay a
dog as his old father. Marriage, however, to Charlotte Cradock of
Salisbury, sobered him. Fielding could almost certainly have supported himself and his growing family as a hard-working dramatist
and journalist, but Walpole brought a stop to his career by instituting
a censorship of plays and theatres in 1737.

This drove Fielding into the career of a lawyer. He was called to
the Bar and practised with indifferent success for many years on the
Western circuit. He eked out his living by continuing his vituperative
attacks on Walpole in the chief opposition newspaper *The Champion*
which he edited.

After Walpole's fall in 1742 the opposition came to power and
after many years of devoted work in their support Fielding at last
obtained a crumb of patronage. He took the oaths as a magistrate on
January 12, 1749, and remained at Bow Street, Westminster, until
ill-health drove him to seek a blander climate in Portugal. By then,
1754, he was a dying man.

These years as a magistrate were the years which established

Fielding as one of the greatest figures in English literature. He worked hard and long on questions of poverty and crime. He pressed the government for reforms, he produced the rudiments of an effective police force for the metropolis. He was tireless in his struggle with the terrible human conditions which his duties constantly brought to his notice. Yet this work proved insufficient for Fielding: neither his success nor his fame gave him sufficient satisfaction. There was in Fielding an unease which neither happy marriage nor a successful career could allay. The happy marriage was blighted by his wife's early death and his marriage to her servant, Mary Daniel, assuaged but did not eradicate his grief. Knowing the force of his own genius, the fact that he had to earn his bread and butter doling out punishment for thieves, rogues, whores and ne'er-do-wells probably fed rather than soothed his restless nature, and drove him to create.

Fielding was haunted by a sense of life's injustice—good men were battered by misfortune, yet bad men prospered; society itself conspired to help the sly, the corrupt, the superficial and the cynical and to blight the search for simple happiness which Fielding felt should be the reward of a life well spent. His work underlined the truth of this attitude time and time again. And it showed him another facet of human nature that he returned to in his books over and over again. Fielding was fascinated by those human characters whose spirit remained cheerful and unsullied in spite of disaster— Parson Adams in *Joseph Andrews*, Heartfree in *Jonathan Wild*, Tom Jones himself and, of course, Amelia. Cruel misfortunes, brought about by the inhumanity of others, were a commonplace in Fielding's day when a rabid competition for gain flourished unchecked by law. Corruption sprouted like a weed: and justice for the poor or the weak was not easy to come by. Too often power was enjoyed by men with inclinations to tyranny. A few virtuous, generous human beings remained unsullied in this harsh world or succeeded in withstanding its temptations or its tyrannies. Less morally well-endowed men and women overcame the buffets of fortune either through sheer animal spirits (in Tom Jones virtue and animal spirits were combined) or by an ironic attitude to the human condition. This was Fielding's own armour against the cruelties and disappointments of life. For those who remained good or stayed happy

Fielding felt not only affection and respect but in his novels he
endowed such characters with an epic quality.

Unlike his contemporaries, Richardson and Defoe, Fielding did
not despise the epic. Not only was he devoted to Homer and Virgil
but also to Cervantes. Fundamentally Fielding loved life far more
than he was horrified by its cruelties and deceits. His morality was
conventionally Christian, his philosophy sincerely stoic, but his
instincts were sharp and urgent. Tom Jones, whose nature was
virtuous, could not resist women of easy virtue who wanted him
ardently. A broad tolerance came easily to Fielding and few of his
characters are unrelievedly vile. Even Jonathan Wild, in whom
Fielding set out to portray the worst of men, is made human by his
gusto, by the huge enjoyment he derived from being himself.

Fielding's novels met with immediate acclaim but neither his
novels nor his unremitting journalism brought him sufficient financial reward and day after day found him sitting in his court dealing
with the riff-raff of London's most vicious quarter—Covent Garden.
Although he was widely admired and possessed many friends in
society as well as in literary circles yet he lived a retired life. In early
middle age ill-health seized him, and he died on October 8, 1754, in
Portugal where he had gone in the hope that a milder climate might
relieve his sickness. He was forty-seven years of age yet his achievement places him with Defoe and Richardson as one of the great
prose writers of the early eighteenth century.

———

Jonathan Wild is not his best book; some critics place it third, others
fourth, although Saintsbury preferred it even to *Tom Jones*. It is
closer to Defoe than any other work of Fielding, and, as with so
much of Defoe's work, it is a mixture of fact and fiction. There was
a Jonathan Wild. He did lead a gang. He was a fence. He did suborn
witnesses, secure the conviction of Blueskin, and ruin the innocent.
Jonathan Wild was hanged at Tyburn before one of London's
largest crowds. But there was no Heartfree, no Tishy, no Count.
The historic Jonathan Wild had aroused tremendous public excitement during his hey-day in the 1720's. Before Fielding, journalists
had begun to use the story of Jonathan Wild as a parable and one

that was easy to read. Wild equals Walpole. Both are 'great' men; one heads a gang, the other a party; both live by corrupting and bribing others; both are without public or private morality. But most of the ephemeral literature, even when used for political ends, was poor stuff compared to Fielding's masterpiece where the parallel with Walpole, never explicit but always implicit, is handled with splendid irony and dexterity. Fielding castigates greatness, the pursuit of power and riches at the expense of virtue; he belabours indifference to evil and to suffering. Fielding also seeks to lay bare the cruelties of London's underworld which even by 1742 he knew well enough. Fielding brings alive Wild's world of highwaymen, cut-throats and cut-purses, pimps and whores, perjurers and false witnesses. He paints a terrifying picture of justice as well as jails in Walpolean England. We are never left in doubt of the terrible fate which could quickly overwhelm not only the feckless and the wicked but also the innocent. In this savage jungle Wild moves with the certainty of a leopard; killing without compunction, never missing a chance of a swindle or a theft, even to picking the Ordinary of Newgate's pockets as he was about to swing into eternity.

In contrast to this world of Wild's, Fielding depicts Heartfree a good man with a monumentally virtuous wife and a dedicated apprentice as noble as himself. As a simple foil to Wild these are excellent but they remain pasteboard characters, unbelievable in their simplicity and their virtue. Wild may be an ironic caricature but he radiates life and at times illuminates the ferocious human scene with shafts of savage wisdom: such as, 'Not to trust him who hath deceived you nor who knows he hath been deceived by you'; 'To forgive no enemy: but to be cautious and often dilatory in revenge'; 'That a good name, like money, must be parted with, or at least greatly risked, in order to bring the owner any advantage'. All wise maxims that must have been second nature to the politicians of Walpole's day, in which men rather than measures dominated politics. And so *Jonathan Wild* is one of the odder great books of English fiction. Like Defoe's *Journal of the Plague Year* it is partly true, an incredible story, based on facts. It is also a brilliant political satire on Sir Robert Walpole at the moment of his fall from power. And it acquires universality by being yet two further things—a straightforward portrait of London low-life, high-pitched in the manner of Hogarth's satirical pictures, yet realistic and close to Fielding's own experience. Finally it is a morality, an ironic, bitter condemnation of human weakness by a man whose experience as a lawyer and whose insight as an artist gave him a rare knowledge of the follies and wickedness of mankind. To appreciate this fine book at all levels needs a little knowledge and a little patience but the rewards more than compensate for the effort. Once read, *Jonathan Wild* is never forgotten. Like Falstaff or Pickwick, Wild is larger than life but essentially of it. He is a savagely personalized human instinct—the ruthless thirst to live even at the expense not only of a fellow human being's happiness but, if need be, of his life.

1962

OLIVER GOLDSMITH
AND *THE VICAR OF WAKEFIELD*

DR. OLIVER GOLDSMITH was a very great man. This his contemporaries agreed on yet none of them knew quite why. He
baffled Dr. Johnson with his absurdities: Horace Walpole dismissed
him as 'an inspired idiot': David Garrick immortalized him in the
biting lines

> Here lies Nolly Goldsmith, for shortness called Noll,
> Who wrote like an angel, but talked like poor Poll.

And even Sir Joshua Reynolds, who saw further and deeper into
Goldsmith's character than anyone else, realized that no man could
get such a reputation for absurdity without there being reason for
it. And all agreed that the absurdest thing about Goldsmith, absurder
even than his asinine and inappropriate remarks, was his transparent
envy. He could not bear praise of any man. The adulation rendered
to Samuel Johnson gave him acute pain. Sometimes he tried to
discharge his envy by making a joke of it and a mock of himself, as
when he leapt on to a chair to show that he could deliver a better
speech than Edmund Burke and dried up after two sentences. Yet
the envy was there; as unmistakable as it was painful. And naturally
his friends rubbed salt and acid on the raw, aching heart. Solace he
found for his strange nature in jokes, in absurdity and in writing.
He was driven by the deep urges of his personality as much as Dr.
Johnson or James Boswell but their urges were powerful, sensual,
religious, locked in a massive, virile framework of passion. Oliver
Goldsmith was blown about like a butterfly: his character seemed

to lack core or mass. He longed for applause, love, affection, to be known to be good, to be wholesome, to be wanted. And the effect became ludicrous. The urgency of his desires, the immediacy of his response, the unawareness of their excess, made him foolish; his features and his manner rendered him ludicrous. People laughed at him but wanted to be with him, so what began as an absurdity, became a practice in folly. Notoriety and laughter, even against himself, were better than isolation and neglect.

Yet despite the disintegration of his personality, the foolishness of his actions, his excessive drunkenness and incurable extravagance, Goldsmith was, and is, a great man, a man of rare talents that bordered on genius, one of the finest natural writers in the English language. This reputation is based on, and justified by, some half a dozen books, essays, plays, poems and one novel, *The Vicar of Wakefield*.

He was an Irishman, born probably on November 10, 1730, at Palice, in the County of Longford, the son of a clergyman in the Church of England. Goldsmith grew up in genteel poverty in rural isolation in a society in which the barriers of class were as firm as the Great Wall of China; in which riches and poverty, benevolence or tyranny seemed as wayward as the winds of heaven. He acquired an education at Edgeworthstown School and Trinity College, Dublin: but he got into scrapes, went wandering and was somewhat lucky to get his B.A. in 1749. Off he went to Edinburgh to study medicine; there he began to discover his true predicament. That he was a poor man, wretchedly poor, so poor that hunger lived with him like a wife and starvation became not a fanciful trope but a threat. And he was an ugly man, really ugly and never desired. As he himself wrote, 'An ugly man and a poor man is society only for himself, and such society the world lets me enjoy in great abundance. . . . I may sit down and laugh at the world, and at myself, the most ridiculous object in it.' For years he drifted, living hand to mouth, begging his bread by playing on his violin, giving lessons in English, entering into formal disputations for the sake of a meal. By such means he did the Grand Tour on foot—the Netherlands, France and Italy and finally washed up in 1756 at Peckham, a London suburb, as a junior schoolmaster, an experience which he so detested that the memory of it drove him into a passion.

Yet his short stay at that school had been comparatively happy compared with the first few months after his return from Europe. He had eked a living partly through practising medicine—usually his patients were poorer than himself and could not pay—and partly through hack work with publishers, including possibly Samuel Richardson, the novelist and printer. 'Nothing,' wrote Goldsmith, 'is more apt to introduce us to the gates of the muses than Poverty.' Once hunger had driven him through, the gates closed and there was no other life for Goldsmith. Having thrown up his usher's job, he became what was in effect an assistant editor of the *Monthly Review*. The work put him in a state of euphoria. He worked hard; reviewed everything—plays, satires, mythology, philosophy, botany; tired rapidly; evaded his work or did it in a slipshod way, and within five months had given it up—as feckless and as restless as ever. But literature had him in its grip: true he went on with his medicine for a time and even did another spell at Peckham, but it was too easy to make a sort of living in literary London of Goldsmith's day for him to be able to resist for long such a pleasurable, drifting, talking, drinking life. He tried to. He planned to go out as a surgeon to India and make his fortune: the prospect of riches, the certainty of status, enticed him. Yet he always prevaricated; he was born to write and the opportunities were not hard to come by.

The London book market was expanding fast, very fast: publishers' profits might be uncertain, but they were usually large. The trouble was to get enough copy. Translations naturally were in great demand, Goldsmith was willing to translate anything. The compilation of factual educational books of a general nature, histories, books on the natural world, compendiums of philosophy, helped to slake the middle-class thirst for knowledge. Goldsmith wrote with confidence, if slight accuracy, on all branches of knowledge. Subscription lists for innumerable projects floated about London, drawing in guineas for needy authors and prosperous publishers: and sometimes but usually many, many years later, producing a set of volumes. For a man of Goldsmith's inventive genius, projects were a godsend. In this world Goldsmith hacked along—sometimes flush with guineas, more often chased by debtors. And still he clung to his Indian adventure. In times of misery, when the world of debt and poverty closed in on him, he tried to summon up courage to go to Coromandel, to gamble on the chance of a quick death or a certain fortune—a dream that was finally shattered in 1758 when the French took Madras. It did not matter. In 1760, Goldsmith began to publish *The Citizen of the World* in the *Public Ledger*, a magazine run by a really great publisher, John Newbery, whom Goldsmith afterwards introduced into *The Vicar of Wakefield* as the 'philanthropic bookseller'. These essays, purporting to be written by a Chinese philosopher—Lien Chi—about London and the English, established Goldsmith's reputation. The method was not original: not only had Montesquieu used it in his *Lettres Persanes* but so had Horace Walpole, as recently as 1757, in his *Letter of Xo-Ho, a Chinese Philosopher in London*. And often the matter was no more original than the method, for Goldsmith tired quickly and found deadlines odious, so he lifted passages wholesale from several writers on China or Persia. Nevertheless these essays deserved their success and they remain one of the most dextrous and ironic comments on society of Goldsmith's day. They are, like all that Goldsmith did, written with grace and although they reek with commonplace morality, the general drift is towards tolerance, kindliness, a mitigation of savagery, tyranny, poverty and pain. From this time on, Goldsmith became a figure of literary London—the friend of Reynolds, Johnson, Garrick, Burke, Percy and almost everyone else who wrote or painted or talked about art and letters.

His output for the next fourteen years was as extensive as it was uneven and the quality of his books was almost in direct proportion to their size. His eight-volume *History of the Earth and Animated Nature*, his four-volume *History of England*, his two-volume *History of Rome* are now worthless and unreadable. In their day they provided a vast amount of information for the general reader, some accurate, but a great deal false, in easy gracious prose. In them, there was little of Goldsmith but tens of thousands of other writers' words: few have plagiarized so remorselessly as Goldsmith. During these years, however, he created as well as compiled. He wrote two long poems, *The Traveller* (1764) and *The Deserted Village* (1771), both of enduring value: two plays, *The Good Natured Man* (1768) and *She Stoops to Conquer* (1773), that changed radically the direction of the English theatre, and one novel of genius, *The Vicar of Wakefield* (1766). These works have lasted: the plays are acted year in, year out: extracts from the poems embellish the majority of anthologies: and the novel has a rare and special place in English literature.

No one knows when or why Goldsmith wrote *The Vicar of Wakefield*. Certainly it was composed before 1762 when the manuscript saved him from the bailiffs. Samuel Johnson found him about to be arrested by his landlady for debt. Naturally he asked him if he had any marketable manuscript and Goldsmith dug out *The Vicar of Wakefield*. After a hasty glance, Johnson went off to Newberry, the bookseller, and sold it for sixty guineas. It remained unpublished for four years. Newberry was so doubtful about its worth that he hedged on it by selling a share to a Salisbury bookseller. Out at last in 1766 the critics handled it warily: the public bought it hesitantly. Dr. Johnson impatiently called it 'a mere fanciful performance'. The mood of the 1760's did not suit it; gradually, however, its popularity spread. During the Victorian age it was translated into a dozen languages and its characters became a part of the English literary folklore. And yet by any standards it is a slipshod piece of work. Improbability is heaped on improbability until the mechanics of the plot become quite outrageous. The characters, too, will scarcely bear analysis. The good are very, very good and most of the wicked damnable: only the rogue, Jenkinson, is allowed to be betwixt and between, otherwise the heart is overwhelmingly in the right or the wrong place. And the dialogue, considering Goldsmith possessed a good ear for music and wrote excellent plays, is remarkable for its artificiality. Yet millions of people have loved it, tens of thousands still read it every year with immense pleasure, alien as it is to current literary interests or techniques. Why?

Primarily because it radiates *goodness* and goodness most writers have found almost impossible to convey without being either sententious or tedious or both. Dr. Primrose, the hero, however, is a very good man. Of course, he is silly, gullible, too prone to charity, and a natural victim of all who are tyrannical and vicious. So he suffers, and how he suffers. The whole novel is an odyssey of undeserved disaster. Primrose is stripped of everything—home, daughters, son, reputation—only through trusting human beings. Yet he never loses hope; never, even in jail, tires of life. His spirit proves unbreakable. He retains a relish for living in the worst of times. And that, of course, is the experience of humanity. Men and women do not break under public disaster or private grief: they endure and maybe as they go on, they find they still like living. And that is the moral of *The Vicar of Wakefield*, of Dr. Primrose. The buffets of a wanton Fate cannot destroy the human spirit. This is the theme of the novel and although it still appeals deeply to its readers, probably it appealed even more intensely to the rougher, more uncertain world of the nineteenth century, where feudal tyranny still flourished. Men at that time could still violate justice, suborn witnesses, browbeat the poor, and stamp on the humble. Men by the very nature of their status were at the mercy of their social superiors and much that seems wildly improbable to us appeared not so singular to our grandfathers. That a rich squire should get his way not only with girls but also with the law might be the material of melodrama yet it was never a figment of the imagination. It happened. Doubtless Goldsmith could have given chapter and verse, for many of the blows that Dr. Primrose suffered, from his memories of his father's time as a country parson in Ireland. And, of course, Goldsmith himself knew the outrages that the powerless and the poverty-stricken had to endure at the hands of their richer superiors. Also he knew the reverse of this. How a man of generous instincts could shower unexpected blessings on those inferior to himself as Sir William Thornhill did on the Primrose family. In Goldsmith's day, and for long after, the wheel of chance could whirl with astonishing speed. *The Vicar of Wakefield* may be light, romantic, improbable but embedded in it is both moral and social comment. And this, as well as its charm, gives it enduring worth. And it contains many incidental felicities: there are excellent lyrics, charming anecdotes and one of the best expositions of Toryism in eighteenth-century literature. And every scene is beautifully written. Goldsmith wrote like a bird sings: the words flowed from his pen as naturally as he breathed. No wonder that the envy was not all on Goldsmith's side and that Dr. Johnson found it hard at times to restrain his malice. And perhaps the jealousy that Goldsmith roused ran deeper than this. His irresponsible spirits, his fecklessness and absurdities indicate, like his gifts, a direct response to life that most men of ability find hard to achieve.

And so Dr. Goldsmith was a very great man. In his own day the hallmarks of his fame were his 'laughing' comedies, so much more robustly comic than the sentimental plays in vogue, and his poetry in which much of the warmth and tenderness of the future romantic movement was expressed with a technical dexterity that could keep company with Dryden and Pope. The fine clothes, excellent food, plentiful wine, the condescension of the great and the applause of the common folk which his success brought him, Goldsmith enjoyed openly and immoderately. He could not have enough adulation. Resplendent in satin and as ugly as sin he became one of the great luminaries of the literary scene, noticed even by Horace Walpole who refused to be introduced to Dr. Johnson. Goldsmith, however, lived too hard: played too much, worked too much. His health broke and stupidly he treated himself, rejected good doctors and followed the advice of indifferent apothecaries. At the age of forty-three, on April 4, 1774, Goldsmith died.

He was still young. So inventive, so natural a writer must have produced further works of distinction had he lived, yet most probably his place in literature would have been neither higher nor lower than it is for he was unlucky to be born in Johnson's day. His wayward spirit would have been happier in the full flood-tide of romanticism: his achievement then might have been far greater. The greatest heights, however, could never have been his. He lacked depth of passion: the fierce overriding passion that darkens the world of true literary genius. Nature, which had given him so much, denied him all capacity for it. Even though he looked like Caliban, his spirit was all Ariel.

1961